CAROL COMES HOME

D1357447

CAROL
COMES HOME
Carol White
with Clifford Thurlow

NEW ENGLISH LIBRARY

A New English Library Original Publication, 1982

First NEL Paperback Edition November 1982

NEL Books are published by
New English Library,
Mill Road, Dunton Green,
Sevenoaks, Kent.
Editorial office: 47 Bedford Square,
London WC1B 3DP.

Made and printed in Great Britain by
Hunt Barnard Printing Ltd, Aylesbury, Bucks.

British Library Cataloguing in Publication Data

White, Carol
  Carol comes home.
  1. White, Carol   2. Actors   Great Britain
    Biography
  I. Title   II. Thurlow, Clifford
  792'.028'0924   PN2598.W

ISBN 0-450-05528-0

DEDICATION

To my mother and father, my sons Sean and Stephen, and a special dedication to my husband Michael for his love, encouragement and devotion always.

ACKNOWLEDGMENTS

Grateful thanks are due to the many people who have helped in the preparation of this book. I am particularly indebted to Mike King, Rona and Barry White, Mary Phillips at Aquascutum, Tess Farrington at Diagem, Nigel Midwinter a devoted fan who has helped so much in providing photographs; to Doug Grant and my mother- and father-in-law, Dorothy and Richard Arnold, and Len Rossi at Essanelle.

The cover photograph is by Brian Aris, with hairdressing by Joseph Bernadello.

Hold fast to dreams
for if dreams die,
life is a broken winged bird
that cannot fly.

Langston Hughes

Foreword

A TELEPHONE rang annoyingly in the distance.

We sat in the shade of a banana tree in Hollywood, the table strewn with notebooks and newspaper clippings and the winter sun reflecting warmly in the swimming pool.

It was an unlikely setting for a story that began in the grey, working-class streets of London, but Carol White had no ordinary tale to tell. It had a rags to riches quality, but while she spoke of her feelings for John Lennon, Warren Beatty and Frank Sinatra, it was clearly so much more than a glimpse into the lives of the world's most interesting men; this was an insight into the life of one of the world's most interesting women.

While we worked, the telephone was left to ring, but somehow that day it seemed more urgent. Carol dropped her pencil and, flicking her hair from her eyes, she walked into the apartment.

She was gone for a long time and when she returned her eyes were brighter and her lips formed just the faintest of smiles.

'We'll have to finish up another day,' she said. 'When we get back to London.'

The call had come from Carol's agent in England and she had accepted not one, but two leading roles. Rehearsals for the West End stage play *Steaming* were to begin almost immediately and there was pre-production work to be done on a new film called *Nutcracker*. The quiet, poolside days had come to an end.

This is the life of an actress, the autobiography of a woman of our times; it is, in her own words, the story of a star.

Clifford Thurlow
London, March 1982

One

IF THERE is a moment in everyone's life when time stands still and we are able to see ourselves as we really are, for me that moment appeared at the end of a confusing period of drug withdrawals.

I looked at my face in the mirror. It was weary and drawn, my pale green eyes had lost their sparkle, while my body still craved the drugs that had been my means of escape. For now, there was nothing: no pills, no glamour and no purpose.

The Hollywood dream had come to an end.

I had earned and spent millions of dollars. I had starred in twenty motion pictures and the world's most famous men had shared my life. But what had it all been for? I had scorned the best opportunities, divorced two husbands and finally turned my back on the chance of being Mrs Frank Sinatra.

I had never thought of myself as an actress who would end it all in panic, but there seemed to be no new challenge to meet, no new day to begin. I looked for the last time at the figure before me. It was all another dream, a nightmare that went on from one day to the next. My skin was dusty white and my long blonde hair had been betrayed by a band of dark roots. Again, I was the broken, disillusioned character in *Cathy Come Home*, but this time it wasn't my children who were being taken from me. It was something misty and uncertain: my soul, my destiny and my reason for living.

Above the mirror was a bare light bulb. I looked at it for many minutes, touching my fingertips to the warmth of its glow, my face fading as my hand found the light switch. The

11

house was silent, the moon seeping through the clear night windows and reflecting my shadow as I moved on tired legs to the last room in the corridor.

The room was small and shone in the darkness. Everything was white: the walls, the ceiling, the carpeted floor, the cover that lay uncreased upon the narrow bed. Scenes from the life of Christ were in picture frames upon the walls, there was a desk, a wooden chair, a pile of thick cards and a single book. The book was the Holy Bible and the cards contained prayers and psalms, so many words that, for me, had no meaning. The room was used for meditation, but to me it was more a chamber of horrors, my own private morgue.

That night, I knew I was going to die.

The room was airless, the closed windows trapping the late summer day to burn on through the night. I was hot from the long slow walk along the corridor. I had been trembling uncontrollably, but now, apart from the heat, I felt at peace. My eyes were tired, my hair was wet and clung to my cheeks and my legs were like lead weights as I stumbled and fell to the bed. I opened my eyes one last time and saw that above me hung a large crucifix. My mind spun madly and I glimpsed everything that was old and forgotten, the past racing before me like a film at the wrong speed. The crucifix was falling from the wall and would crush me beneath it; but is it a dream or a memory, a scene from a movie, or a scene from life?

Everything was distorted, a disorganised carnival where the real and the unreal had blended into a grotesque monster:

The Ghost of Carol White.

I was conscious of the struggle going on within me, but only as an onlooker. I was watching opposing forces lure me towards death and tempt me with life, yet I cared so little about the result. I was soaked in my own sweat, but the heat had become an intolerable cold. It passed, as the pain had passed; my mind swung between the real and the unreal, until it came to rest at the line that divides the two: my body was weightless and I moved into another dimension.

I had the feeling that I was the assistant in a magic show, the magician creating the illusion of levitation, but as I looked down at my own discarded, physical self, it became clear that it was no cheap circus trick. A part of me had taken on an ethereal body that was now completely separate, a floating white form with all the emotions and all the senses that had lived in that fading, far away figure below.

A great force was drawing me away, but still, something clung on, the breath of life was still beating in my soul.

It was warm and peaceful above, my new body languishing in the comfort, my mind climbing through the eye of the spiral and shooting into the freedom of time and space; islands of the past grouping and scattering, the black velvet sky turning upon the arc of a rainbow, the dancing shafts of red light now London in flames: people running for shelter, a little girl in pigtails, strapped to the side of a taxi cab, her eyes reflecting the shadows of German planes, as they passed in waves above the rooftops.

The taxi becomes a horse and cart, dad leading Snowy with a load of scrap iron, the little girl waving in the distance and running across the leaf-patterned grass to pathways that lead to rockeries and sleeping flower beds, thickets where trees stretched fingers through the night, onyx silhouettes against power lines, hour-glass chimneys, dark eyeless warehouses, the wharves and Hammersmith Bridge. On she travels, past St Paul's Church and the high walls of the convent, where rows of red bricks listen for the chanting prayers, guardians over the waiting nuns, sad Juliets wedded to Christ.

The words of each psalm and prayer interweave with my life and accompany my wanderings, lending strength and meaning, a reason to carry on. The crucifix upon the wall remains in position, but its reflection spins with me, as bright and as luminous as any shooting star.

More of my life goes by, a screen kiss from Peter Sellers

13

and a real-life kiss in the secrecy of his dressing room; Richard Todd behind the wheel of a gleaming Rolls Royce, but no, it's my first love, Richard O'Sullivan, in his pea-green tights, dancing a *pas de deux* on Chiswick Green. One part of me cherishes the fame and success, while another part, perhaps the inner me, the real me, hides in the wings, at one with the poor, the homeless and the dispossessed. My face filled the posters for Shelter and that same face and those same posters now decorate the vastness of space.

I'm slipping now, slipping further away, the fingers that reach out for the motionless corpse below growing pale and tired. So much that I didn't understand is clear. The whole world passes by – John Lennon with his words of wisdom; Warren Beatty creeping from Julie Christie's bedroom to join me across the street; Mike King, with the sound of wedding bells chiming a bond between us and Paul Burke bringing another woman to our room and bed in Las Vegas.

Las Vegas.

The scorched grey rocks of the desert appear through a curtain of cloud, the city like a child's toy, building blocks tossed randomly together, monstrous signs scribbling meaningless words into the heavens. The private jet sweeps like a bird of prey onto a runway and comes to rest at a silent terminal.

An air-conditioned limousine, tireless machines humming their electronic tongue, chandeliers and thick carpets, the white faces of those who come to lose; the fall of chips, the call of numbers and a spinning wheel like a space craft that beams me to the windy, wintery streets of New York. I'm in the city of endings. A secluded alcove, low lights and the man who sang to me at Caesar's Palace with me once again.

'It's him or me,' he said and suddenly, Frank Sinatra is walking out of my life forever. A faint image remains and I stare into those famous blue eyes, but the picture grows misty and the eyes belong to another man who played such an important role in my life.

My father.

The flashes from the past fade away, while my father and the city of New York both roll into focus.

Of course. That's where it all began.

Two

'OPPORTUNITY ONLY knocks once!'

'Of course it doesn't, Dad,' I replied. 'You say that every time I don't want to do something. You said it when I went for the part in *Never Let Go*. Don't you remember?'

Dad became silent. He was standing at the head of the Christmas table, carving the largest turkey in London.

'Never mind what I remember, my girl, this is different. This is America.'

'It's no different,' I said meekly, my words disguising how I really felt. I was suddenly unsure of so many things; the fuss, the success, I was now even afraid of flying.

'What about Sean and Stephen?' I said, using my two young sons as an excuse.

Dad sensed victory and resumed his carving. 'They won't be any problem,' he said. 'You can leave them here with us. We'd love to have the kids, wouldn't we, Joan?'

Joe White had been a market spieler, a rag and bone man and a prize fighter. He was a big, powerful man and few people disagreed with him.

Mum was the exception.

'Of course we don't mind,' she said. 'But if the Americans want her to go over there, they can pay for the kids and Mike as well.'

Dad acknowledged mum's words with a satisfied smile and started to pass the turkey-laden plates along the table. He had made sure that his children went to stage school, but in her subtle way, mum's influence on our lives was just as important.

16

'Here's to you, Carol,' she said, sipping her wine.

The whole family did likewise and, in response, I lifted my glass and finished the drink in a single gulp.

The morning sun sent a ripple of silver light across the cabin as the Pan Am DC-10 lifted into the grey winter sky.

It was a cold January day in 1968 and I was on my way to promote Jo Janni's hit movie *Poor Cow* in New York. The film had been sold for a small fortune to National General Pictures and they were sparing no expense in having me behind the advertising campaign.

But there was more to it than that. My name was synonymous with the age: the sixties, Swinging London, long hair, Purple Hearts, mini-skirts, the Beatles, that spectacular, roaring tidal wave that carried a new era and a whole new way of life across the Atlantic.

An army of airline officials eased our luggage through the departure formalities and escorted us across the windswept strip of runway at Heathrow. We were travelling first class and were the last to board the loaded plane. A forest of arms waved from the viewdeck; friends, fans and the press. Mike disappeared with the boys into the warmth of the cabin, but I remained, framed in the oval doorway, waving farewell to London and saying goodbye to the past.

There had never been any doubt that I would go, the part of me that had worked for success carried the most muscle, although then, as always, there was a second self who found just as much satisfaction in cooking the Sunday dinner, walking with the children in Hyde Park, the part of me who had married and had never stopped loving Mike King, although the ambitious, determined, selfish me that struggled to reach the top was the part of my personality that was to betray him many times.

These thoughts joined me on the long flight to America, a journey that was an event in itself, like an omen of what lay ahead. Halfway across the Atlantic, a stewardess said over

17

the speakers that there was no need for concern, but one of the engines had developed a fault and we would not be landing directly in New York. She had one of those laid-back 'Fly me' voices that sound great in commercials, but aren't at all convincing in an emergency. It was like a scene from a disaster movie, a stunned silence, the sky suddenly darkening and the passengers all staring ahead, or up at the little signs that said 'No Smoking'. The children sat there with open mouths. It was only the second time they had flown and this wasn't what they had expected. I consoled them with the story that we were landing outside the city just long enough for them to be able to see a real cowboy.

'The stewardess had to say that, just in case the other people complained,' I said.

They sat back with wide grins. They were getting used to being privileged.

One of the passengers wasn't quite so lucky. He had a heart attack and collapsed. There wasn't a doctor on board, but true to the disaster-like script, a Roman Catholic priest appeared and said prayers. In time, we did manage to land safely; we spent nearly two hours in a cold waiting room and when the fault was repaired, we all trooped back to the same DC-10 and took off once again. I don't know if it was the last rites that the priest had said, but the heart attack victim was no longer with us.

Sean and Stephen, though, were very happy. The cowboy I had promised was waiting at the small terminal. He was the standard caricature of a Texas oil man, but he played his role to perfection.

The initial set-back flooded into the past as the silver jet came to rest at Kennedy Airport. Another cluster of officials welcomed us as the door slid open; baggage men from the airline, film company executives, scores of eager cameramen and show business reporters who all talked at the same time. We were exhausted, but the reception made the journey and all the preparations worthwhile.

Preparations? Once I had agreed to go, I determined to

arrive in style. Sean and Stephen were dressed like miniature rock stars, with tailor-made black hipster cords, wide belts, ruffled shirts and Afghani sheepskin waistcoats from the King's Road. Sean was five and Stephen had just had his fourth birthday, but they had quickly become acclimatised to the pose. Mike had bought a khaki suit at Cecil Gee's, tight trousers with a short, jean-style jacket and high, black leather boots. Like me, he was wearing dark glasses, though we had arrived at night, in worse weather than we had left behind in London. As for me, I was the symbol of stardom in a lavender and cream mini-dress from Biba's, lavender suede boots and a long scarf that I wrapped in careful folds over my shoulder-length, honey blonde hair. I looked sensational, my dress barely covering my knickers and the excitement shielding the sub-zero winds that had chased us into the VIP lounge and an impromptu press conference.

It lasted for about fifteen minutes and was stage-managed by Herman Kass, the publicist for National General, who glowed throughout the reception and whisked me away at its height, so as not to give too much away all at once. He was a short, balding, Jewish man with a crooked smile that he balanced with an unlit cigar butt. A real professional. His eyes danced through the lounge as he manoeuvred me through the barrage of questions, smoothly past customs and immigration and out into the cold city night.

A long, sleek black limousine was waiting and I climbed in to find a bouquet of flowers and a bottle of champagne.

'From Mr Levin,' Herman Kass said from the open door. 'With his compliments.'

Mr Levin!

The name had taken on the aura of a myth. I had never met the man, but whenever his name was mentioned, the speaker sounded in awe. I imagined him to be a larger and older version of the publicist, with a matching, but much longer cigar.

The door closed and the limousine was soon leaving the terminal lights and whispering along the highway to the

Sherry Netherlands Hotel, where a platoon of uniformed valets took control of our Woolworth's suitcases and guided us to the reception desk in an elegant, oak-wood lobby. The walls were dark green and white, the furniture was a deep golden velvet, there were tapestries and paintings and marble pillars supporting a high ceiling.

For a second I lost my cool and felt thankful for the dark glasses. The hotel was a citadel of wealth, the people who passed by on silent feet oozing a self-confidence that I could manage in front of the cameras, but evaporated the moment I forgot I was an actress. The hotel was like a castle in a fairy tale, the dark green carpets so thick that each step was cushioned and comforted on to the next. Compared to the hotels in Brighton, even the Ritz, in Paris, where I had stayed when I was fourteen, the Sherry Netherlands could have been on another planet.

But of course, it was. This was America.

'Miss White, Mr White and children,' the desk clerk said. 'Your suite is waiting. On the fifth floor.'

I noticed Mike wince and he had all my sympathy; there had been a time when I lived in his shadow. The family trio, the King Brothers, had twice been voted the nation's top vocal group, but when the Beatles were climbing the charts with 'Please, Please Me', the King Brothers and their brand of music were left in the echo of their own best known song: 'Standing on the corner watching all the girls go by'. I first met John, Paul, George and Ringo at an Abbey Road recording session in 1962, although Mike's relationship with Paul McCartney went back much further. When Paul was a teenager, he waited outside the Liverpool Empire to get Mike King's autograph.

That's show business.

Still suave behind my dark sunglasses and highly conscious of the cheap suitcases, we were escorted to an old-fashioned, black iron lift and were soon ensconced in a suite of rooms overlooking the fairy lights in Central Park. The suite was huge, a vast lounge with antique French furniture, two bedrooms and two bathrooms, each complete with bath tubs and separate showers. The boys each had a bed as large as an English double and the master bedroom contained a king-sized bed. I had never seen one before. There were Persian carpets over polished wood floors, bowls of fresh flowers, a golden glow from concealed lighting and each of the three rooms had its own television set. Sean and Stephen were in paradise. Suddenly, I wasn't so sure. My lavender dress clashed with the subtle colours all around me. I may have been labelled the paragon of London fashion, but I felt distinctly out of place. Mike and the boys had bought new clothes, but I had worn the dress the previous summer when I made *I'll Never Forget What's His Name*, with Oliver Reed and Orson Welles. In London my rig out was the latest thing, but at the Sherry Netherlands Hotel, I was way too far ahead of the fashions.

The doubts were fleeting and the result of our in-flight drama. Sean and Stephen had forgotten their momentary fears as soon as they saw their Texas cowboy; the dark-windowed limousine made them excited, but once they discovered the number of TV channels that served New York, they were overcome by a sort of ecstatic mania. All three televisions were now blaring at full volume, while the boys ran wildly from room to room.

I was exhausted. It was 8.00 p.m., but with the time change, all I was fit for was about twelve hours' sleep. Some food appeared on a large-wheeled trolley and with two of the TV sets finally quelled, I was lying in the luxury of a fan of soft pillows within the hour. Mike ambled in and out, squeaking in his Cuban-heeled boots, a tall-stemmed glass in one hand and a bottle of champagne in the other. Mike loved it. At heart, he was just a playboy. It took some time, but eventually the children did go to sleep and Mike joined me in the king-sized bed. I don't know why, but the extra space seemed more conducive to being close together; we made love amidst the opulence and everything was good between us.

We had been apart the previous summer, but had got back together in the October, when Mike joined me on the trip to Budapest. I had a cameo role in Bernard Malamud's haunting story *The Fixer*, with Alan Bates and Dirk Bogarde. We travelled by road across communist Hungary without proper papers, assisted by a vodka-drinking peasant who looked over eighty and who stopped every fifteen minutes for a fresh bottle. I played the Jewish wife of the main character, which I thought was a strange piece of casting, but I enjoyed the role as much as the unique experience of working in the grey conformity of East Europe. Everything about the production had its funny side; everything from the bone-shaking journey, to Alan Bates importing his own make-up man from the Royal Shakespeare Company.

The Fixer came at the end of the most challenging period of my life. It started with Jeremy Sandford's *Cathy Come Home*, a dramatised TV documentary that highlighted the housing shortage in Britain. When it was shown late in 1966 it caused not just a storm, but a furore, a tempest, an earthquake. Questions were asked in the House of Commons, the 'Shelter' organisation was formed to help fight the problem, the cast and production crew signed over their royalties to the cause and Carol White became a household name.

I was twenty-three years old and my life's ambition had been achieved. I was a star.

I was a star, but not in the traditional mould. *Cathy Come Home* was seen by everyone in the country, it was shown in schools and colleges and helped influence the attitudes of Britain's social workers. Cathy's very name became a symbol for the homeless and I was associated with their plight; I was Cathy. Playing the character in the title role, I received most of the praise. My reviews couldn't have been better if I had written them myself, but just as essential was director Ken Loach, whose sensitivity and feeling brought an honesty and a reality into people's living rooms. 'The most important piece of dramatised documentary ever screened,' as Frank Norman wrote in the *Sunday Times*. I felt proud that I was doing something worthwhile. Shelter used my face for their poster and Jeremy Sandford did the same with his book. I spoke at rallies, I helped to raise money and I relived the past. My family had never been without a home, but there were times when there was no food on the table.

It was inevitable that my role in Shelter would come to an end and in time the film successes would lead me to the world of fame, fortune and the easy life. It was a complete contrast, but being able to encompass those opposites is what marks people for stardom. In a world where everyone is ambitious, nothing and no one are how they first appear.

I was criticised by some for leaving Cathy behind and moving my career to Hollywood, but life is a continual process of change, of doing one thing and then moving on to the next. All that we do becomes the sum total of what we are and it appears that, ultimately, destiny carves the path and there is nothing for us to do but follow it. I wasn't Cathy, I was Carol White, putting my soul into the part. That's what acting is all about, though for all the acclaim and all the appreciation, there is a price that has to be paid.

That price is demanded by the men who mould your personality from the movie screen, and often precipitate the mental problems which result from living a double reality. This knowledge took a long time coming and only crystallised during the crisis of my second nervous breakdown. I had been committed to a hospital in California and needed a court order to be able to leave. Being screamed at by people who had totally flipped and going through pathetic tests that caged mice would scorn was enough to drive anyone crazy, but when I woke one night to find a man urinating over me, I knew it was time to cling on to my sanity and get out.

The confusion seemed to be an inherent part of success, although when I was working towards that goal, everything went my way. After *Cathy Come Home*, Michael Winner signed me for *I'll Never Forget What's His Name*. Shooting was to commence in the summer, so when Ken Loach asked me to take the lead in *Poor Cow*, it appeared that the spring starting date would leave time for a break between films. In the movie-making business such plans are apt to go wrong and for more than two weeks, I was rushing from one set to the next, slipping in and out of roles and dividing my active social life between an endless stream of parties and a lecture tour I was giving to raise money for Shelter.

After *Cathy*, I was a celebrity. Mike and I shared night club tables with people who would soon become legends: Brigitte Bardot, Rudolf Nureyev, who was staging his own version of *Don Quixote*, Clint Eastwood, top model Jean Shrimpton, Mike's long-standing friends Dudley Moore and John Junkin, the members of that up-and-coming rock band, the Rolling Stones, the comedian Ronnie Corbett and John Lennon, who was usually out with his wife Cynthia and not the other Beatles.

Like John, I was beginning to question it all. What does it mean; where are we going, why us? We talked for hours about fame and money and why we seemed to lead such 'charmed lives', as John always put it. Thirteen years later he wrote in one of his last songs: 'Life is what happens to you when you're busy making other plans.' I heard it in the autumn of 1980. On 8 December, John Lennon was gunned down in the streets of New York. I cried for two whole days.

I had the same mental, rather than physical, relationship with Stones' guitarist Brian Jones and, several years later, with the Who's drummer Keith Moon. Each in his own way was a hero of the sixties, but so, too, were they all its casualties. They shared an element of self-destruction and it is only now that I can see how this trait was a major ingredient in our mutual attraction.

The seed of that ingredient first seemed to find fertile soil at the beginning of 1967, when I started work on *Poor Cow*. Mike and I had been married for five years; it hadn't always been easy, but suddenly our relationship slipped to its lowest ebb. Terence Stamp was signed as my co-star and our brief but consuming affair was inevitable. We had slept together before, when I was seventeen and at the height of a wild period of promiscuity. In those days, I was more concerned with numbers than feelings. I wanted to sleep with as many men as possible and Terry happened to have been one of them.

It's true, I was cheating on Mike, but it worked both ways. In tandem with Dudley Moore, he often went out on the town with dancers and models, and for some months he had been having a hot romance with the highly celebrated Miss Keeler, whose reputation was soon to spread all the way from Westminster to the Kremlin. That little affair came to an abrupt end the night an anonymous caller telephoned the warning that Lucky Gordon was on his way over to kill Christine. Lucky was a West Indian musician renowned for bravado and pantomime, but Mike was soon dressed and on his way ... just in case.

There was no excuse for either of us, but it was the sixties; free-love was the catch phrase of the times and we weren't just saying it, we were living it!

Once I started work on *I'll Never Forget What's His Name*, my romance with Terence Stamp fizzled out. Oliver Reed was my new co-star and we were both immediately attracted to one another. Once again, we had met in the past, way back in the foggy ruins of the fifties when we made *Beat Girl* together with Adam Faith, John Barry and Shirley Anne Field. I was in love with Adam, Adam had a thing going with Shirley Anne, I ended up with John Barry and Oliver Reed was happily married with a baby son. That was eight years ago and things had changed.

Mike and I didn't stop loving each other, but we didn't stop arguing, either. There were a couple of spare weeks after filming finished when we took the boys to Albufeira, in Portugal, but the holiday was a disaster and the day we returned Oliver Reed arrived on the doorstep with a case of Dom Pérignon champagne. From that day on, he started to appear at all hours, his bright yellow E-type racing into the street and advertising his arrival. My marriage to Mike had long been hanging on by a tenuous thread and now it crumbled into non-existence. He went away with his brothers on tour and I spent several happy weeks at my own private party.

Oliver had a vast appetite for pleasure: eating, drinking and tumbling between the sheets. We went from one to the other, leaving little time for sleep. My only restful hours were spent taking driving lessons. Oliver wouldn't let me drive his Jaguar, it was so special he called it by name – the 'Yellow Banana' – but he did spend his afternoons babysitting the boys, awaiting my return.

'And how were you today, my little angel?' he would ask as we walked along the garden path, continuing before I had a chance to reply: 'Have I got a surprise for you!'

He always remained in the house while I was out with the driving school, so the surprise had to be one of his three favourite activities. Not that I cared. Oliver's capacity for excess was only matched by my own.

The pattern continued through the summer and suddenly it came to an end. Oliver Reed had more adventures to attend to and I had signed for *The Fixer*. I spent a week alone in the house, watching the trees in the garden turn gold and maroon, the small birds gathering in the high branches and the chubby neighbourhood cats all dreaming of winter fires. Mike returned from the summer tour and I asked him to join me on the trip to Budapest; my younger brother, Joey, flew out to Hungary to be with us before filming was completed.

Sean and Stephen were left with a nanny and we set out on the train for Vienna, the European countryside flooding past in endless colours and our feelings in tune with the season. If nothing else, Mike and I had a flair for forgiveness. We had known each other for so long that our souls had found perfect harmony, like parts of a Chinese puzzle that appeared to be identical but only fitted together in one place. By the time we crossed the Hungarian border we were

26

childishly in love again and we each promised to remain faithful from then on.

Six months had passed, but Hungary was light years away.

All these thoughts chased into my dreams that first night at the Sherry Netherlands, although it seemed only minutes later when I was awakened by an awful noise coming from the adjoining room. I leapt out of bed, I was bleary and stiff with sleep, suddenly afraid that someone had entered the suite and was torturing Sean and Stephen. I found them sitting up in bed, both fully rested and dressed in their Afghani waistcoats. It was 4.30 in the morning and they had discovered the first cartoon show. I turned the television set to its lowest volume, closed the door and stumbled back to my room, Mike looking so small in the king-sized bed and the vast space already cold with the morning chill.

I surfaced again for breakfast at ten and entered the day with a greater feeling of self-confidence. I chose an even shorter mini-skirt and commenced my role promoting *Poor Cow*. Each day there were TV and radio shows – the *Today Show*, the *Tonight Show*, the *Saturday Show* – until in the end I didn't know if it was yesterday or the day after tomorrow. The chauffeur from National General took me all over New York. I went to cocktail parties, receptions, fashion shows and one day I even opened a new supermarket.

My agent in the United States was Richard Gregson, who took us out to dinner with his wife, Natalie Wood, and Alan Ladd Junior, his agency partner. The city was alive with activity and although I seemed to bump into big stars everywhere I went it was at Albert Finney's party that I saw them all gathered under the same roof. Paul Newman was there with Joanne Woodward, Shirley Jones, Jack Cassidy, producers, directors, gossip columnists and the deans of New York society. The party was to celebrate the success of

27

Peter Nichols' play *Joe Egg* on Broadway. Albert, as the play's starring performer, was the main guest, but I was the centre of attention. With the shortest of dresses in the world and with all the publicity behind my part in *Poor Cow*, rumour had it that I was to be nominated for an Academy Award, and the whispers that I was bound for Hollywood became so loud, that I read about it in the *New York Times* long before the first firm offer was made.

I may have been the talk of the town in show business circles, but to the average New Yorker I was just a crazy person whose skirt was too short for the winter. The point was ably demonstrated before the opening of *Poor Cow*, when Julian Holloway took us to Sardi's restaurant in Manhattan. We were placed in a dull corner, the spot, as Julian explained, for the hopefuls and the has-beens. I was livid and vowed never to return, although as Sardi's is a place to be seen at, I soon changed my mind.

When we went with friends the second time, we were shown to the very best window table. *Poor Cow* had opened and everyone knew who I was. People recognised me in the street, I was an overnight success; all doors opened and I was able to watch the traffic while I ate my meal.

A week had gone by since our arrival in the city. We had met everyone on National General, from the publicist to the shoe-shine boy. More champagne and flowers arrived daily, but the hallowed figure of Irv Levin was still just the cigar-smoking tycoon of my imagination. That image persisted right up until the time I donned a checked Mary Quant skirt and blouse and rode the hotel lift to the final press conference on the ground floor of the Sherry Netherlands.

A display of flashing camera bulbs blinded me for a second, but when I opened my eyes I had the surprise of my life. Irv Levin was at the far end of a long, highly polished table. I wasn't introduced, but then it wasn't necessary, since the vibes and chemicals that sparked between us were both very animal and basic.

Herman Kass placed me at the opposite end of the table

and, from there, I stared into Irv Levin's dark, deep-set eyes. The show business reporters went through their usual round of questions and, somehow, I managed to say all the right things.

Irv Levin was nothing like the picture I had drawn. He was a slim, handsome man in his early forties. He was immaculately dressed, perfectly composed, with even features and jet black hair. As I answered the questions, those dark, blue-brown eyes glittered their secret code and I felt like the sacrificial virgin going happily to the altar stone; a symbol of fertility, everything woman, everything that's steeped in danger. My Mary Quant blouse was tight and revealing, but before those motionless dark eyes, I felt naked.

The questions went on and on, but in my mind I was painting another picture, a portrait of myself upon silken sheets, my arms outstretched, eager for that first embrace, my voice whispering words that are saved for a lover.

Irv Levin's charisma settled about him like an aura. Few men had it since it came from success, wealth and the ultimate aphrodisiac: Irv Levin exuded power.

When the press conference was over, he asked me to join him for lunch.

I knew then that my promise to Mike King would be broken.

Three

MY STOMACH filled with butterflies as soon as Irv Levin took my arm and guided me from the conference room to the small restaurant at the Sherry Netherlands. The reporters disappeared to meet their deadlines, Herman Kass left with his assistants, and suddenly we were alone, staring into each other's eyes.

'You handle the press very well,' Irv said, his wide, thin mouth breaking into a smile. 'It's rare to find brains and beauty all in one person.'

'You must be surrounded by beautiful, intelligent women all of the time,' I replied, continuing to play a role and trying to be what Irv Levin thought I was. I had noticed that he was impressed with my response to the reporters' questions, especially when they went into the routine over my so-called rival.

'Are you worried about being labelled the "new" Julie Christie?' someone asked. I replied: 'Of course I'm not worried. Julie should be worried about me!'

The reporters all laughed and scribbled notes in their pads. They asked more questions about Julie Christie and I went along with them; the publicity was good for both of us, even though no real rivalry existed. We were both under contract to the producer Jo Janni, as we had both signed with Beaconsfield Studios as teenagers. If there ever was a feeling of competition, it came much later, when Julie and I owned houses opposite each other in Fulham's Neville Terrace and Warren Beatty kept himself fit by running between the two.

My affair with Warren Beatty was only physical. It ended as casually as it begun and continued as if there had been no break when we both moved to Beverly Hills. That wasn't the case with Julie and there was even talk of them getting married. It never happened, but even when the rumours were at their height, Julia and I never came to blows.

The only nasty taste left from that period comes not from Julie or Warren, but the gossip writer Rona Barrett, who describes me as the 'poor man's Julie Christie'.

But back to January 1968 and the tall, dark stranger smiling at me through the candlelight. He said he had fallen for me the moment he saw my performance in *Poor Cow*. I wondered at first who exactly it was he had fallen for, me, or the trouble-bound character I played, although the longer we sat there, the more that fear diminished in my mind.

'You're a very lovely girl and I like you very much,' he said.

There wasn't a lot I could say, so I sipped my wine and remained silent.

Sean and Stephen were five floors above with bad colds and Mike was looking after them. I had hurt him many times with my brief exploits and I didn't want it to happen again. I was unsure about so many things, so I just closed my eyes, relied on my intuition and moved along with the flow.

Irv Levin asked me to continue promoting *Poor Cow* in Los Angeles and that is where we went the following day.

Irv Levin had to leave immediately for the west coast, but overnight his private Lear jet returned to collect us. This was the real thing; this is what I imagined a film star's life was really all about. It was so removed from the draughty dressing rooms at the BBC and film budgets that counted every penny. In America it was different. Once you reached the top, you were treated like royalty and expense was no object. I sat back in the tiny plane and watched the tall Manhattan buildings grow smaller, leaving the cold city for another appointment with fate.

31

A limousine was waiting for us in Los Angeles and with palm trees and blue skies as the backdrop, we were driven to the Century Plaza Hotel, on the Avenue of the Stars.

The car returned that evening and, from a private plane and a private limousine, we were driven to a private estate overlooking the Beverly Hills. It was my first taste of winter sunshine, the car moving slowly through a pink and orange haze, Sunset Boulevard, the famous Sunset Strip, alive and teeming; the clubs with their gigantic signs, the open-topped cars, the beautiful hookers, the hustlers and the neatly dressed people all waiting to be discovered. Pretty girls and pretty boys from all over the world were there in search of the myth and even while I sat protected behind the limousine's dark windows, a part of me was still on the sidewalk, waiting for the dream to end.

We left the lights behind us, the car climbed a hill and then passed between a pair of black iron gates, where armed guards watched our progress until we arrived at a rambling, single-storey house. The chauffeur opened the car doors and once on the porch we were greeted by a black butler. It felt as if I had walked on to a film set, the image persisting as Irv Levin introduced me to his guests.

Raquel Welch was there, Bobby Darrin, Sandra Dee, Patty Duke, the gossip ladies, Hedda Hopper and Rona Barrett, Warren Cowan, who is now my American publicist, and three men who immediately made me feel at ease. They were Jerry Belson, Gary Marshall and Jerry Paris, who were all wearing large Ban the Bomb badges, an outrage amongst the ultra-conservative clique of Hollywood film people. Jerry and Gary, who wrote the hit TV shows *Happy Days* and *Laverne and Shirley*, worked with the director Jerry Paris on *The Grasshopper*, the film that put a black mark against my career, as I shall explain later, and made Jacqueline Bisset a star.

Apart from my meeting the Ban the Bomb trio, the party was a bit of a disaster. Irv Levin followed me everywhere; Mike in turned followed Irv following me; and Irv's wife,

Lenny, joined in by following Mike. I pretended to be oblivious to it all. I kept my party grin in place and thought more about my host, whose personality was coming alive against the background of his home and friends. Red-jacketed valets parked the cars and black maids served food, but everything remained tasteful and underplayed. The house was modern, but the contemporary furniture was set off with well-placed antiques, Indian rugs and paintings. My attraction to Irv had dulled a little after our brief luncheon, but seeing him in his home made my feelings soar once again. With it came the confusion. I broke up the senseless round of follow the leader, took Mike's arm and forced my infatuation with Irv to wait for another time.

The rest of the week was filled with more press conferences and television talk shows; the highlight was the Golden Globe Awards, at the Ambassador Hotel, where I was invited to make a presentation to Sophia Loren. It was fun pulling open the big envelope and reading out Sophia's name; she beamed with pleasure and I knew just how she felt.

Before I reached the United States, I received a best actress award from the Variety Club of Great Britain, for my performance in *Poor Cow*. I was absolutely thrilled even though in time the honour became just one of many from all over the world, including two American tributes for the best newcomer. I enjoyed the thought and didn't bother to send them back with a note explaining that I had starred in my first movie fifteen years earlier, when I was ten years old.

The week went by without further upset, but I tempted fate by agreeing to take Mike and the boys for a weekend of real sunshine in Palm Springs. We stayed in a bungalow in the Gene Autry Lodge, with Irv and Lenny and their two children next door. From Palm Springs, we returned to Los Angeles, only not to the hotel, but the Levin family home, where I had the shock of my life. Everyone treated Irv Levin like an emperor, but not Lenny. They had a house full of servants, but still she ordered her husband about, whining in a high-pitched voice and going into fits of histrionics over the smallest thing. It was the first time I had stayed with a American couple and I wasn't aware that this was how Lenny showed affection and, more to the point, that she was Irv Levin's wife. Lenny was a typical Beverly Hills American princess who, along with the other wives of the film executives, formed the cornerstone of Hollywood society.

But that wasn't the case with Irv Levin.

As a movie boss he was an enigma. He had all the trappings, a sort of lord of the manor with his hillside retreat, private jet and endless assistants. Yet somehow he didn't fit the image and looked more at ease in the combat fatigues he had worn during his stint in the Israeli Army. He was proud of being Jewish and proud of his country, and while he was a man with no vanity regarding his film business, he spoke happily of Moshe Dayan, the Israeli Defence Minister, as one of his best friends.

After two days fraught with minor complications, the car carried our cheap suitcases to the airport and I left the blue California skies with mixed feelings. Mike and I had little to say to each other on the long journey to London. My reception in the United States had been a sensation, but what was that going to do to our shaky marriage? I had returned to filming in 1964 after a break of two years, a cure for the motherhood blues, but Mike was still the bread winner and preferred it that way. My comeback had taken three years of hard work and it was obvious that *Poor Cow* was only the beginning.

Our four months' second honeymoon from Hungary to Hollywood was about to come to an end and it did so a lot sooner than either of us expected.

About a month after our departure from Los Angeles, Irv Levin was again in London on business. He called from his suite at the Dorchester and invited Mike and I out for a night on the town. Mike got in touch with Sue Baker, an actress who had appeared with Tony Newley in *Stop The World I Want To Get Off* and she agreed to join the party. We went to the Club Les Ambassadeurs and on the the Club D'ell

Artusa, Mike's usual stamping ground. We had gone to the opening night with Tom Jones, Richard Harris, Roman Polanski and Sharon Tate, Brian Jones, Rudolf Nureyev, in fact, almost everyone who was in show business. That night the club was filled with stars, although our quiet foursome became just as memorable, for different reasons.

Before we had finished our second bottle of champagne, I was dancing closely with Irv and Mike was almost eating Sue Baker. They had known each other for a long time. Sue had once been engaged to Mike's brother Denis and she was a beautiful young starlet. She and her sister Jennifer made up the famous Baker Twins.

When we got home, Mike and I had a huge row, each of us dragging up the past and saying words that would ultimately commit our fragile union to eternal rest. We were so similar to each other, caught up in an age and a way of life that created disharmony. Peace and love were the subjects of every song that made the charts, but they were spread far too thinly for such old-fashioned concepts as marriage to survive.

The King Brothers were working a few days later in Bootle. No more had been said after the fight and instead, we lived like strangers. When Mike finally left, I was relieved. With my own space I was able to think, although the solitary hours weighed heavily and far from taking a fresh look at my own life, I fell into a state of boredom and depression. I knew my personality was made up of a whole bunch of different characters and I was equally aware that none of them functioned that well without a man. I looked through my address book, reliving the previous summer and fighting the temptation to call my former lovers. It would be degrading and probably pointless. Terence Stamp was back with his model girlfriend Jean Shrimpton and Oliver Reed may have soared away to another planet. They were both memories and the real temptation I struggled with was the telephone number at the Dorchester. I had to wait until Irv Levin called me. Thankfully he did so before I went crazy with waiting, his voice changing my mood from despondency to instant bliss. Would Mike and I like to go out for dinner?

'Mike's away working, but I'd love to come.'

'Mike's away,' Irv said, his voice fading into a windy telephone noise. Then he added, 'Do you have his number so I can call him?'

'Call him?' I said. 'What for?'

'To ask if he minds us going out for dinner together,' he replied.

'Irv, I don't need anyone's permission to go out,' I said. 'This is 1968 you know.'

'I ought to ring him, though, just to be fair.'

I gave Irv Mike's number in Bootle. We had lunch together that day at the White Elephant, in Curzon Street, and that evening we went to a cocktail party at Nat Cohen's penthouse opposite Green Park. At the time, Nat Cohen was the head of EMI, the company that had made *Poor Cow* and sold it for a huge profit to Irv Levin, for distribution in the United States. We didn't learn how big the deal was until a few months before the time of writing, when Mike King bumped into Nat Cohen in the lift at the Beverly Hills Hotel. They smiled and shook hands and talked with nostalgia about those long ago times.

'Tell Carol when you see her that I'd like to thank her very much,' Nat said as they parted.

Nat Cohen made a million dollars on the sale of a movie that had only cost half that to make.

Me? I was paid £7,500 which, with some more cash from *I'll Never Forget What's His Name* went towards buying a tiny, two bedroomed town house in Putney.

The cocktail party was for the launching of another young star, Susan George, who had just made *All Neat in Black Stockings*. She was then going through the same press ritual as I had undergone with Julie Christie, Susan being described in the tabloids as the 'new' Carol White.

The only other young person there was the actress Fiona Lewis, the latest Jo Janni protégé, and the rest of the guests were tycoons with their big cigars and wives. I was glad when it was time to go.

'Shall we have a drink at the hotel before I take you home?' Irv asked. He was such a gentleman.

'Of course,' I replied. The city lights pierced the night and sent shadows chasing through the car. Irv drove slowly and with great care, which made me think of Oliver Reed, who drove his 'Yellow Banana' as if London was his own private race track.

When we arrived at the Dorchester, the bar was full of noisy people; we went straight to Irv's suite and he ordered drinks from there. There was a long, embarrassing silence, and for the first time since I had met Irv Levin he seemed unsure of himself. I had been seduced by an older man when I was a teenager, and judging by that experience if this was now Irv's plan, he was completely at a loss. He hated the idea of being unfaithful to Lenny and he considered my being there as unfair to me.

'I'm sorry, Carol, we shouldn't have come here,' he said. 'Let me take you home.'

'Don't be sorry. There's nowhere else in the world that I would rather be.'

My words opened the floodgates. Irv pulled me into his arms, the embrace sending a warm sensation tingling through my body. All the passion and desire that had filled my mind in the conference room at the Sherry Netherlands Hotel was with me again, crystallised into that second. That night, I didn't go home.

Everything about our relationship was a bit like a fairy story – Irv the rich and handsome prince and me a Cinderella with glass slippers and a late night pass. That was how it started out, although the next morning it moved on from being a fairy tale into the realm of romantic fiction.

After breakfast, we walked from the Dorchester to Park Lane. Irv stopped and looked at a row of new cars in a show room.

'Which one do you like?' he said.

37

I thought it was just a game, but went along with it by choosing a navy blue Mercedes. We went in, Irv said: 'We'll have that one,' as if it were a cauliflower we were buying. He signed a cheque and the salesman said I could drive it away that afternoon. It was as simple as that. The previous summer, I had passed my driving test, and the sleek 280 SL was my first car.

Wonderland? It didn't end there. I had told Irv over breakfast that my marriage to Mike King had been finished for a long time and that we only stayed together because of the children. It wasn't strictly true, but after such a romantic night it seemed like a nice thing to say.

'Do you have any money pressures?' he said.

'That goes without saying,' I laughed. 'We're not all millionaires, you know.'

Irv laughed, too, but he had obviously listened. From the car show room, we walked to the small bank next door to the Dorchester.

'I've got some money from my Swiss bank account that I can't use,' he explained. 'Would you like to keep it in a safety deposit box and use it if it becomes necessary?'

The suggestion was pointed and dangerous, but without hesitation I nodded my head and replied, 'That'll be great!'

He paid for the box, we each had a key and Irv Levin stored away $20,000 in American currency, just so there were no pressures.

If that wasn't enough, the story had one more twist to make it complete.

I was suddenly a greedy child, taking all that I had been given as if it were my right and then wanting more. At least, that's what I think was the case. The alternative is that my next ploy was totally shrewd and calculating. I told Irv that I had a girlfriend who was selling a sable fur for £750.

'It's really fab,' I said, using the latest word popularised by John Lennon and amusing Irv.

'Then buy it, I'll give you the money,' he replied. 'You're a

38

star, you should have nice things, and anyway, it's winter and you need a warm coat.'

He was very paternal.

We collected the Mercedes, Irv gave me the cash, leaving the dollar bills undisturbed, and off I drove to Hammersmith. I had to talk Irv out of joining me. He was a man of unswerving honesty and buying the coat wasn't quite as straightforward as I had made out. It was new, it was worth £3,000 and it was in the possession of a shady character from the back streets of my childhood. Had I asked, Irv Levin would have bought me a new coat, but buying hot goods was an adventure and it kept me in touch with my roots.

The coat's history didn't end there. Some time later, when it had been long forgotten in a cupboard, it was discovered by Mike King and I let him have it. He gave it to a girl he wanted to impress and she promptly sold it for £250. Cause and effect, maybe, but I don't think so. If I sowed any bad seeds in acquiring the coat, I reaped my just deserts tenfold, when I returned from another trip to the United States with three furs and was arrested for smuggling. The episode cost me £10,000, or, translated into dollars, almost the exact sum Irv Levin had left in the safety deposit box.

The final act brings us right up to date. At present, I am a vegetarian. I don't eat meat and I have no desire to own a fur coat.

But just imagine how I felt that crisp March evening in 1968, wearing a crochet-work mini-dress that showed that I had a great figure, my long blonde hair falling heavily into the upturned collar of my sable and my hands gripping the wheel of a gleaming Mercedes, the mile clock moving from 12 to 13 as I turned into Park Lane and headed for the Dorchester. My children were safely at home with a nanny and I had a dinner engagement with one of the most powerful men in the film industry. As I parked the car, the odometer clicked to 14; seven was my lucky number and it felt good to have two of them.

Dinner that evening was a private affair. Bottles of champagne sat in ice buckets, like small birds at the edge of a nest, a silent waiter served food from silver dishes in the suite and classical music played in the background. We made love and I felt like a princess.

The next morning, Irv Levin flew back to his wife in Los Angeles.

When Mike returned from Bootle, I kept the nest egg a secret. He was incensed by the car, so what the $20,000 would have done, I didn't even want to imagine.

'You're just a slut, Carol,' he yelled. 'You think because you're a star it's different. Well it isn't. You're no different to the girls who hang out in Wardour Street.'

'And you know all about them, don't you Michael!' I shouted back. 'You're just a damned hypocrite. You have one rule for yourself and one for me. We're not living in the reign of Queen Victoria any more, so you'd better get used to it.'

'What's that supposed to mean?'

'It means, Michael, that I sleep with who I want to because I want to and not for anything else.'

'So what's the car in aid of?'

'The car isn't in aid of anything,' I replied. 'It's the way Americans do business. Irv Levin wants me to sign with him and the car is just a sweetener.'

'Just a sweetener,' Mike said mockingly. 'And you didn't have to sleep with him?'

'I slept with Irv,' I replied. 'Not for a car, but because I wanted to.'

Mike and I were like brother and sister and he knew what I said was true. He was hurt and jealous, but it worked both ways and the upset eventually passed.

With my new car and plenty of money – my own money, that is, from the previous year's films – we were both eager to be out and about; clubs and discos and select in-spots where sixties' stars could hide from the madding crowd. During the day, there were expensive coffee houses to visit, and with all that money burning holes in my pockets, I went on endless shopping trips in the West End and along the King's Road, in Chelsea.

It was on one of these expeditions that I met Yoko Ono for the first time and, to say the least, I was impressed. I was in Patsy Booth's boutique, a hole-in-the-wall bazaar of flashing lights, black carpets and chromium rails filled with the latest fashions. I had a fetish for silver lurex and Patsy always had something special. As I idled my way through the dresses, I noticed John sitting on the steps that led up to the changing rooms.

"Ello, luv,' he said. 'On your own?'

'Course,' I replied. 'I can spend more that way.'

John was still laughing when Yoko appeared in a short black dress. He immediately became serious. John was wearing black jeans and a black sweatshirt and it appeared that gloom was the bond between them.

'Well, what do you think?' Yoko said, completely ignoring me. 'Do you like it?'

'Not a lot,' John said lightly.

'You never like anything,' Yoko snarled.

'Well it's not that bad, luv.'

Yoko Ono returned to the changing room and John just shrugged. I was astonished. Everyone in London was talking about John's Japanese girlfriend, but she was nothing like I had imagined. I have to admit to being a little biased against her; I liked Cynthia Lennon, a pretty blonde from the working class streets of Liverpool.

I said goodbye to John and left the boutique without buying anything. I had a strange feeling as I walked through the spring sunlight. The big wheel of time was about to move on and I didn't know if I was ready for it. John Lennon was entering a new phase in his life and there was me, dressed to the nines and driving a flashy car. The sixties were at their height, everyone had turned on to psychedelic drugs, the

41

immortal 'Lucy in the Sky with Diamonds', but with the era reaching its peak, there was only one way for it to go.

London seemed different, smaller; even the scenes shown in *Cathy Come Home* were no longer apparent. The period I had spent helping to raise money for Shelter had receded, time was racing ahead and, like John Lennon, I realised that I, too, had to take a fresh look at where I was going. It was April and I had just had a birthday. I was twenty-five, one quarter of a century, and I was eager for whatever life had in store.

I had been shopping for summer clothes to take on holiday to Majorca, a trip Mike had organised with the composer, John Barry. He was staying in a beautiful villa that belonged to a French nobleman with his girlfriend, Polly Williams, and a staff of domestic helpers who wore white gloves at all times and served the most amazing feasts. They treated us all like members of the aristocracy, even the children, and made a big display of presenting John with dusty green bottles of wine at sunset, for him to approve before they were served with dinner. He had come a long way since we did *Beat Girl* together and that very year he won an Academy Award for the music in the *Lion in Winter*. His career had soared and he moved in different circles, but who was the mystery nobleman?

'He's just a friend,' John replied cryptically. 'He's a count.'

'A count?'

'Well, not just a count, he's The Count!'

We never did find out who the count was and we talked away the days reminiscing about the early sixties. John and I had had a fleeting affair when I was seventeen and we had come out of it as good friends. Mike and I, though, had carried our problems with us and I ended up spending most of the holiday talking with John about marriage and its drawbacks.

The scenery was impressive and the days were warm; it was nice to see John again, but by the time Mike and I arrived back in London, the problems between us had reached a climax. We talked about it until there were no more words to say and finally, on 29 April, Mike left the house in Putney and moved back to Hammersmith. It was our sixth wedding anniversary and we had split up once again.

This time, it was for good.

I would have been depressed, especially as there was no man to fill Mike's shoes, but there simply wasn't time.

Within a few days of our parting, my agent, Jean Diamond, was on the phone, bubbling over with excitement. I had been asked at the last minute to open the Cannes Film Festival. Would I like to do it?

'Like it?' I replied. 'I'd love it.'

'There's only one thing,' Jean said, her bubbles going flat for a second. 'Can you speak French?'

'Like a native,' I quipped. 'It was my best subject at school.'

I had a lot to do, hunting through the boutiques for something startling and, with the more womanly awareness that had settled about me after my brief meeting with John and Yoko, I found myself lured to the select shopping malls in Knightsbridge and Kensington, where ladies with Buckingham Palace accents eased me into the haute couture models befitting my new image.

At the end of the week, the air smelling fresh with the coming summer, the boys entrusted to their nanny and my outrageously expensive suitcases packed with new things, I was back at the airport, en route for the South of France. A car was waiting at the airport, doors opened for me as soon as the hotel came into view and everyone I saw gave me a welcoming smile, as if I should know them. I was only just getting used to being a star.

The opening took place the following evening and I spent about six hours getting ready. I applied my make-up with infinite care, the hairdresser shaped my every curl to

43

perfection and finally, I stepped into a black, very tight, very low cut evening dress. I looked at myself in the full-length mirror and burst into tears. I looked fantastic, the lines of my figure like razors against the fine material and the halter holding my boobs like ripe fruit that was ready for plucking. It was an image, for sure, but it wasn't me.

Jean Diamond arrived to find me sobbing on the bed, the opening of the 1968 Cannes Film Festival due within minutes.

'There, there,' she said. 'There, there.'

I cried and she there-there'd; I smoked half a dozen Rothmans' cigarettes and finally pulled myself together. I had tried to be what I wasn't and so I returned to the new suitcases in search of the real me. And there I was in a single neat fold, ready and waiting. I repaired the splattered make-up, sprinkled my cheeks with silver sparkles and climbed into the shortest dress I had. It was as white as the driven snow, it made me look about sixteen and, with my love of opposites, I felt great.

With my short, short dress and a big smile, I arrived amongst Europe's rich and royalty to perform the short ceremony, a ten minute soliloquy that I had five minutes to study before I was on. I looked down at the type-written sheet and my mouth nearly fell open. My schoolgirl French was rustier than I thought. I could read it, but I could only understand half of the words and the general meaning was cloudy, to say the least. The first film to be shown that year was the classic *Gone with the Wind*, in honour of its leading lady, Vivien Leigh, who had just died. The speech mentioned the movie and Vivien by name, but what I didn't realise was that the whole thing was actually about her life and career. The audience was quiet and respectful and there I stood, the shortest dress in the South of France, silver sparkles shining in the lights, delivering a sad speech about a fellow performer with a cheerful voice and the biggest smile I could manage.

A thin wave of applause followed my exit and I took my seat between Princess Grace and Prince Rainier. It was such hard work, being a star. The excitement, my nervousness, the last minute dress change, all had combined to tire me out. I sat back in the darkness and the full, four-hour, uncut version of *Gone with the Wind* commenced. My eyelids became heavier and heavier, the theatre filled with smoke and gradually I drifted off to sleep.

The first I knew about it was a gentle shake and the refined countenance of Princess Grace outlined before me.

'You're snoring, my dear,' she said and suddenly, I was wide awake.

That was my second blunder and I only learned of the first when we retired for a midnight dinner and I shared my table with the French actress Jeanne Moreau and an illustrious group of gentlemen, who had all found my approach to the speech the most entertaining part of the evening. I sat that night with Danny Kaye, Marcello Mastroianni and Omar Sharif.

By the time I got back to my room, I felt wonderful. If all the snobs and all the people with titles found my mistake an embarrassment, that was their problem. I had meant no offence and my approach in no way reflected my respect for Vivien Leigh.

The end result came the next day when a dozen photographers got together and invited me to a picture session on the small pier in Cannes. I wore skin-tight pink jeans and a white shirt without a bra and made everybody's day by falling into the sea. The Italian and French photographers thought it was great, me appearing from the water with my hair over my face and my clothes stuck to every curve, although my infamy was spreading and Jean Diamond was getting angry.

'What do you think this sort of thing is going to do to your career?' she said. 'You're an actress, not a glamour girl.'

I pouted and stormed off. I hated travelling with another

45

woman, they were no fun at all. I went back to my room and locked the door. I stood under the shower for a long time and re-entered the day with a fresh smile. I immediately telephoned Irv Levin and told him I was unhappy.

Two days later, he was there in Cannes. We sat out the end of the film festival and left together for the small airport in Nice, Jean Diamond's parting words still ringing in my ears: 'I'm warning you, Carol, you're playing a dangerous game.'

I didn't know what she meant and I didn't care. I was happy to be with Irv Levin, flying south to Naples and on to a small village where we found a secluded hotel on a deserted beach. The week that followed was one of the happiest of my life, long hours of sunbathing and swimming and warm nights shared in the arms of a man who loved me. I wanted the freedom to last forever, but the house of playing cards we built came tumbling down when responsibilities called from the outside world. When I telephoned Mike to inquire about the boys, he threatened to take them away with him, and when Irv called Lenny the picture became even blacker. She had guessed that Irv was with me and had tried to commit suicide. That was the end of our secret holiday. We left immediately for Rome, Irv flew to Los Angeles and I returned to London to commence divorce proceedings.

I was soon bored being in London by myself. My relationship with Irv had been left hanging and I had no intention of waiting, just in case. Jean Diamond was relieved, for Irv Levin was the 'dangerous game' I had been playing and she set about ending it once and for all by introducing me to the Jugoslavian actor Bekim Femu, who had just been cast in Harold Robbins' *The Adventurers*. Bekim was absolutely gorgeous, which was just what I needed. His English, although better than my French, wasn't that good, and the night we met I offered to give him English lessons. He had an apartment in Park Lane, which is where I went the next day and for many afternoons that summer. I made sure Bekim's pronunciation was correct and he made payment in ways other than in cash. He was fiery and filled with Slavic passion. Even more important at that time, I managed not to take it all too seriously; I didn't think I was being unfair to Irv Levin and I wasn't cheating on Bekim Femu when Oliver Reed turned up on my doorstep one evening.

It was marvellous to be so free, to go where I wanted and to spend my time with the people I chose to be with. It was a new and refreshing feeling. When I was young and first making films my parents were strict, or at least I thought so, and by the time I was nineteen I was pregnant and married. Now, I was my own boss. The little house in Putney was fully paid for, I was released from the responsibilities of marriage, free from the ties of a permanent relationship and I was ready to throw myself into any adventure that came along. Oliver Reed standing on the doorstep with his mischievous grin and the bottle of Dom Pérignon that he carried like a calling card was just what I had been waiting for.

'And what's my naughty little girl been up to?' he said, kissing me lightly on the cheek and pacing through to the kitchen.

'I spent my whole life dreaming of you, Oliver, what else?' I joked.

'I hear tell you were the talk of the South of France,' he continued, popping the champagne and spilling the drink into two glasses.

'Bad news travels fast,' I said.

He held out the two glasses and I took one. 'Bad news, little one?' he said. 'On the contrary. I was told you were sensational.'

Oliver always spoke to me as if I were a child; I think he did it with all the ladies. He was like a great big cuddly bear and it didn't matter what he did or said, it was impossible to get angry with him. We finished the champagne between us, Sean and Stephen stayed with a babysitter and we went out that evening for a meal. The yellow E-type that Oliver had

47

been so fond of had been exchanged for a Rolls Royce; a mark of success, another sign that the age was passing? For Oliver, perhaps not.

The house where I lived was in a quiet square, with a central garden of neatly clipped grass and flower beds. On the grass was a blow-up paddling pool where the children played; the mums all sat in deck chairs, reading and talking, and the sun set across the square's one open side and remained warm until early evening. My middle-class neighbours were used to Oliver and his antics, although nothing quite surpassed the time he arrived in one of his inebriated stupors and plunged fully-dressed into the pool. The children thought it was great fun and the housewives had a dinner party story that would last them a lifetime. He seemed quite pleased with himself as he dripped his way from the square and into my kitchen, although his smile became a look of absolute shock when he discovered that I did not own a clothes dryer. Still dripping and smiling once again, I led Oliver to my car and drove him to the laundromat in Putney High Street. He stripped to his underpants, to the amusement of everyone doing their laundry, and while the clothes spun round in the dryer, he formed all the old ladies into a chorus and coaxed them into joining his song and dance routine. Everyone knew who we both were, which I found embarrassing, but Oliver was always too well lubricated to care.

The paddling pool incident wasn't the first time Oliver had gone for a swim with his clothes on. When we were making *I'll Never Forget What's His Name* the previous year, he fell into the river at Cambridge and ruined the suit that had been specially made for the film. It shrunk in the dryer and there was a week of delay in filming while another one was made. We spent that week snuggled up warmly in an hotel bed.

I thought at the time that Oliver's ducking had been an accident, although now, I'm not so sure!

When I wasn't busy with Oliver's escapades and my part-time Slavic romance, I had the divorce to worry about. There was a dispute over the custody of Sean and Stephen and the proceedings seemed to be getting nowhere. The lawyers sent squadrons of letters and I watched the bills creep from three figures to four figures and on into telephone numbers. I was used to having agents and managers dealing with the little problems of life and I elected to go the same way, changing from one firm of solicitors to the next, in the hope that a new face would speed the process to completion. I thought I knew what waiting was all about, being in show business, although I now learned that the men of law have made adjournments into an art form.

In July, I had my second brush with the nobility, when I was invited to the Royal Command Performance of *Romeo and Juliet* at the Odeon, in Leicester Square. This time, even I didn't dare wear my mini-dress and went all formal in a yellow chiffon gown. The dress was Grecian-style and very low cut, the same as the dress I had rejected in Cannes, but now I felt a lot more secure. Hobnobbing with the Royal Family was one of the by-products of success. I lined up alongside Tommy Steele, Joan Collins, Richard Attenborough and Lynn Redgrave, all tense and excited as the Queen and the Duke of Edinburgh moved slowly along the red carpet, with Prince Charles and the other dignitaries in their wake. The Queen and the Duke had reached the entrance to the auditorium just as Charles was shaking my hand.

'I loved *Poor Cow*,' he whispered. 'I had to sneak out of school to go and see it.'

I replied with a blush and, as Charles said something else, the press photographers captured us sharing a smile. We were still speaking when the Duke of Edinburgh returned back along the red carpet with the message: 'Do come along, Charles, your mother is waiting.'

'Coming, father,' he replied, turning to me with a last smile. 'Well, it has been jolly nice talking to you. Good luck with your next film.'

The next day, nearly every newspaper in the country carried the picture of the prince and I on their front pages with the traditional question mark hanging in the air: Will this be the next Queen of England?

Dad had pushed me to aim for the top, but that was going a little bit too far!

Following the performance, there was a late dinner at the Dorchester. I went in with Bekim Femu, but I was introduced to Chaim Topol and spent the rest of the evening dancing with him. Like Irv Levin, Topol, as everyone called him, was an Israeli and exuded all of the charm and magnetism that went with success. He had opened in *Fiddler on the Roof* the previous year and the play had been one of the biggest things ever to hit London. From dancing in his arms that night, we met the next day for lunch and lunch turned out to be even more exciting than I expected. He was a fascinating man.

The summer was turning out to be very full and when I wasn't speaking with the solicitors about my divorce, I was juggling times and places with my men friends. It all went quite smoothly until I spent a night away from home and the telephone rang at two in the morning.

I was with Bekim Femu, but my instincts told me that something had happened to one of my children and the call was for me. It turned out that I couldn't have been more wrong. The call was from Bekim's mother, long-distance from Jugoslavia. While we had spent the night making love, Bekim's wife had given birth to a son. He had never told me that he was married and somehow that seemed dishonest. The relationship had never been serious, but now I felt tainted and dirty.

The next day, Bekim Femu flew to Jugoslavia and I didn't care if I never saw him again.

* * *

I was due for another disappointment to offset the good times of that summer, although I had few spare moments in which to brood over anything. Since parting from Mike, I had slipped from one man's arms to the next, keeping alive the myth of the sixties and creating deep-rooted problems that time would make manifest. I should have sat down right then and worked out who I was and where I was going, but my career had reached another set of crossroads and the dilemma of making the right choice overshadowed any doubts I may have had concerning the way I lived my life. It appeared that, for me, nothing was ever going to be simple. The previous year I had made two films at the same time and I would have done so again, but for the Atlantic Ocean that separated the locations!

Shortly after the Royal Command Performance, I had gone to a meeting with the director Ken Russell, a man whose work I admired tremendously. He wanted me to play opposite Glenda Jackson in the D.H. Lawrence classic *Women in Love*. Oliver Reed had already signed for the male lead. It was a great opportunity and the right move in my career, but at the time, I wasn't so sure. I was used to playing strong, independent women and Ken had cast me as the weak-willed, unsure female, against Glenda's all-powerful, domineering role. It was a compliment that Ken Russell believed in me and was aware that I had the ability to put myself into such a part, but while I thought it through, Irv Levin called from Los Angeles. He had said that he wanted me for his next film back in January. It was now August and the right one had appeared.

He sent the script on the overnight plane; I read it and I still wasn't sure. As screenplays go, it wasn't that bad, but compared to the D.H.Lawrence story, it was trite and mediocre. One advantage in Irv Levin's *Daddy's Gone a Hunting* was that I had the major role and would receive star billing. In *Women in Love*, my name would appear second, or even third in the list of credits. Performers are always concerned with this condition in their contracts and

51

leave the money wrangles up to their agents and managers. I was torn between the Hollywood glitter and Ken Russell's reputation for brilliance; my name carved in neon tubes and the flawless treatment of a piece of literature; the devil and the deep blue sea.

The advantages and disadvantages popped up and down like carousel horses spinning in my head. I talked to all my friends, even Topol while I was at his flat, and he tried to advise me, but everyone's advice had been different, which made me more confused and added to the bitterness I felt towards Bekim Femu. Suddenly, I felt so depressed I started to cry, and with Topol's strong shoulder to lean on, I blurted out my long tale of woe. When my sobs finally died down, he cupped my cheeks in his hands and stared into my eyes.

'You are a very complicated girl, Carol,' he whispered. 'I cannot see why such a thing should make you so unhappy.'

'Why not?'

'Well, I too am married.'

For a few seconds I was speechless. I pulled myself away and said angrily, 'Then why the hell didn't you tell me?'

'I didn't tell you, because I introduced you to my wife; the first time we met.'

No doubt it was true. That night at the Dorchester I drank a lot of champagne and friends' wives or husbands were not people I tended to remember.

The long hot summer had come to an end. I had a lot to think about as I drove slowly home from Maida Vale; it was raining and the windscreen wipers flowed back and forth in wide, mesmerising arcs. I couldn't recall having used them before. Bekim Femu, Topol, Oliver Reed, all were suddenly forgotten and my mind lifted away from the grey streets and grey skies of London as I remembered the pink glow that washed the night sky over Sunset Boulevard. I was through with playing the dumb blonde with married men. I felt that I had been used and mistreated and I now yearned for a new direction. California had opened its arms and I longed to go.

There was one more factor in my choice between filming

in England and going to the United States. It hadn't been that important, but then, perhaps it was an indication of where my career might go. Ken Russell had offered me £10,000 to appear in *Women in Love*, half what I had been paid for a cameo role in *The Fixer*. National General were talking in terms of a three picture contract and I was offered $150,000 for *Daddy's Gone a Hunting* which, in 1968, was staggering.

By the time I parked my car in the little square the decision had been made. I called my agent, contracts were signed and on a leaf-blown day less than two weeks later, I was flying Pan Am flight number 171 to Los Angeles. With me were my Irish nanny, Mary and my two sons, Sean and Stephen. Hollywood beckoned, like the gold at the end of the rainbow.

It was the biggest mistake of my whole life.

Four

THE SPINNING slowed to a stop; my limbs ached, my eyelids were heavy and my mouth tasted awful. I felt as if I had been through a long illness; I was weak and drained, but I was completely relaxed. It was many minutes before I was able to work out where I was; for I hadn't merely awoken, I felt reborn. My memory was a blank, but I was sure of one thing: I was at peace with myself and I was happy.

I remained in the same position, staring at the ceiling above, searching for the part of myself that had been there. It now seemed such a long time ago. I had been through the toughest test of my life – and I had survived. Now, piece by piece, the jigsaw puzzle of the past formed a rough pattern; it would remain vague for months and some of the pieces would be lost forever, but one thing was clear, I knew what had led me to that small, white-walled room.

Nothing had been going right. I felt that I had failed as a mother, failed as a human being. Success? Yes, I had made a lot of movies; I had slept with a lot of men. But what did it all mean; what was it all for? Inside, there was no peace. I had worked to reach the top, expecting to find something special; Eldorado, Shangri-la, Nirvana, heaven upon life's yellow brick road. But it wasn't there. Money and recognition found you at the same place that you left behind, only now everything was coated in a bright plastic gloss. The people weren't more exciting, in fact in Hollywood they were usually more boring. The only escape was the unlimited supply of drink and drugs that combined to make the plastic seem like glitter, the tiresome parties where, by going over the top, even the ageing executives became more interesting.

While the bottle and the bank account remained full, there was always tomorrow.

I was living in a big house on the beach with my ex-husband. Not Mike King; we had parted so long ago that we were once again close friends. In the April of 1972, I married Stuart Lerner, a Beverly Hills psychiatrist; it was a mistake from the beginning. I married Stuart because he happened to be there at the right time and he married me because I was an actress. We had broken up and come back together too many times for me to count, but Stuart's home was now the home of Sean and Stephen and it was to them that I always returned.

They had been dragged around the world for nearly ten years and I was reluctant to move them away from their permanent home and friends at the Malibu Park Junior High School. I was doing the right thing by them, but it was no good for me. The unhappiness became depression and the safety valve was a drinking and drugs binge that I couldn't escape. I lived a strange, nocturnal existence, Stuart going off to his practice while I slept, only for me to arise as soon as he entered the bedroom. I was slipping further from reality. I had always worked and it was important to me, but now there was no point. The money I had earned in Hollywood was growing dusty in the bank, while Stuart's introduction to the disillusioned world of show business created a full diary and more of what we already had – money.

For a while, I thought I had everything under control. I wasn't happy, but I was sure that even this was temporary. The drugs made the days pass more quickly, but in time I became dependent on them; the bright colours became gloomy and the euphoria withered into an anxious, painful craving. I needed cocaine to make me alert, Quaaludes to relax, Valium to sleep and vodka to handle the people who came to the house.

My own friends had vanished and most of the visitors were Stuart's psychiatric patients; people in the same state as myself. What they couldn't see, what I couldn't see, was that

55

we were all suffering from the same thing: Boredom. During the struggle to reach the top, every second was important. Life was fast and dangerous, but the long heady climb up the ladder was the very thing that kept you sane. Success results in too much time and too much money and the combination is disastrous. I had reached the stage of not caring. It didn't matter what drugs I used, so long as they got me high and helped me to forget myself.

People came and went at all hours; I didn't know who they were and it didn't even matter. Dope dealers arrived when Stuart was out. We would smoke a joint together and I would hand over a wad of notes in exchange for little packets of pills and powder. The house became a 'scene' and strange, pointless parties blossomed and faded without plan or pleasure. I was crossing the road from being a drug user to an addict, and would have taken that final step had it not been for the fact that one night an old friend turned up at the house and took it upon himself to save me.

His name was Craig Shipp, a born-again Christian, who left the party early, but returned the next day with all the dedication and zeal of the newly converted. He read me parables and gave me prayer cards and I listened with the patience of one who had given up caring. His words seemed wise while he sat there, but the second he left it was back to the bag of pills and the cabinet of alcohol. The world only looked fine through the distortion at the bottom of a bottle. Craig was joined by a reformed heroin addict named David, I never learned his second name, and a young man named Michael Arnold, who appeared as a sort of symbol of youth and vitality. Craig kept up his daily sermon and David joined in with words he quoted like a mantra: 'If I can do it so can you.' It went on for days and weeks, I no longer noticed the divisions, but when Michael Arnold saw that it was making no difference he took it upon himself to 'save' me. With his reluctant friends in tow, he came to the house when no one else was there and insisted that I left with him.

'What is this, some kind of joke?' I said.

Michael Arnold looked at me with clear, steel-grey eyes and replied, 'If you like!'

He was a man of few words, but I knew he wasn't joking. I went to the bedroom and stored my precious bottles of drugs with a few clothes in a shoulder bag. I looked at the wardrobes, all heavy with fur coats and designer dresses from Paris. I was wearing white shorts and a yellow tee-shirt and the other things suddenly seemed stupid. I wasn't sure why I was going, but I shrugged, looked at myself in the mirror and joined my escorts. We drove from Malibu to Newport Beach; I hadn't seen so many cars and so many people for months.

I was happy to be in a different environment, but soon after my arrival Michael saw my bag full of drugs and snatched them away from me. He strode to the bathroom and flushed the whole lot down the lavatory. Everything that kept me alive was there, the uppers, the downers, sleeping pills and speed, pills of every colour, shape and size and suddenly they were gone. I went berserk. I punched and scratched my tormentor, but he just laughed. In that second, I had never hated anyone quite as much as I hated Michael Arnold.

When my anger subsided, I collapsed into my first fit of withdrawals. My throat was parched, my stomach was knotted and twisted, the cramps making me roll into a ball and scream out for help. Craig was still trying to sell me Christianity; David repeated the same words over and over again: You can do it. You can do it. I pleaded for a drink and threw the glass across the room when I saw it was only water. I ran around in circles, pulling books from the shelves and tearing pictures from the wall, but the three young men remained passive and ignored me. I needed a drink, I needed sleep, I needed so many things and I was given nothing; nothing but prayer cards and quotes from the Bible.

'Jesus freaks, that's all I need,' I shouted, throwing the cards across the room. Craig patiently picked them up and I collapsed with an even greater pain in my stomach.

'I was a heroin addict,' David said again. 'If I can do it, so can you.'

He sounded like a worn-out record and I now hated him as much as I hated Michael.

Hours passed into days. I was there with the three of them and then I was alone again. It was all distorted and confusing, the withdrawals becoming worse, my head spinning through unknown depths of depression. I begged for some Valium so that I could relax, but there was none. Each day the withdrawals became worse and each day my gaolers denied me drugs. I now felt that I was in prison. I asked for a telephone, so that I could speak to my sons, but it had disappeared.

'They'll worry about me,' I kept saying, only to be given the same reply.

'You'll be no good for your sons until you learn to love yourself,' said Michael.

It was Craig, still reading me psalms and Bible quotations, while I lay in pain upon the floor, crying and sweating and wishing that I was dead. David disappeared and Michael remained distant and out of reach. He looked at me with his passive, dark eyes, but I was unable to see what was behind them.

The withdrawals went on for a week and finally I felt the same old breakdown symptoms swimming into my mind. I knew if I went back to the Camarillo State Hospital that I would never get out again. Now, it no longer even mattered. I had gone beyond the need of drugs and only yearned for peace. Suddenly I was left alone. I thought about escaping, but what was the point? It was dark, a silver half-moon waltzing eerie patterns upon the wall. I went to the bathroom and looked at myself in the mirror; I was worn out, the flicker of life now missing from my eyes. As I started out for the meditation room, my room, the corridor seemed so long and I had the fleeting glimpse of an old elephant, wandering off alone into the jungle to die!

Nothing was clear except the narrow bed and, as I curled up into the foetus position, my thoughts became a surrealist movie with time juggled into abstraction and me both the main character and the audience of one. I appeared neither as good nor bad; simply human. There was no one to judge me but myself and, ultimately, that was how it should be. Life was a trial, for me, for everyone, but in the final analysis, it was too precious a gift to discard so readily.

The drugs trip had been a result of boredom, but there was more to it than that. I suddenly realised that I had no friends. Success only comes to those who constantly strive to reach it and when that plateau appears beneath your feet, you look around and find yourself in a very lonely place. The people from the past may look upon you with awe or envy, which is no foundation for friendship, and the new friends who appear on the high ground are like members of a very private and exclusive club – we love you while you're here, but it goes no deeper than that. I had gone from rags to riches along the traditional path, but I had never lost sight of my roots; amidst the glitter, I was haunted by the riddle: Why me? I expected to find peace at the end of the ladder, and the knowledge that there was no peace or happiness anywhere but within yourself had been a long time coming.

The prayer cards that Craig Shipp had given me suddenly assumed greater meaning. To say that I was a born-again Christian when I awoke that morning wouldn't be strictly true, but I certainly had greater empathy with Craig's beliefs and I had surely been reborn. The ghost of Carol White had been my shadow and a death wish had been my driving force since I was sixteen years old. The out-of-body experience had all the elements of a vision and out of the confusion I had found the light. The past had been cut from me like a tumour and I knew my life would start once again.

I remained staring at the white ceiling above me for a long time until suddenly, I felt ravenous.

I walked slowly to the kitchen. My legs were tired and I felt very weak. Michael Arnold was sitting at the table.

'Want some orange?' he said. I sat down and took the glass of juice. 'How is it?'

'It's wonderful,' I replied, my voice barely a whisper.

Michael cooked eggs and American pancakes and I ate with a new appetite, everything tasted so good. He sat down with a pot of coffee and as I looked into his eyes, I saw that they were not cold and grey, but the brightest blue I had ever seen.

Everything then happened very quickly. Within a few days, my London agent, Michael Linnit, called with the news that I had been nominated for the *Evening News* Best Actress Award, for my performance in *The Squeeze*. There was nothing for me in Los Angeles. Stuart Lerner was busy with his practice and wealthy, rock-star patients; Sean and Stephen had their own lives and friends. I packed my bags and, with Michael Arnold as my companion knight, I flew first to Boston and then home once again to England.

We stayed at the Kensington Hilton, the atmosphere and spirit of London like a tonic that made me feel alive and prepared for whatever life had to offer. Michael was fired with the same feeling. It was his first trip to London and he spent days going out and getting lost, then returning to the hotel by taxi. It was on one of these excursions that he met a gregarious cabbie who said in the course of conversation that his main interest was boxing.

'That a fact?' Michael said. 'My lady friend's father was a boxer in London.'

'Was he? What was his name?'

'Joe White.'

'Joe White? Not from Hammersmith?'

'I think that's the place,' Michael said.

'Me and Joe White were friends for years. His daughter's the film star, Carol White.'

'I know. That's who I'm with.'

'Well, I'll be ... '

Michael invited the cabbie for a drink and we met in the hotel lounge, where I was having tea. He went to the bar to order two brandies and the taxi driver just stood there and looked at me in a bewildered silence.

'Carol White!' he said at last. 'I'll tell you something, I've known you since you were four years old.'

Five

SOMETIMES I would sit on the back doorstep for hours, staring at the sky. Even as a child, I knew that something was going to happen.

The winter had been endless, very grey and very cold, but suddenly it was spring and everything was growing.

It was March 1948. People had stopped talking about the war and although there were still food shortages and rationing, the streets were filled with big prams and new babies. I was four, very grown up, and I would soon be having a birthday.

The yard was in shadow, but a small square of sunlight found its way onto the step and I was able to warm my knees and look upon all the exciting things. Dad was a rag and bone man, so instead of flowers and fruit trees, my world was filled with scrap metal, old bicycle frames, brass taps and wash-tubs, door handles with beautiful patterns and a big pot like a witch's cauldron that bubbled with melting lead. As I grew older, it became my job to stand there and stir it. In the corner of the yard was a large bench, where the metal was sawn into shorter lengths, and below this there were tea chests filled with hardback books and framed pictures of fine ladies and important-looking men. The brass bedstead that had been saved for something leaned sideways against a wall and served very well as a ladder. I also had great fun building pyramids with the half-filled paint tins and there was a cracked, willow-patterned teapot that looked just right for makebelieve tea parties. There were buckets of rusty nails, ancient gardening tools, toilet seats, sinks, chests with missing drawers and a mountain of useless gas masks and dented tin helmets. Everything was interesting, but most of all I liked the clothes.

Dad cleared houses when people died, so there was always an endless supply of costumes, dusty old things that had been forgotten in wardrobes, Victorian dresses with fine lacework, hats with veils, army trench coats with brass buttons and leather boots that smelled terrible and went mouldy when it rained. There were parasols, strange pieces of underwear that amused the boys and plastic jewellery that couldn't be sold in the shop.

When I was by myself, I was happy just to sit, polishing the step thin, as mum would say, gazing up at the clouds and laughing at the startled faces they formed. I'd be wearing a long flowered dress and smart shoes, mum only bought the best, my face usually streaked with dirt and my hair cut in the latest post-war fashion. I was tubby, had a big smile, bright eyes and was happiest when I was getting into mischief.

This usually required the assistance of the swarms of children drawn to the adventures only found in Joe White's scrapyard; although little did they know that the adventures were always theatre and they were the supporting cast.

My daydreams had always been visual and I'm sure I was acting by the time I could walk. Now, as a four year old who was about to have a birthday, my stories had become complicated sagas; I always cast myself as a love-lost heroine and the best looking boy as my Romeo. The performances went on for hours, there were lots of scene changes, constant dressing and undressing until, finally, I wilted into the arms of my beloved and everyone lived happily ever after. The war years had made a strong impression on me and in most of the plays the boys would have missing arms and awful limps, and the girls would nurse plastic babies with bandaged heads and gaping holes where legs should have been. I had hundreds of dolls, but none of them was complete.

My stories had plenty of action, sword fights, charging cavalry, fighter planes, wounded soldiers who took hours to die and whose mums would thrash them for ruining their clothes in the scrapyard, double crossings and subterfuge, Hollywood upon the London streets of Hammersmith and always, but always that element of romance – me loving two men at the same time and creating a pattern that would haunt me in the years to come. My plays were invariably serious and a little sad and it took me a long time to realise that life wears the same two masks as the theatre, a comedy, as well as a tragedy. Such thoughts, though, never touched those early years. Everyone was poor and everyone had big dreams; all small children imagine themselves as film stars, their stage the twelve-by-twelve living rooms, with overlarge furniture, plaster ornaments, flying ducks, china dogs and a half-moon rug often filled with a recumbent greyhound – or, in our case, an ancient Alsatian named Nell.

Our house was a little different, with the shop on the corner, the scrapyard and an old garage where Snowy the cart horse lived. Next to the garage was a bomb site and opposite stood the Royal Napier, the local pub and focal point of all the grown ups. Dad went there every day for his pint, even when there was no money for food. Everyone in Hammersmith knew Joe White and his influence on my childhood was immense. He was a carefree, life-loving man who felt that he had missed out by not making a career in show business. As a young boy he ran away with the circus, he travelled with gypsies and over the years he learned to turn his hand to anything. As a teenager, he was making secret potions, like the Mid-West snake-oil men, the elixir of life that may have been laughed at by the sophisticated Cockneys, but cost a penny a bottle to make and sold for £1 a bottle amongst the farming peasants of Devon and Cornwall. He then became a prize fighter, slogging it out with bare fists and only taking home some money if he was lucky enough to have won. The living room and the shop in Great Church Lane were filled with trophies and me-mentoes.

Dad was always looking to make his fortune. He realised

that prize fighting outside the pubs wasn't going to be the way; he had one good win, put all his money together and acquired a barrow in the local market, calling out his wares in true Petticoat Lane fashion and assuring the public that everything had just fallen from the back of a lorry ... which wasn't far from the truth. Needless to say, he did not become a millionaire, unlike Lord Cohen, who started out with a stall in Ridley Road market and ended up owning Tesco's. Dad's progression was to vaudeville, a good grafter is more concerned with his act than the takings, moving on to the variety hall circuit and even forming a double act with Tommy Trinder, a life-long friend who went on to become the compere of *Sunday Night at the London Palladium*, the highlight of the week's television when I was growing up.

Unlike Tommy, dad never hit the big time, money was always tight and when he got the chance to make a better living collecting scrap iron, the way he had learned in his travelling days, he took it. He was a talented man, capable of doing almost anything – and capable of the most violent temper to match his kindness. As a child, I was embraced by his strong limbs and boundless charisma; I remember the smell of sweat and manliness, his powerful legs when he sat me on his knee and the faces of people who greeted him in the street.

Jane came along when I was two, Barry was already a big boy and going to school and, three years after Jane, Joe Junior was born. Dad loved us all, but in his eyes I saw a special feeling that he saved for me; an anxiety and pride, a love that bordered on passion and was to come between my mother and I in later years. Since childhood, I have seen the look of love many times, but if there was ever a man who would have laid his life on the line for me, my father was that man.

His death was drawn out and very sad, but that, too, was way in the future and during those early years, dad was the centre of everything that was important to me.

I can see him now, telling his stories, surrounded by

workmen in their cloth caps and mufflers, or the little boys in the yard who watched in awe as dad lifted the moulded blocks of lead on to the back of his cart. Even when there was snow on the ground, and it seemed to snow every winter when I was a child, he would work in his shirtsleeves, his bare neck and arms always red and filled with muscles. Everyone enjoyed his company, he would do anyone a good turn and, nine times out of ten, when he got drunk he would give all his money away. But there was also that dark side to his character, a violent, uncontrollable temper that may have been useful in prize fighting, but frightened the life out of me when he brought it home with him from the pub at night. His eyes would glaze over with a sort of schizophrenic madness and a distraught Mr Hyde would yell at the top of his voice and chase mum through the house with a carving knife.

She was able to give as well as she got and some mornings they would both appear festooned in bandages and sticking plaster. Once I remember mum pulling the heavy black telephone from the wall and beating dad over the head with it; another time, they broke every piece of crockery we possessed, throwing the cups and saucers across the kitchen and yelling the most awful curses. They both had strong personalities and I knew they always loved each other.

In those days the fights seemed natural. They were working class people who aired their problems in front of everyone; nobody cared what the neighbours were going to think and the neighbours all went through the same scenes. But people didn't have our modern hang-ups and, although the fights were a part of the way we lived, they lacked today's mindless violence; nobody carried guns, just honest fists and a handshake the next day. Punch ups in the pub happened all the time, it was usually over the ladies, and dad often had scuffles in the shop, although they were for a quite different reason: the class struggle. The dialogue was always much the same:

'So I'm doing a bitta work in the corner and this 'ere toffee nose comes in an' says: "I say my good man ... " So I says:

Don't you my good man me; he gives me some lip, so I wallops 'im!'

Dad would now be sitting at the bar in the Napier, surrounded by admirers, his glass refilling as if by magic. On those days, mum would cover his dinner with a saucepan lid and deliver it across the road for dad to eat while he told his tale.

This was my life: the endless drama in the scrapyard, riding the streets with dad on a Saturday afternoon, collecting junk and talking to the people, working class Londoners, Cockneys from beyond the sound of Bow Bells, but Cockneys nonetheless. They enjoyed the life for what it was, the singsongs and punch ups, pie and mash at the eel shop, dart matches and football, the horses, dancing on a Saturday night, everything and everyone giving London its charm and its colour. So many things which have disappeared forever: the knife grinder with his bicycle, the chestnut man with his brazier of glowing coals, the Pearly King and Queen, the organ grinder with his little monkey and tin cup, the old soldiers selling matches, the street actors and sand dancers – everyone so filled with life that it was impossible to see that they lived in a world that was changing.

Nowhere has the same atmosphere as London, the poverty, yet the humour, the huge markets with their bustling crowds, the smell of fish wafting from the Thames and settling on the street stalls, the piles of polished vegetables, trucks rumbling over cobblestones, women in pinafores, workmen with calloused hands and lots of children still not wearing shoes. Maybe the whole world isn't a stage, but London, the London beyond the mansion houses and stockbroker suburbs, was, for me, the biggest stage of all.

Now, my home is in Hollywood and my sons have American accents, but still my heart remains with that tide of back-to-back houses and the people who make London a very special place.

I think of London, but in those days, it was only Hammersmith, a village where everyone knew everyone and neighbours had a warmth that went beyond the occasional fist fight. They had all lived through something together. Great Church Lane led to the Broadway and on to Hammersmith Bridge. The docks and warehouses were a regular target for Hitler's Luftwaffe, but countless stray buzz bombs and doodlebugs found their way into the maze of small houses. There were lots of bomb sites where the children played and, after the war, the council finished the Luftwaffe's job and most of the area was pulled down. The house, the shop and the garage that sheltered Snowy have all gone and a block of flats now fills that same corner.

I was born on 1 April 1943 at six minutes past midnight – just long enough to become an April Fool and find myself a constant butt for jokes, especially from childhood boyfriends. Germany's spread across Europe had already been stemmed, but the air raids on London continued and many times I would wake to the sound of falling bombs, mum checking the blackout curtains and staying beside me until the danger passed. I missed her comforting hand when, towards the end of the war, she had complications with the birth of my sister Jane and had to spend several weeks in hospital. Dad's rag and bone business wasn't earning enough to feed us and he spent every evening travelling the streets of the West End on a bicycle, acquiring the 'knowledge' and finally getting a more regular income behind the wheel of a Hackney Carriage, London's world-famous taxis. Dad passed the test while mum was in hospital. There was no one to look after me and so I spent long, cold days in the taxi's open luggage area, strapped in with the suitcases and coats. It was a good way for dad to earn extra money. The passengers would look at me, my ears red and my teeth chattering, they would pay dad the fare and give me a large tip.

The war was coming to an end, but still there were days when the sky was bright red, the fires burning through the night and on into the day; fire engines with ringing bells and people standing on street corners, their faces blank and their homes just a pile of rubble. It was all so ephemeral, but it taught me not to worry about money and possessions.

Millions of dollars have slipped through my fingers, but like my father, I was always sure that something was just around the corner. All through my childhood, there were times of plenty, when we were all bought new clothes and taken for long holidays in Brighton; the money would go and a period of poverty would set in. We would spend three months eating nothing but potato stew and dad would complain because he didn't even have enough money for a pint. Something always turned up and, if it took too long, mum was versatile enough to weather the storm. Joan White was just as adaptable as her husband. I didn't really notice the shifts in our finances, but felt especially lucky that dad had always been there. Most dads were away 'in the war' and lots of them never returned. My own father joined up in 1939; he was an obvious leader and soon rose to the rank of sergeant, but he was a man with no regard for discipline. He went AWOL several times, he was busted to private and eventually given his marching orders. When I was nine and went to the Corona Stage School, I discovered who I took after!

When I wasn't out collecting scrap iron with dad, I played street games with the other children: hopscotch, skipping, Tin Tan Tommy, which was a sort of glorified hide and seek, war games, chase games and one amusement that was favoured by us all. It was called Knock Down Ginger and really required the cover of darkness. I was an eager initiate, although it was a few more years before I became a regular player. There were only two rules: 1: Be as daring as possible; 2: Don't get caught. The rest was easy. You went down the street banging on all the doors and ran away before the occupants realised it was 'those bloody kids again'. Our leader was a little spotty boy named Johnny, who took all the children to the flats by Hammersmith Bridge and improved upon the game by looping all the door knockers together and knocking down whole rows of Gingers from the entrance to the flats. A dozen men in braces and carpet slippers would chase down the stairs, but we always had a good head start.

When I wasn't out knocking on doors and being a tomboy, I found the role as mother's little helper just as easy. I would wear my pretty clothes, comb my mousy, oft-cut hair and act as if butter wouldn't melt in my mouth.

Sunday mornings I would spend hours in the kitchen, up to my elbows in flour, cutting the corners off potatoes, shelling peas and trying not to make a mess; Jane was just a toddler and getting into everything, Barry out back trying to make a bicycle without sufficient parts and dad wandering in and out in his baggy trousers, slapping the newspaper with the back of his hand and threatening to vote Conservative next time ... we lived in a Labour stronghold. Mum would be wearing an apron over one of her good dresses, stockings and shoes, even if she wasn't going out, the radio playing the big band tunes popular after the war and mum singing at the top of her voice.

The radio was still called a wireless and we had owned one for as long as I could remember, which wasn't the case with some of our neighbours. Those people who were too poor to afford such a luxury would come to our house on special occasions and listen to the speaking crystals as if it was an act of black magic. At Christmas there were plays and royal messages and those same people would don their Sunday suits and look very funny, wearing serious faces below brightly coloured paper hats. The floor would be littered with small parcels and bottles of brown ale and dad would hand out cigars to all the men, the smoke filling the small room and making patterns through the paper chains and pine tree. They were good times in spite of the shortages, although that whole post-war feeling of togetherness seemed to fade very quickly. By 1953, nearly everyone had their own

70

nine-inch television set, bought in time to see the coronation of Queen Elizabeth, and neighbours were spending less time in each other's living rooms.

When they weren't listening to the radio, mum and dad and their friends would amuse themselves by telling stories and having a singsong, as much a part of London life as the cobblestones and black taxis. One of the men played an accordion and there was always somebody who could coax a tune from the ancient, upright piano. The pubs were always full, the kids hanging around the door and the boys creeping in to take a swig from unguarded pints. At home it would be the same, everyone taking it in turns to perform their special piece, no one inhibited or bothering to make judgements; it was the doing that mattered, not being best.

It was upon this stage and with everyone's encouragement, that I premiered my own charades and musical offerings.

After we had all taken our turn, all eyes would turn to George, a Cockney pensioner who, to me, seemed to be at least one hundred years old. He had a long, dangling moustache, a thick black waistcoat, a white silk scarf and a flat cap that never left his head. The room would go quiet and George would stamp his boot and sing endless verses of Cockney rhyming slang, stories and ballads and in a language that no one down the road in Knightsbridge would understand. I heard the songs hundreds of times, but only this short piece has remained in my memory:

> She was walking' danna street
> On 'er fancy plates of meat
> Wiva summa sun shine smilin'
> Frough 'er golden barnet fair,
> Bright as angels from the skies
> Were 'er bright blue mutton pies
> In me east and west Ol' Cupid
> Shota shaft and left it there ...

71

Like most pieces of good poetry, it loses too much to make a translation worthwhile.

At the end of the summer each year it was time for the pub beano, when everyone clubbed together, hired a coach and exported their bottles of beer to the seaside; hours of promenading, jellied eels, rock, winkles and mussels, more beer, fishenchips from yesterday's *Daily Mirror* and the seafront at Southend or Margate littered with drunk Londoners. The purpose of the excursion was to see the lights, ride the merry-go-rounds and big dipper and smell the salt sea air, but more important was that sense of belonging that everyone felt on the coach ride home.

Most of my memories are jumbled and my early childhood years form one brightly coloured collage without space for anything drab or grey. So many events in our life improve with age and are better on reflection and, as I now think back, I find a lump in my throat and tears in my eyes. Whenever I return to London, I can't resist taking a drive through Hammersmith.

But I am still only four years old and this is a bright Sunday morning, dad tossing his paper across the room in disgust, Barry covered in oil and cursing the multi-holed inner tubes, mum still singing and rich gravy smells creeping from the gas stove and filling the kitchen. Again, unlike many of our neighbours, our Sunday dinner table was usually full. During the hard times, it was potatoes, three times a day, but when we were better off, mum would find enough money for a joint of beef or lamb, Yorkshire pudding made with the meat fat, apple pie and custard for dessert and rock cakes at tea time. Mum showed me how to bake scones, cook lamb's hearts with stuffing, boiled pork, pease pudding and carrots, pies with parsley sauce, liver and bacon, leftovers on Monday, fry ups on Tuesday, bubble and squeak, toad in the hole and fish and chips on a Friday night. I could recognise the days by what we were eating.

I don't want anyone to get the impression that the cupboard was forever overflowing. Apart from our own lean times, there was still rationing in the shops and lots of things would disappear for months at a time. Mum would spend hours in queues, because sausages were available off the ration card or a fresh load of Dutch Edam had arrived from the docks. What you could and couldn't get this week was one of the main topics of conversation. Everything we had was made at home, which meant shop-bought things seemed much more attractive. When off-the-peg trousers and suits first appeared, it was like a revolution.

It was the same with shop-bought treats, like the white-iced birthday cake that appeared mysteriously one day on the kitchen table. I saw it first, all creamy and tempting. Barry arrived with one of his friends, then Jennifer from the next street, then someone else and then ... it really was too much of a temptation. The cake had been left there by one of mum's friends, while they went off to the shops. When they arrived back with their shopping bags, not even a crumb could be found on the table. There weren't any children either; they were hiding somewhere with full tummies and vivid imaginations. Nobody in those days said it was unhealthy to give your kids a good hiding.

Clothes, too, were rationed, but even the very poor had clothes to wear, second-hand and hand-me-downs, but what really seemed to matter were shoes. There had been a time when inspectors visited the schools and checked the children's footwear, giving out tokens to children whose shoes were worn through and to those whose shoes were non-existent. The token shoes they received were all identical, sturdy boots with thick soles and straps; they lasted forever and they marked you as being destitute. I don't remember those times, but I do remember that mum would only buy the very best in footwear.

It was typical of mum; she was proud and strong and didn't want anything she hadn't worked for. Even with four children, for young Joseph was now on the way, she remained slender and attractive, tall with well defined features and wide cheekbones. She always looked immaculate, for when she·could afford it, she only bought the best and when she couldn't, she went without. Saturdays we would go shopping in King Street, Hammersmith, looking at price labels and trying on the dresses. Once a month, Jane and I would have our hair trimmed by the student hairdressers at Littlewood's department store and mum would have her hair done nearly every week, so that she looked her best when she went out dancing the same evening.

Throughout their lives, mum and dad went ballroom dancing. It was how they met and through the fights of my childhood, if nothing else, it kept them together. Every Saturday, rain or shine, air raids or empty larders, Barry would be left in charge of us littleones and off they would go for an evening of competitive dancing. Dad would transform into a dashing Fred Astaire with a silk piped evening suit, cummerbund and bow tie and mum would appear like a Christmas fairy in yards of chiffon and lace, frills and sparkling sequins that she sewed herself. They must have been good, for the dance trophies filled every room in the house.

The life and routines were a part of me and I wanted everything to go on forever. People were always busy doing something and though I liked to join in, I really looked forward to sitting in that square of sunshine, polishing the step thin with my woollen knickers and watching the clouds sail by overhead. It was the last day of March, the house and the yard were silent and I had every reason to be daydreaming. There were simply hundreds of things that I wanted for my birthday; I knew there would be a surprise, but in my mind, there was only one thing that would make my dreams come true.

I went to bed early and when I woke up it was still dark and everyone was snoring. I put on my long dressing gown and crept down the stairs. The sun was coming up and the birds were out in force, singing from the grey slate rooftops and pecking about amongst the rags and scrap iron. I looked in the kitchen, the cupboard under the stairs, the larder and out amongst the hardbacks of Shakespeare and Dickens. Nothing. Across to the garage; still nothing. By this time, I was getting a bit concerned. Then it dawned on me.

I rushed back to the house, through the kitchen and entered the best room. It was still dark, the curtains drawn, the big armchairs dusty and asleep, the chiming clock tapping its tick tock, tick tock. The dark oak dinner table was draped in a white cloth, with triangles of lace falling from each side. I looked beneath the table and there, hidden in the shadows, was a twin doll's pram, the birthday present I had wanted so much. It was shiny, even in the darkness, with gleaming chrome wheels and blue and white lacquered paint, there were two tiny pillows and two navy blue hoods that went up and down on folding arms. I had seen the doll's pram in a toy shop window every Saturday afternoon for months, but I never imagined that one day it would be mine.

It was twenty years later that Irv Levin bought me the Mercedes 280 SL. It was exactly the same colour as that twin-hooded doll's pram, but it never had quite the same magic.

Six

WHEN I was at stage school I had two idols. Marilyn Monroe and Brigitte Bardot.

For me they epitomised everything that was perfect. They were sexy and seductive, but remained coy and charming with their whispering voices, bodies that moved like rolling surf, eyes that sparkled and flashed a thousand mysteries and both were sunny, buttercup blondes   which I wasn't!

When the algebra and history lessons began to drag, I would inscribe their initials on my books and look out upon a world where everything was more interesting than the classroom. I never did find out what x was worth, but by the time I was thirteen, Marilyn and Brigitte had both touched upon my life, although in very different ways.

It was a time of moves and changes. We all loved the old house with its creaking floor boards and dusty trophies, but only Nell, the ever faithful Alsatian, derived any pleasure from the numerous rats that sniffed and nibbled their way through books and boxes and everything edible. Nell would chase them through the scrapyard and return triumphant to the kitchen with a bloodied corpse dangling from her teeth. Since her skill was not enough to drive the rats away, we left instead.

The move was to Fulham Palace Road and at first we all hated it. The old house, with Snowy on the corner, the shop and the memories wasn't exactly Windsor Castle, but there was a feeling of space, the scrapyard out back, the pub so close that the smell of malt and barley tingled through the air, the best room with its huge pieces of furniture, all the props to my theatrical productions and my childhood.

The house became a giant store, the best prices of scrap were being called antiques and our family of six were all squashed into a flat above a gentlemen's outfitters. Dad had opened a greengrocer's further down the road and now, instead of collecting old iron, he used the horse and cart to fetch fruit and veg from Covent Garden; mum ran the shop and dad called himself an antique dealer. In time, the horse and cart were replaced by a lorry, dad bought the outfitters and reopened it for mum as a children's clothes shop, and the greengrocer's was transformed into an upmarket version of the junk shop we still had in Great Church Lane.

Dad still hadn't made his fortune, but we never ate potato stew again.

All this time, I was going to St Paul's, a small Church of England school beside the graveyard in Hammersmith Broadway. Like the church on the other side, the school was sort of gothic, with dark bricks and small windows. During the winter it looked very eerie from the outside, but inside there was a warm glow and a friendly atmosphere. I had lots of friends and was able to continue playing starring roles in playground scenes and the many minor intrigues that surround school life. Reading, Riting and Rithmetic filled the days; there were no elaborate toys, but we made papier mâché puppets and put on Punch and Judy shows, which I liked best of all.

Saturday was routine, shopping with mum, a trip to the hairdressers, tea and television; we had a minute screen in a vast box and the flickering black and white images were magnified into grotesque elongated shapes by a plastic bubble. It was dreadful and we loved it. On Sunday we would visit relations, we had scores of aunts and uncles, and on sunny days all the kids would clamber onto the back of dad's truck and off we'd go for a picnic at Maidenhead. Dad kept an old sofa on the back of the lorry so everyone had a seat, but we found it more fun hanging over the side of the tailgate and waving at the cars.

A great number of changes had taken place since my fifth birthday. The flat in Fulham Place Road was nothing like the crumbling tenement we had left behind, all the old things replaced with bright rugs and G-Plan furniture. The fifties were rocking along with a new optimism, unemployment was a thing of the past, rationing had come to an end, the shops were full of new things and everyone had shoes on their feet. Dad had taken the changes in his stride, but although money was no longer in short supply, he still had big ambitions for his children. Joe White hankered for the smell of greasepaint.

Nothing happened until a rainy spring day in 1953, when mum had taken Jane and I to have our hair trimmed at a new place. The hairdresser's name was Karen and she altered the course of our lives. She asked mum it we were at the stage school.

'They're such pretty girls, they certainly should be,' she said.

'I've never really thought about it,' mum answered.

'You should, the stage school's right here in Hammer-smith.'

Mum repeated the conversation to dad when we got home, although at first he wasn't prepared to listen. Fulham, his favourite football team, had taken a thrashing and he was studying his paper in silence. The angry lines gradually changed to a faint smile and suddenly, dad leapt from his chair, took mum in his arms and led her in an elegant waltz around the tea table. Had the school been open that evening, he would have rushed us there immediately.

His excitement grew throughout Sunday and first thing on Monday morning, all scrubbed and polished, off we set for the Corona Stage School, situated, ironically, less than two miles from where we lived. Jane and I were in our best clothes, Joey, who was only five and even a reluctant Barry, who had already left school to run the scrapyard and had no desire to enter show business. He also turned out to be too

78

old, but photographs were taken of us all and Jane, Joey and I were accepted.

It sounds almost too easy, which wasn't the case. Corona was a fee-paying school, but we were among the few children given places because the agent, Hazel Malone, considered that we would get enough work to pay our way. The school principal was Hazel's sister, Rona Knight, a fiery and attractive woman who took one look at me and decided we were not going to be friends. I was almost ten, just like my dad and afraid of no one. I looked back at Rona and silently declared war.

As far as Rona Knight was concerned, I was never going to make it. I was too short and too tubby, my voice projection was lousy and that endearing little Cockney accent was the passport to nowhere. Jane's accent was overlooked, for even at seven she was slender and tall, with lighter hair and pale amber eyes. She really grew up a stunner. On top of my physical defects, I was soon to give Rona plenty of occasions to complain that I was too cheeky and a continual troublemaker.

It was a big load to contend with, but if until that time it was mainly dad's ambition that I should become an actress, Rona's lack of faith was all the challenge I needed.

We settled down to dance lessons, Shakespeare and mornings of algebra. I didn't take the ordinary school lessons too seriously, but managed to stay at the top end of the class when we had exams. To me, the drama classes were all that mattered; I worked hard and within just a few weeks a slim opportunity appeared. The Children's Film Foundation were producing an adventure film called *Circus Friends* and planned to give the lead role to a little girl at Corona.

There were 300 of us.

We were all lined up in the playground and the selections began. At first it was all very hit and miss; a point of the finger, a nod and a shrug. Those who were left had to say a few words. We were asked silly questions and slowly the numbers dwindled to just ten small girls. Jane and I were among them.

Judy, the little girl in the script, was seven years old, which placed Jane in the right age bracket and made her the obvious choice. But it wasn't to be. I was shorter, saucier and was destined to ride Pinto the circus pony across the silver screens of Saturday morning pictures. Rona Knight seemd just as disappointed as Jane. She continued to say that I would never get anywhere, but Hazel Malone kept putting me up for cameo roles and I kept getting them.

After *Circus Friends* I had the taste of things to come in the giant shape of *Moby Dick* an MGM American production made in England, with a somewhat slimmer version of Orson Welles and the stunningly handsome Gregory Peck. He was everyone's heart-throb and made me the envy of stage school. The production was like a vivid dream, hundreds of people rushing everywhere, gigantic sets and dressing rooms that were plusher than the best hotels in Brighton. I only had a few lines, but the American performers made me feel like a star. I enjoyed the taste and crossed the channel to France a few years later to make *Bon Voyage*, with Fred MacMurray, Michael Callan and Jane Wyman, the ex-wife of US President Ronald Reagan. Tommy Sands, who was married to Frank Sinatra's daughter Nancy, was also to have been in the film, but dropped out before shooting began. Mum also came as my chaperone, we were supplied with our own suite at the Ritz and I had the time of my life.

Cameo and extra work with American companies was rare, but I had small speaking roles in dozens of English films throughout my early years at Corona. The ones I remember best are *An Alligator Named Daisy*, with Kay Kendall and Kenneth More and the two St Trinian's romps, when I was typecast as a troublesome tearaway. I befriended the endless list of *Carry On* stars when I appeared in the Teacher, Doctor and Nurse films of the fifties. Jane also had a part in *Carry On Teacher* and for a while we returned to being friends. I had a larger role in *Prize of Gold* with Richard Widmark, when I played a German refugee fleeing across Europe. Richard remained solemn all the time we were on set, but when work was done, he was full of jokes and high spirits. I was beginning to learn what being a professional was all about.

For me acting was like living and breathing and came very easily but, inevitably, the successes were to have an adverse effect on my personal relationships. Rona Knight called me a five minute wonder, which didn't worry me, but in continually promising Jane a great future, she was the source of a new rivalry that evolved between us. Jane seemed to lose heart when I got the role in *Circus Friends* and although she did get small parts in several of those ancient, black and white movies, she never reached the heights that Rona predicted.

The final straw came when I got *Never Let Go*, a part I didn't even want. About the same time, Jane had been cast in the more prestigious *A Town Like Alice*, with Virginia McKenna. Jane played a malaria victim and in a scene where she was being carried across a swamp in a stretcher, the stretcher broke and Jane got a ducking. Unfortunately, it wasn't part of the script and although Jane wasn't badly hurt, the whole thing terrified her and the last of her ambition evaporated.

She turned from acting to singing – on top of her willowy good looks and fair hair, Jane had a beautiful voice. When she was fifteen, she entered the *Search for a Star* competition and won first prize. But Jane was obviously not destined to remain in show business and finally, she returned to school, passed all her exams and became a nursery school teacher in Putney.

Like Jane, Joey had a number of small movie parts, but when he finished school, he went into the family business. The scrapyard moved from Great Church Lane to Fulham

Palace Road and when it made way for the Charing Cross Hospital, Joey opened a much larger concern at Iver Heath, near Slough.

Barry avoided show business and had some success as an ABA amateur boxer. He now keeps a sixteenth century pub called the Tite Inn and a string of horses at Chadlington, near Oxford. It is in the heart of the Cotswolds in a village of only three hundred people, a far cry from the bustle of west London, although tourists and the faithful fans of Carol White give him a good business. The Tite Inn? The spelling's right and it's got nothing to do with drinking too much.

Everyone did what they wanted to do, or at least I hope so, which left me to carry dad's greasepaint banner. I did and I loved it. After *Circus Friends* I was hooked. I had no intention of being anything but an actress. My Cockney accent was an asset and, as I grew older, it changed to fit the needs of the time. That's what being an actress is, after all.

I loved working with the stars. Just imagine, me, a tearaway ten year old, and Gregory Peck walking across the set, smiling his radiant smile and teasing me when my eyes bulged like organ stops. I watched the way the ladies sat and the way everyone walked and held themselves; the performers all seemed so upper class in those days. Kay Kendall and Kenneth More were more like members of the Royal Family than movie actors.

It was a bit less serous when I did the *Carry On* films, everyone ad libbing their lines and laughing. Sometimes it was more like drama class than movie making, but the films got made and the cast earned their living by enjoying themselves. I was still only a little girl, but I made a lot of friends who remain sweet memories: Sid James, Barbara Windsor, little Kenneth Williams, Dora Bryan, Fenella Fielding, Bernard Bresslaw, Terry Thomas and the young and handsome Jim Dale, who dropped back into my life a generation later at Lynn Redgrave's Welcome to Hollywood Party at the Beverly Hills Hotel.

Gregory Peck was my heart-throb, but after *Moby Dick* I had an even more exciting encounter with an overseas performer. I had a small part in *Doctor at Sea*, all the *Carry On* team were there, it was the same crazy comedy as ever, but when I arrived to do my little bit, none other than my long time idol Brigitte Bardot walked casually from her dressing room. I almost fell over, I was so surprised.

Brigitte kept very aloof from the rest of the cast, but I must have showed by my wide eyes and hanging lip that I was over-awed to be in the same film. We didn't speak for days, but finally, she invited me into her dressing room and we had a long talk. I asked her daring questions, marvelled at her eighteen-inch waist and thought her accent the most sexy thing in the world. She had perfect, cupid lips, bright blue eyes and the most startling blonde hair I had ever seen. How did she keep it such a beautiful colour? That's a secret we share.

After talking with Brigitte Bardot, movie making and star meetings became such a way of life that my eyes stopped popping every time I saw one of my idols, and at home in Hammersmith, I even enjoyed my own small measure of fame. Life with my family, though, went on unchanged, there were still conflicts to come, but while I remained a child my only unhappiness came when Snowy, the cart horse, had to be sold and Nell, our ancient Alsatian, was put down. She never adjusted when we moved from Great Church Lane and when she bit Joey, dad took her to the vet. I think she missed the rats that still lived in the scrapyard.

In a way, *Doctor at Sea* was the last film of my childhood. I loved working with Brigitte Bardot, I admired her style and her chic. When I returned to London, the change in me was obvious. That dull, mousy hair that I had always hated was gone.

Carol White was a blonde.

Something else was beginning to change. My little boy's

flat chest had suddenly started to lost its flatness. I was pretty excited about the idea of having breasts and spent hours every day looking in the mirror to see how big they had grown. I also stopped eating chocolate bars, spent more hours touching my toes and was happy to discover that I had a figure.

Trouble was, the boys at Corona discovered it at about the same time. I never did manage to grow as tall and beautiful as Jane, but a bubbling blonde with a figure I was happy to show off was much too much to handle. I was still forever in trouble with the school principal and when a gang of boys held me down and tried to rape me, I was sent home as the instigator.

Rona expelled me at least three times. I didn't care. I bounced back each time and still managed to get more film parts than anyone else.

The boys didn't manage to rape me, but I was well aware that my small prize wasn't going to last that long and I was quietly excited about the idea of giving it away. Men were always to be my downfall. I just revelled in the idea of being in love, although then, as so many times since, I was always in love with being in love, rather than anything else.

Even my scrapyard antics were fated to contain a major love scene and I managed to embarrass the hell out of half the small boys in Hammersmith. Playing doctors and nurses behind the horse trough was one thing, but kissing! At the stage school, my flirtations assumed an even greater momentum. I became a detached and waif-like ballerina, a jilted Juliet waiting for her Romeo, a wilting flower in need of love. I would walk around the school with all the nobility and sadness of Marlene Dietrich; then Rona Knight would spot me and send me home.

I flirted with all the boys at Corona, especially the good looking ones, and there was one mischievous little fellow who soon became my best friend. He had a saucy smile, curly brown hair and his name was Richard O'Sullivan, the star of *Man About the House* and *Robin's Nest*, both of which could only have been written with Richard in mind. He fell in love with me during my *Circus Friends* triumph and our childhood romance flourished with all the passions of torrid fiction, though our stolen seconds in the stock room cupboard were only used for a few unsure pecks and the squeezing of podgy fingers. Things did mature, only that was much later, when mum and dad caught us in a somewhat awkward position. Richard was banned from the house and I was called all sorts of biblical names. Our relationship cooled for a while and Richard went off with my rival, Francesca Annis, the lovely Lady Macbeth in Polanski's film version of Shakespeare. It was a big blow to my fourteen year old ego, although I turned the tables a little later, when Adam Faith turned up on the scene..

It wasn't all passion and intrigue at school, but jolly hard work. The mornings were set aside for scholastics; three hours of maths, English, French and science, with lots of homework to make up for the afternoon drama curriculum. Lunch was from 12 to 1.00 p.m. and we then faced a solid four hour wall of stage training: ballet, tap, modern dance, speech, reading, straight drama, improvisation, comedy and Shakespeare. It was hard work and the best training in the world.

Rona Knight was as tough as they come. She gave me six years of constant battling; we never did become friends, but she did win my respect and perhaps helped to make me one of the finest actresses today.

At about the same time that I had the constant fascination with my figure – and a bit before my infatuation with Richard O'Sullivan – dad started paying me rather too much attention. He treated me like a film star. I was given lots of small gifts and taken out more often than the other children. Every Wednesday evening we went to the movies and on Fridays he took me all over London, to watch Barry compete in boxing matches.

We had been extra close since the horse and cart days and

now he was just so proud that he wanted to take me everywhere and show me off to all his friends. Jane was still the prettiest, but while she was only eleven, I was already the blonde bombshell. I was the embodiment of dad's wildest dreams. Now, I could even be mentioned in the same breath as the great Carole Lombard; she was dad's favourite actress and I had been named after her. I was christened Carole Joan White, but as a teenager, I dropped the e from Carole, forgot about the Joan and started my career as plain Carol White. It was nicely rounded, with exactly ten letters.

Unfortunately, all the time that dad and I were getting on so well, mum and Jane were feeling left out; mum acted as if I was competing with her for dad's affections not as a little girl, but as a woman. It soon passed, but just as one day I turned the tables on Richard, mum was to leave me in the shadows when the actor Ian Hendry came to call.

Being thirteen was a time of great turmoil; in a word: puberty. I wanted to be suave and sexy, the only trouble was I didn't know a thing. It was true, I had been kissing and cuddling Richard O'Sullivan since I was ten. I took one look at his skinny legs and his pea-green ballet tights and it was love at first sight. It's true that mum and dad caught us in bed stark naked – BUT, I was still a virgin. I wanted to be a chic starlet, like Brigitte Bardot, but I maintained my working class morals and hung on to what the wouldbe rapists were so eager to steal. Dad had taken me back to school after the classroom assault, Rona Knight finally believed my story and, after further investigation, it was the boys' ringleader who was expelled. I really wasn't as bad as Rona thought. I did enough to get by in the schoolroom and earned my stage fees by doing plenty of film work. In a way, it was a big game, for when I wasn't getting into trouble, I would be sent home to polish my shoes. We wore immaculate uniforms, green blazers with yellow piping, green and white striped dresses and little straw hats. The boys wore grey shorts and ties and everyone was finished off with brown leather shoes. We all slipped on occasions, but I was always spotted and sent home to do the job again. Those little Kiwi tins with their butterfly handles and the smell of dark tan boot polish form one of the best memories of that time.

The battle with Rona continued to simmer; I was still insolent and Rona still insisted that I would never get anywhere. The last time I was expelled was for playing truant with Richard O'Sullivan but by then I was fifteen, *Never Let Go* was just around the corner and I no longer cared. School was behind me.

I went back to visit Rona Knight some years later during a school reunion; I had just won the *Evening News* best actress award and I delighted in showing it to her. It was a bitchy thing to do, but I still hadn't grown up.

While the White children went to school, dad's new role as an antique dealer went from strength to strength. After buying the shop and flat in Fulham Palace Road, he resold the old building and bought our first smart house, at Ashchurch Grove, in Shepherd's Bush. The Corona Stage School had opened an extension in Ravenscourt and when we moved, we changed to the new school and walked there each day across Ravenscourt Park. We moved again soon after to another house nearby in Goldhawk Road, a beautiful building with bay windows and high corniced ceilings. Barry was still running the scrap business, but dad had found his forte dealing in paintings and genuine antiques. He was still a wheeler dealer, but what he dealt in was better class and earned him a lot more money.

The summer had arrived with bright weather and weekends at the seaside. Brigitte Bardot had taught me how to walk and how to hold myself. I was thirteen, with flowing blonde tresses and a healthy young body that turned the head of every man who passed by. A year later I would feel uncomfortable with my sexy role, but for a while I loved it. I imagined that the handful of movies I had made put me in control of all the answers. I was in a world where everyone lived by the shark ethic and, as a newly blossomed teenager, I imagined that my teeth were the sharpest.

Through the summer we went to Brighton every weekend, it was London-by-the-Sea and still dad's favourite resort. We stayed at a bed and breakfast place near the sea front and on Sunday afternoon, Jane, Joey and I did an act at 'Uncle Jack's', a little theatre built on the pebbles. Shows went on every day and children on holiday were given their chance to be performers. Dad took us to make sure we didn't forget our stage training; we were featured so many times we were virtually part of the bill.

It was during one of those weekend outings, that the *Sunday Mirror* held a Marilyn Monroe lookalike competition on the beach. All the girls had to wear swimsuits and climb into a strange cardboard shell, made to the exact measurements of Marilyn. We had to walk and talk and wiggle our hips, everyone clapped and cheered, the girls all giggled, but with my 36-24-36 figure, wavy blonde hair and boundless, thirteen-year-old self-confidence, there was little doubt that I would be the winner.

It was like a beauty competition and I was pleased to have won. I went home that weekend with a cheque for £15 and a white vanity case filled with cosmetics.

But it wasn't good enough for dad. In the following weeks, we travelled to Margate, Ramsgate and Hastings to enter the same summer competition and, in each place, I won first prize. Winning was nice, but with the newspaper publicity and all the fuss, it started to be less fun and more confusing. The role of a sexy woman was too much for me to handle; a web had been spun and I was suddenly the fly surrounded by lecherous predators, the crowds, the cameras and the dirty old men.

Dad was the proudest man in the universe. He called me his 'Pocket Venus' and took me everywhere to meet his friends. I was thrown into a world where everyone was interested in my body, not Joe White's daughter who was going to be a fine actress. The attention only sucked me deeper into that same web. I started to see myself through other people's eyes and started being what they thought I was, while inside, I remained just another little girl from Hammersmith.

When I won the four Marilyn Monroe competitions, naturally, I gave three of the four cosmetic sets away, to mum, Jane and Auntie Cath, who was married to dad's brother Jim, but it made no difference. There was a cold wind blowing between us and it would only disappear in its own good time – or never.

I wanted to be a beautiful sexy woman, I wanted to be admired as an actress, but I was just as happy running barefoot in the park, playing on the swings, looking at the distant chasing clouds and reliving those long-ago days in the scrapyard.

While all these conflicts were going on inside me, the movie makers took it upon themselves to choose my direction by casting me as an awful little Lolita in a warped sort of comedy called *Surprise Package*, an American extravaganza starring Yul Brynner, Mitzi Gaynor, Noel Coward, Claire Gordon and Evie Bricusse, whom I met again during the casting for *Never Let Go*, and Kenneth J Warren, the Australian character actor who must have made more movies in his time than anyone else.

My child acting days were over.

Never again would I run to the sound of *The Bells of St Trinian's*, or gaze wide-eyed as I watched Brigitte Bardot apply her make-up.

There would be no more tips from beautiful actresses, for now I, too, was a competitor in the biggest rat race of them all.

In *Surprise Package* I had one scene where I had to do a sexy, titivating dance in front of a grinning, dirty old man – played by Kenneth J Warren. In it, I wore a clinging satin jumpsuit, with black and white beading and glistening spangles of glass. It was the most revolting outfit I have ever worn, designed to get as much of me past the censors as possible.

I had a nice scene with Noel Coward, but I was back again as the 'bad girl', fluttering across a boat in the shortest shorts that were made in the fifties and a tee-shirt that was more off than on. The movie was supposed to be a comedy, but at this point, the Svengali-like old man buys me for a small fortune and carries me off to reveal the secret of the universe. I hated Kenneth for the character he played, but off the set he was a very sweet man.

The part gave me a stronger resolve to let the secret remain a secret and I continued with the notion that my husband would be my first lover. I wanted a white wedding and a candy house cottage and a bed shaped like a love heart! By then, my body was fully developed, I was a young woman with all the instincts that are natural: a tummy filled with butterflies when I thought of Gregory Peck and sleepless nights when I tried to imagine what it was like to really be in love. Some of the girls in my class had already lost their virginity and they said I was really missing out! Perhaps I was, but there was another factor to consider. I didn't like the way older men looked at me; they made sex seem dirty, which did not relate to the way I was feeling. After the film, I rushed back once again to Richard O'Sullivan. We could take our clothes off, climb into mum and dad's big bed and remain the innocent children we still were.

Until this time, the roles I had been playing were all for saucy little girls and now here I was, shaking myself like a Turkish belly dancer for an over-enthusiastic cameraman and cinema audiences all over the world. It was a very strange feeling, but I was happy to be working with Americans again and assumed that the trauma was all part of growing up.

I had played my role as the juvenile seductress to the best of my ability; that's what I was paid for and, as an actress, I was only willing to give my best. But at the same time, I continued to feel uncomfortable, for it seemed that as soon as I found myself with a body, the agents, casting directors and producers were compelled to fit me in a neat little box and stick a label on it: dumb blonde. This mould haunted me for several years. In front of the cameras, they dressed me as a tart and when the day's work was done, men still looked at me in the same light. I started to live not two lives but three: the movie star with more body than brains, the off-the-screen good time girl and the real me, who remained a working class drama student, viewing it all with the detachment of a psychiatrist. In a way, it's hardly surprising that my second husband turned out to be just that.

The one big advantage in it all, was that I did get plenty of work. As a teenager, I played lead roles in a whole list of movies: *Linda, All Night Long, Jailbreak* and *Never Let Go.* I featured in just about everything that was going during the late fifties and even showed my face in the classics *Around the World in 80 Days, The 39 Steps* and the Beatles' first film, *A Hard Day's Night.*

Every director in every film said it was great to get a sexy young actress who was also able to act, but it took *Up the Junction, Cathy Come Home* and *Poor Cow* before I was taken as seriously as I thought I deserved.

There were both good times and bad times ahead of me, but during *Surprise Package* there was so much going on that wiggling my boobs seemed a small price to pay for all the fun we were having. Apart from myself, there were several other young girls in the cast. Together, we spent days speculating on why a large cylinder was carried each morning to Yul Brynner's dressing room. We knew that some Americans actually used drugs, it was terrifying but added to their mystique. When we discovered that the cylinders only contained oxygen, it was a bit disappointing, although Yul Brynner, with his shiny bald scalp and muscular body, remained just as high in our estimation.

The oxygen? The star would not appear on the set each day until he had filled his lungs – and cleared his head. Years later, I learned that pure oxygen was a good way to get rid of a hangover. Yul Brynner liked his drink and left drug-taking to the next generation: mine.

The Americans always had something which set them apart. Yul's was a dependence on oxygen, while Mitzi Gaynor, his co-star, required something even more outrageous. She had been one of my favourites since the Fred Astaire dancing days and now there she was, still amazingly beautiful and wearing the tightest clothes in the business. Her dresses and skirts were so tight that, between takes, she was unable to sit down and rest. Somebody in the props department came up with the answer and built Mitzi a leaning board, a sort of life-sized stand up chair. Someone was employed to carry the thing wherever she went and when it was time for her to rest, she simply stepped backwards and spread herself out.

This was too much for us up-and-coming young starlets. We spent hours hanging around the props department, complaining that our clothes were too tight – though mine were about ready to fall off – and finally the boys succumbed to our pressure and built us all our own mini-leaning boards. Mitzi Gaynor found it highly amusing.

The music for *Surprise Package* was supplied by the John Barry Seven. John and I did little more than exchange glances, but we met again soon after during the filming of *Beat Girl*. For me, it was a disaster in every sense. I had lost the lead role to Gillian Hills, because I was considered too young for a striptease scene, and when I fell head over heels for Adam Faith, he went off with Shirley Anne Field. I'm not exactly sure how it happened, but that particular night, I didn't end up with Adam or John Barry, but stayed with Shirley Anne at her flat in Maida Vale.

Such intrigues were still to come, although I was beginning to feel grown up after *Surprise Package*. I now returned to school with a new attitude. I had battled with Rona for so long that it was wearing me out. I started to act like an adult and, suddenly, everyone treated me as one. I no longer attended school classes, but the senior school, which was completely devoted to drama. I didn't have many friends amongst my contemporaries; there's nothing your classmates hate more than success, but I had one close friend by the name of Mia Karam, an Egyptian girl who was nearly twenty-one, which I considered ancient.

Dad didn't like her. He called Mia 'The Manx Cat' and said she was a bad influence on me, although he was really objecting his little girl slipping away from childhood and discovering the world beyond Hammersmith.

Mia took me to a jazz club called 'Cy Laurie's', on shopping trips in the King's Road, and to coffee bars where young film people and rock musicians gathered. Dad had always warned me about drugs, but everyone was smoking pot, passing reefers and gulping down Purple Hearts so they could stay awake all night. It was another new world, made exciting because my father was so much against it. It was the working class ethic that you could pickle yourself mindless with barrels of booze, but one puff on a joint was the sure road to doom.

I approached drug taking with my usual ambivalence. The inner me wasn't really bothered, but the curvy blonde starlet I showed the world puffed away in the dark corners of jazz clubs as I listened to the saxophones straining on the high notes and danced away until the early hours. Dad soon realised, by my red eyes at night and the black eyes by day, that I had broken my word and smoked pot; the word dope came along years later. Dad was outraged, but he bided his time and got his own back by storming into a club one evening and dragging me off home. The young starlet was shown up as being no more than a naughty little girl.

Dad blamed Mia and said I must never see her again, but I was outgrowing his discipline and within a few weeks I was out again, acting out my role. Mia and I continued to be good friends. She is now a travel agent in London and visited me at my home in Hollywood last time she was in the United States. It's funny, but old friends are often the best friends.

93

Not long after the club incident, Mia and I were invited to a reception at the Savoy Hotel, where the photographer David Bailey had an exhibition of work. Jean Shrimpton was there, along with lots of models and fashion people and the new James Dean of the movies, my latest heart-throb, Steve McQueen. The party was all cocktails and orange juice, people saying nice things with their nice accents, but when the exhibition was over, the real party moved on to a luxury flat nearby. Everyone was drunk, everyone was smoking pot and everyone seemed prepared for an orgy – except me.

There was lots of noise, bottles were broken and Mia was dragged off to a bathroom to play a more definite part in the revelry – but then, she was old enough to enjoy it. That left me, fifteen and beautiful. However, by the time Steve McQueen had decided that it was my turn to receive his attentions, I had fled the house and got a taxi home. Richard O'Sullivan and I had come so very close to making it and that night at the party, the chances were that someone was going to take the choice from me. I had held out for so long that the last thing I wanted was to be raped.

Steve McQueen was no longer my dream man and I was now completely against drugs. The resolve didn't last very long, naturally, the two Carol Whites were forever interchangeable.

It was during this time that I had my first television part, as a minor guest in *The Avengers*. I felt very grown up going off to Manchester, my school uniform all pressed and neat and my suitcase filled with tight blouses and sexy underwear. I stayed in digs, at the home of the renowned Mrs McKay, an awful tyrant who cooked great food, acted as a surrogate mother and waved her bony finger at every itinerant performer from Sir John Gielgud to Max Bygraves. It was there that I first met Ian Hendry, although my appearance in knee socks and pigtails frightened him into limiting his courtship to a glass of cider and a kiss on the cheek. We didn't meet again for another three years and by then a lot of water had gone under the bridge.

Like *Bon Voyage* and *Surprise Package*, my role in *The Avengers* contains only happy memories. I was slipping in and out of two very different worlds, my childhood where everything was easy and secure and that tempting, attractive universe peopled only by adults. I had no great desire to take the final step and, while I remained with one foot planted firmly in the world that I knew best, everything continued to be straightforward. The confusion didn't start until the summer after my sixteenth birthday.

After the period of late night jazz clubs and pot smoking parties, mum and dad were pleased when I met a young French boy on the beach at Brighton. His name was Alain Rentz, he was seventeen and he was spending one month in the town to improve his English. We met every weekend and when it was time for him to return to France, mum and dad consented to my joining him. His parents owned an hotel in Le Havre and it all seemed very innocent – which, in fact, it was.

With my suitcases once again filled with frilly underwear, I thought of myself as being very sophisticated as I set off on the ferry for France.

Sophisticated!

I didn't know a thing.

Richard O'Sullivan and my other boyfriends had always respected my wishes. In Woody Allen's words, we may have 'petted heavily', but that wasn't what the amorous Frenchman had in mind.

One day when his parents were out, he forced me into an empty room and raped me.

My childhood dreams were shattered. I hated Alain Rentz, I hated everyone in France and I hated myself. The experience made me feel bitter, angry and abused. I returned to England and when I looked at myself in the mirror a new face looked out. The little girl had gone.

95

At the end of the summer, I found myself with the lead role in *Never Let Go*. All the men wanted me and I took them on what I thought were my own terms, a makebelieve adult playing games in the real and ugly world.

My intention was to leave every man I met with a broken heart, but any suffering I gave out was to return ten times over.

Seven

EVERYTHING I did during the next year of my life was a runaway success – and I hated myself.

I returned from France feeling dirty and cheated. Summer was coming to an end, but while everyone was out enjoying the last of the fine weather, I remained in my own room, cocooned with my private unhappiness. All my illusions had been destroyed. I had been protected by an image, the unreachable actress who graced the silver screen, the schoolgirl maiden with her pride and her secrets; ten minutes in an unused hotel room and the dream had come to an end. I moped around the house, I avoided my sister and even neglected the creams, perfumes and tiers of make-up bottles that lined my dressing table.

Dad kept asking what was wrong and mum would answer by saying I was growing up. I never spoke of Alain Rentz, but mothers always know anyway. Had I said anything to dad, he would have taken Barry on the first ferry to Le Havre and given the whole town a good seeing to. Richard O'Sullivan called several times, but I didn't want to see him. In a way, I felt that I had let him down. I remembered the ballet lessons, Richard's legs so skinny that they barely filled his green tights, his constant grin and the twinkle in his eye. It all seemed so long ago.

My childhood had gone, vanished. It was all so sudden that I already missed it. I looked at my tattered and crestfallen dolls and wanted to play with them. I wanted to be back in the scrapyard with Snowy, all grey and dirty white, like London snow. I missed the coal fires and bottles of brown ale, and the old man who sang Cockney songs. He was dead now. The big house in Goldhawk Road appeared unreal and foreign with its fitted carpets, the seventeen-inch television set and an electric fire with false logs and a little fan that sent shadowy, imitation flames across the room.

I searched through the old Hammersmith streets for my childhood, the places where we had played Knock Down Ginger, the scrapyard where so many ghosts still mimed my daydreams, the wooden fence where someone had painted 'Churchill Out', the letters as neat and as faded as they always had been. The same warm beery smell still hung in the air outside the Royal Napier and, opposite, the old house looked inviting with its fresh coat of paint and bright curtains. I envied Barry, for he had married a girl named Rona and moved back. He was twenty-one and a grown-up.

But much had already changed. Whole rows of back-to-back houses had gone and new shops and large buildings stood in their place. The Georgian houses were being restored and converted into bedsits. Hammersmith was suddenly becoming fashionable, and the old community had scattered and gone. Barry's home would soon be demolished and so would the Royal Napier.

Goldhawk Road was part of a new era. Dad was well off. The big house with its four bedrooms stood detached amidst a large garden of flowers and fruit trees. The cart horse had been replaced by a flashy American car, a station wagon with wooden sides; mum and dad still danced, but they hardly ever shouted at each other. We had two dogs, two cats, a parrot and, at the end of the garden, dad kept chickens, which were a bit out of place in such middle class surroundings, but a reminder of other times.

But something was missing. I didn't know whether this was part of growing up, or if the world really had changed.

Perhaps it was both.

The trees in Ravenscourt Park spread a knee-deep carpet of maroon and golden leaves across the grass, the flower beds were black and turned with peat, each curving mound like graves that entombed the past. The park backed onto the house and for years I had jumped the fence and ran to school, the damp morning easing the shine from my brown leather shoes. It was time to return to school again, but now, instead of skipping through a park, I walked to the corner and caught the bus to the senior school in Hammersmith. My green and yellow blazer had gone and the shine on my shoes no longer mattered. The senior school only concerned itself with drama study; mime and voice production at Hammersmith and dance classes on the top floor of the old church hall in Chiswick.

As soon as I made the move, I missed the junior school at Ravenscourt. It had been a Victorian mansion, but in converting it much of the original decor had been retained; the highly polished stairways, winding corridors, latticed dormer windows, arches of sculptured plaster and heavy oak doors that closed without making a sound. When I first started at the school, the pupils put on variety shows at Chiswick Town Hall, to raise money to build a theatre. It was completed when I was thirteen and with purpose-built facilities, plays and revues were now constantly in progress. As a senior, rehearsals were performed in Chiswick, but most of the finished productions moved back to Ravens-court.

I continued to be aloof and melancholy and channelled my energy into a season of classical plays: Shakespeare, Oscar Wilde, G.B. Shaw and Tennessee Williams. I now only played leading roles and, in making sure I diversified as much as possible, I took the male lead as an aged professor in an American play called *Our Town*, and was even applauded by the girls who didn't like me.

Rona Knight knew that something was up, but I gave her no reason to send me home. We hadn't spoken to each other since the summer break, but one day, almost offhandedly, she praised my skills in mime and improvisation. It was the only compliment she ever gave me.

I enjoyed the plays set in Victorian times, Shakespeare, anything to do with the past. I marvelled at the way the great writers strung their words together, as if each syllable was a careful sculpture and nestling with the others in a sentence, it produced a work of art. One of the teachers loved Oscar Wilde and would make us learn the famous quotes and sayings. One he said often and it stuck in my memory.

'Genius is born; not paid.'

I liked it and, fifteen years later, I began to understand it.

At home I remained silent and at school only the serious stage work seemed important. I became every wilting Ophelia, Marie Antoinette before a glistening guillotine, the damsel forever in distress and every Greek maiden to be turned into a constellation. At the height of my classical aspirations, and while I was still feeling sorry for myself, Hazel Malone put me forward to play a dim-witted Cockney scrubber, in a film being shot at Beaconsfield Studios.

I hated the idea and I didn't want the part. Hazel tried to pressure me by saying it was my big break, but I refused to get excited.

'There's not a girl of your age who wouldn't want the part,' Hazel said. 'Opportunity only knocks once.'

I told her that it wasn't what I wanted and I was still protesting a week later, while dad drove through a frosty cold morning to a screen test in Hertfordshire. The sun was rising somewhere behind us, its glow all grey and damp, the large American Ford shedding the small villages and dad's driving matching his anger. The trees were like frozen statues, their bare leafless branches clinging to armfuls of mist.

'You're so ungrateful, my girl,' dad kept saying. 'I've given up everything to help you and now you get the chance to do something big and you don't give a damn. I'll give you a word of warning: Opportunity only knocks once.'

Mum had said it, Hazel, dad, even Rona Knight. Perhaps for most people it's true. But as John Lennon said to me a few years later, we had charmed lives and for me, at least, opportunity was to knock many times.

Dad's car continued to whisper through the sleeping

countryside, the heater blowing out warm air, the frost and mist wrapped trees like a surrealist painting and dad's humming words so constant and familiar that I drifted upon the waves of fate, unconcerned with where I was going, allowing the stream of events to carry me to success or failure. When we arrived at the studios, I felt confident that I would not get the part; the other girls were older, taller, more attractive. I felt like a little girl, playing out some role that had been added as an afterthought.

There were about ten other girls who had been put up for the part: Evie Bricusse was there, she's now a painter; Jackie Collins, whose new book *Chances* is a bestseller; Claire Gordon – everyone smartly dressed and, in 1959, eager to play opposite Peter Sellers in *Never Let Go*.

We had to wear full make-up and costume and act a short scene where the gangster has found out that his moll had been fooling around. There was plenty of screaming and shouting and face slapping and, much to everyone's surprise, Peter was there to play his part in each screen test. The part required a girl who was young, vulnerable and able to shift from mood to mood. I did my test, removed my make-up and was soon sitting again beside dad as the big Ford drove through a bright autumn day; the mist had gone, the countryside was rich and vibrant with colour and the small houses in Hertfordshire seemed like props for a movie, everything so old and neat and so very English.

'Well, did you get it?' dad kept saying. 'Did you do your best?'

'I always do my best, dad,' I replied. 'But I don't think I've got a chance.'

'Don't worry, I think you've made it. This is your big break.'

We sat in silence, the black and white cottages giving way to the suburbs, London drawing us in like a great sleeping animal. Dad was smiling quietly to himself.

'Do you remember the old gypsy lady?' he said at last. 'At the races?' I shrugged and he continued, 'Long time ago,

101

when you were about four, I used to take you with me to the horses, as my lucky mascot. On one of those outings, we met an old gypsy lady selling violets or something. She bent down and looked into your eyes and said you were precious. That's the word she used: precious. She said you'll do whatever you want to do and one day, you'll be a star.'

Dad seemed very pleased with himself and confident that I would be in *Never Let Go*.

No more was said, but two days later, breathless and excited, Hazel Malone interrupted the drama class to tell me that I had got the part. The boys were all very pleased and the girls acted with mixed feelings, the same as myself. Jane had just been cast in *A Town Like Alice*, a serious and worthy tale, and I continued to have grave doubts about my first starring role as an adult.

My apathy during this period had even reached the roots of my hair, a dark mousty strip appearing to sabotage the hairdresser's craft. I had stopped wearing make-up and I had even had my hair cut short to punish myself. I wanted to be ugly and I wanted to be left alone.

It wasn't true, of course, but a game, a part of growing up. Dad had encouraged me to be a self-possessed glamour girl, a femme fatale who could take anything she wanted. While I won beauty competitions and admiring glances, it was fine, but I still hadn't crossed the bridge that changed the girl into a woman. I stood on the crossroads with a whole gang of Carol Whites and allowed destiny to usher me forward. Had I been cast as a nun in a tear-jerking epic, my life may have been completely different.

I had worn my penitent's sack cloth and ashes for many months and not only mum, dad and Rona Knight had noticed. Richard O'Sullivan watched from afar, while the same old chemicals fused between us. He had a new girlfriend by the name of Jackie Cox, but we were both aware that this was only temporary. Richard was excited that I had been cast in *Never Let Go*; he thought of me as a star and he wanted some of the stardust to rub off on him.

We started to see each other again, my hair went through a phase of being dazzling yellow and, two weeks after Hazel Malone's news that I had the part, a chauffeur was calling at the house to take me to work.

My hair was immaculate. I was dressed to the nines and made-up like a French china doll. I was beautiful and I had crossed that swaying bridge.

At Beaconsfield I was treated like royalty. I was Mitzi Gaynor and Brigitte Bardot, with my own dressing room, a wardrobe mistress to fold my clothes and a make-up man to tease a soft brush over my cheeks.

I was a star – and I was frightened out of my life. Upon the stage at school, I could play any role. When I had been slack about rehearsals, I still managed to remember my lines and, even if I did forget, I could bluff my way through without upsetting the flow. But when I stepped in front of the cameras at Beaconsfield, my self-confidence deserted me.

Peter Sellers saw me wobbling like a jelly and quickly came to the rescue. He cracked jokes and went into his 'ying tong tiddle I foo' routine, my moment of anxiety passed and we were soon whistling through the takes and sending finished film back to the printers.

We were a bit like the couple in the script; Peter a Liverpool gangster trying to make it in London and me, his brainless sidekick going along for the ride. In the story Jackie, that's me, gets involved with a young and ambitious small-time villain and the gang boss becomes jealous.

The small-time villain was Adam Faith and although we had met before, it was a 'love at first sight' feeling that flowed between us; our eyes popped like cartoon lovers and we wanted to grab hold of each other and run away to the sound of violins and pounding surf. Adam was very handsome, with his bright blue eyes and blond hair, and when he looked at me that first day out on location, I went all funny inside.

It wasn't Adam's screen debut, but as his first major

103

dramatic role, he was even more nervous than I had been. It was now my turn to help someone through a moment of stage fright, Adam's brief panic making me feel like an old-time professional, although outside the movie business Adam's record releases were always high in the charts. The latest was called 'What Do You Want If You Don't Want Money', a commodity that Adam has always managed to hang on to!

That first scene with Adam was shot on location in a garage and, at the end of it, Adam had to drive away on a motorcycle with me riding pillion. I was wearing a short black dress and black leather boots and for the first time since my return from Le Havre, I enjoyed the looks that followed my exit.

That night, I sat in my chauffeur-driven car with a lot to think about. Adam had made his feelings obvious, although we parted without saying very much. Amongst the weapons employed by the femme fatale is silence – along with irony, tears, sophistication, wit and inaccessibility, all at the appropriate time. Adam, I knew, would make his move.

He did so, the next day.

He made eyes at me nervously all morning and then he asked me to join him for lunch. I had already rehearsed my response. I remained quiet for several seconds and then replied tiredly, 'Why not?'

And off we went, both secretly smiling and Adam's brother following behind us, just in case! Adam was a big star and his brother was employed as a bodyguard. They were a very close family, as I was soon to find out.

We went to a silver-service restaurant, attached to a country pub, where the camera-eyes of the head waiter roamed over a sea of starched white table cloths and where I felt wonderful, flicking through the pages of a leather-encased menu. Adam ordered boiled fish and when he explained that he had an ulcer and had to be careful what he ate, I forgot my cool and burst out laughing. I'm sure Adam felt silly, but he managed to smile and the ice was broken. We talked about ourselves and what we hoped for in the future. I wasn't sure and I'm still not, but Adam knew exactly where he was going. He knew he wouldn't stay at the top forever, but while he was there, he intended to make enough money to retire.

It was very romantic, miles out in the country, the two of us laughing over our boiled fish and Adam's brother sneaking furtive glances from afar. He was still guarding the door, in case a mob of screaming girls came running over the fields.

The lunchtime outings became a daily routine and a week later, when work finished earlier than usual, instead of going home with my driver, I went to Adam's flat in Acton. We kissed each other and pulled at each other's clothes, but when we finally made it to the bedroom, it became clear that neither of us were as cool as we had pretended. Eventually, like children, we managed to make love and it was great. All my expectations were fulfilled and the French experience was forgotten.

After that first time we went back to Adam's flat every night. Now that a new bounce had found its way into my step, I made sure Richard O'Sullivan knew what was going on; I still hadn't forgiven him for going off with Francesca Annis and revenge was suddenly sweet.

Dad was pleased that I was doing well and happy that I had lost my surly expression. He knew by my high spirits that I was sleeping with Adam, but turned a blind eye. It was show business, after all.

The flat in Acton wasn't Adam's place, as I was soon to find out. It belonged to his mum and dad, who had been away on holiday and returned unexpectedly to find us in bed. Adam's mum went mad. She said I had seduced her son, I was a whore and a hussy. She told me to get out of the house and never come back. Six months earlier I would have been frightened, but now I found her hysteria comical. Adam's embarrassment was just as funny; there he was, a big-time pop star, living at home with his parents and now being caught with his trousers down. 'If only the fans knew . . .' I kept thinking to myself, as we pulled our clothes on and Adam's mum stood with her back to us.

For Adam, it was the last straw. Not long after, he bought his own place and has invested heavily in real estate ever since.

My relationship with Adam Faith was apparent to everyone, including Peter Sellers. He had stopped being paternal towards me and, true to the character he played in *Never Let Go*, he acted like a jealous lover. The motorcycle scene had aroused the gangster's suspicions and when we came to the face slapping scene, I could see in Peter's eyes that his actions betrayed more than just good acting. I don't know what went wrong, but we had to do the shot about a dozen times, and when it was over I was red-faced and just a little upset.

Peter came to my dressing room to apologise. I put my arm around him to kiss his cheek and say it didn't matter and we were soon in a passionate embrace. He said he was madly jealous over Adam, but that time, nothing happened.

I felt like a life-sized Venus, not the pocket version that dad still called me. I was sleeping with Adam, still going out with Richard, and there was superstar Peter Sellers telling me that I filled his every dream. It was enough to go to anyone's head. Still nothing happened between Peter and I, partly because there had not been an opportunity, but mainly because I enjoyed playing one man off against the other. When it was cold, it was now the end of November, I would sit with Peter in his car, making Adam jealous; then, when it was time to go home, I would take Adam's arm and give Peter a cheery wave.

Some days, mum would come with me to the studio. She had always been a fan of Peter Sellers and now they had become great friends. Peter was very overweight during the movie and it was mum who suggested that he should try the latest in diet techniques: plastic sweat bags. They were an awful pink, very fashionable, and you could wear them under your clothes while you were working. Peter thought it was a great idea. He covered his entire body with the bags and continued endless conversations with mum over how many pounds of fat had slipped away that week.

A day came when Adam was not required at the studio; a day full of tears and passion, the gangster and his girl finding their direction, while all around the noose grew tighter. It wasn't unusual for Peter and I to rehearse the coming scenes in his dressing room, and mum would inform us when the set was ready.

We were doing a bedroom scene, and in the dressing room a narrow couch served for the rehearsal. Peter sat there with a silly grin and made all the funny voices I remembered from the *Goon Show*. And there I was, little Carol White from Hammersmith, with a real star, his arm around my shoulders and the words in the script being said in a brand new way. Peter was playing at being a great lover, holding me to him, and seeing how far I would allow him to go. It was still only a game, me Miss Supercool and Peter a parody on an Italian gigolo.

It was daring, naughty, exciting, it was all the things you shouldn't do and more so, as mum stood on the other side of an unlocked door. Peter wanted me and I found it a big compliment – and more. He had helped me through my brief spell of insecurity and I felt I owed him something. No excuses: I liked the fact that most men wanted to make love to me and I had gotten over being raped and I enjoyed being desirable. What woman wouldn't?

But that first time I think Peter felt guilty. He said lots of nice things and passed from the great lover to another of his army of Goon characters.
lover to another of his army of Goon characters.

The call came, mum knocked on the door and Peter and I returned to the set all bright-eyed and breathless. Our lovemaking added to our rapport, which showed when the

107

film was finished. *Never Let Go* wasn't a great script, but the standard of acting was praised by everyone. It won me a five year contract.

Adam returned to work and I played the great lady; the nod, the smile, the little touch, all the tricks that I considered, then, as terribly clever. Peter would act like a wounded lover and Adam would ask what was going on. I, of course, admitted nothing, but made it obvious that I was a free spirit with my own code and my own sense of style.

For so long, my father had been telling me I was beautiful, I was special, I was his 'Pocket Venus' and could have anything – and that meant any man – I wanted. A role had been created for me and I did my best to live up to it. To some extent, I was over-compensating for what happened in France and for not wanting the part in the film in the first place. But that was only in the beginning and while I was making love with Peter and then going home with Adam, I thought I was very clever indeed.

After that first time in Peter's dressing room, I was captured by the very thrill of it. I became warm and excited when I thought about my mother on the other side of that unlocked door and the idea that she or anyone was likely to walk in at any time. Peter called me his 'little raver', although I acted cool and detached, the way only a sixteen year old knows how. It was the same when I went home with Adam. Then, making love was a richer, deeper experience, but still I half hoped that his mother was going to walk in and catch us in the act.

The film crew seemed aware of everything that was going on, film crews always are, but that only added to the plot.

What I failed to do was sit down and take a close look at my own feelings. Adam and I thought a lot of each other. We were great lovers and continued to enjoy each other for a long time to come, but I treated Adam badly, and, in time, he did the same to me.

I also used Adam to make Richard O'Sullivan jealous. I made sure he saw us out together and then contacted him to see his reaction. Richard didn't care. He thought it was great that I was a movie star and we went for walks together in Ravenscourt Park. Richard was a year younger than me and I now thought of him as being very immature. Since we had been on the verge of making love for so long, I decided it was time to show him the ropes.

We made love and it was childish good fun, the same as it was with Peter Sellers. It was a romp, like pillow fighting, doctors and nurses all over again and I didn't consider that I was being unfaithful to Adam. I was discovering myself and being myself and trying to find myself.

All the time it was the image of Carol White that acted out the man-killing role. The inner me was still a highly respectable girl and it was this part that had learned nothing about birth control. Luckily, the good-time Carol was over endowed with good fortune.

While I was playing the game, I felt in control of all the pieces.

Suddenly it changed.

We were halfway through *Never Let Go* when Richard Todd arrived on the scene.

To me, he was the real star, Britain's answer to Cary Grant and Gregory Peck, suave and stylish with clear blue eyes and every hair in place, everything that a fortune teller would find in her crystal ball except feet and inches: without his built-up shoes, he seemed no taller than me. But still my pulse quickened. Richard Todd was immaculate, a pantomime prince whose carriage was a gleaming Rolls Royce and whose smile made me go weak at the knees. My own newly acquired chic drained instantly from my shoes and disappeared.

Richard was the perfect gentleman. He treated me not as a star, not as a beauty queen, but as a lady. I was bowled over. Our relationship remained very professional, but one day, after there had been another face slapping sequence, Richard came to my dressing room and offered me some brandy 'to make you feel better!' Up until that time, I hadn't drunk anything stronger than cider, but being Miss Supercool, I sipped away and fell head over heels into Richard Todd's dazzling blue eyes.

Nothing happened, of course; he was a gentleman.

Later that same day, he came to my dressing room again. This time with a bottle of champagne. We drank from tall-stemmed glasses, Richard told my driver to go and he took me home in his Rolls Royce. I felt great. The best looking movie star in the world taking me home, opening my door and driving off in a Rolls Royce. Dad was just as impressed.

'Anyone who drives a Roller can't be bad,' he kept saying. 'He really is a nice man.'

He continued to be the perfect gentleman on the set and, on another three or four occasions, he drove me back to Shepherd's Bush and saw me to the door. He would come in and speak to my parents and leave them with this huge feeling of pride. Jane was green. She had removed her Adam Faith poster from the wall and now, with Richard Todd bringing me home, it was too much.

About a week later, the routine changed. Would I like to go out and have dinner?

Richard found it necessary to change first. We drove slowly through the countryside, the people at the bus stops looking in to see if it was somebody famous. We skirted the West End, drove through Hyde Park and arrived at a block of luxury mansions. The black iron fences smelled of fresh paint, the buildings tall with imposing columns, ornate balconies and gargoyles that spilled the afternoon rain from the roof. However, it wasn't the smell of paint that pervaded the air, but something that was obviously meant to impress: money. We were in Mayfair, which up until now, I had only known as the best piece of property on the Monopoly board.

I knew that Richard had a farm and bred dairy cows and the place where we were going turned out to be a bachelor apartment owned by his publicist.

Richard moved through the flat as if he were the owner. He switched on lamps, and set the mood with some romantic music.

We became lovers, and I had entered a world where only the best was good enough. Richard Todd was Mr Perfection, the right tie to match his every suit, everything neat and clean and the twinkle in his eye like a beacon that hypnotised me and drew me to its power.

Adam Faith knew what was going on. We kept up the charade of boyfriend and girlfriend, but the fierce passions that had surrounded our lovemaking had already gone. If, as I told myself, I was only trying to make him jealous so that he found me more attractive, the whole thing had gone wrong. I was so busy being sixteen and enjoying my own body, that I was unable to gauge my own or anyone else's feelings.

During the last two weeks of shooting *Never Let Go*, I enjoyed my triangle of lovers and I didn't think about the future. When filming was over, Peter Sellers returned to his wife and our secret adventure was over. I expectd the same to happen with Richard Todd, but it wasn't the case. By this time, I was bored with the affair, but I didn't know how to bring it to an end. Richard continued to call for me and, while mum and dad thought we were off to make the circuit of London's best restaurants, it was back to his publicist's place for a session of drinking and lovemaking.

I still don't know why parents imagine that trouble only happens after midnight but, like Cinderella, this was my deadline. Dad would bolt the door and, if I was late, I would have to wake him up and face his terrible temper before I could get in. But what dad didn't know was that after he had bolted the door, mum would creep down the stairs and unbolt it again. I had my own key, so I could arrive home late and avoid being punished.

But dad wasn't stupid. He knew I was coming in later and later and he was fully aware that the toffee-noses don't take young girls out on the town for nothing. One night, he waited outside the house and when the Rolls Royce came to a standstill, he pulled the driver's door open and threatened Richard Todd with a punch on the nose.

'Your type make me sick,' he said. 'Clear off and don't come back again.'

Richard fled and I stood on the pavement, awaiting the brunt of dad's ill-humour. We stood there for a long time, but finally dad draped his arm over my shoulder and all he said was: 'Watch yourself, my girl, they're only after one thing.'

That was pretty much the end of the affair, although it came to a complete halt when somebody called to warn me that Richard's wife had filed for divorce and it was likely that I would be named in the petition. I was worried for months, but when the case went to court, my name wasn't mentioned. I think Richard's wife was embarrassed that her husband had been committing adultery with a girl young enough to be his daughter.

When filming came to an end, there were only two more weeks of school left before the end of term, but I didn't bother to go back. Hazel Malone continued as my agent, but now, instead of sending me up for any part that came along, I was only to test for leading roles.

It was a family Christmas with everyone celebrating my first major success and me stepping back into the shoes of mum and dad's little girl. Six months had passed since my first experience, but the actress in me was almost as much a woman of the world, as Richard Todd was a man.

After Christmas, I settled down for a long think. I was pleased that the musical beds episode had come to an end. I thought that sleeping with the big shots would enhance my career, which was nonsense, and it was quite apparent that no one had been left broken hearted. The older men were glad to have got a teenager into bed and I was glad to have come through the experience unscathed – and with my mind still intact.

As it turned out, the only big shots who mattered were

Julian Wintle and Leslie Parkyn, the heads of Beaconsfield Studios. I didn't have a lot to do with them during filming, but when it was over, I sat in their office with a cheque for £750 and a contract to continue making films at Beaconsfield. It was very open-ended. I was paid a small retainer and was allowed to take other acting jobs when I wasn't needed.

I had won the contract because of my abilities as an actress. Nobody cared whom I slept with.

I felt rich and successful, not that it made a lot of difference to my father ...

He paid the cheque into a bank account and asked me what I intended to do. It was the working class ethic that everyone had to have a job. If I wasn't making a film and I wasn't attending stage school, I was doing nothing.

'But I'm resting between roles,' I protested.

'Resting my foot,' dad replied. 'All you're doing is sitting on your backside.'

Joe White wasn't a man to argue with and we finally came to a compromise. I have since learned that life is one series of compromises.

Dad fired the Italian cleaning woman, she didn't do anything anyway, and I was employed as the char. I was paid £5 a week, £2 of which I gave to mum for my keep, leaving £3 for me. I thought it was very fair, £3 was a large sum of money to have all to myself. Jane was now fourteen and still had to make do with five shillings.

Easy Street?

Not really. Through the years in dealing in junk and antiques, my parents had built up a vast collection of silver and brassware. It needed a week to clean it all and there were still beds to be made, the washing up and the menagerie to be fed: the chickens at the end of the garden; the poodles, one was black, one was white and both were spoiled rotten; there was Bill, the red and grey parrot that was always trying to bite me; and there was Ming, a neurotic, blue-eyed Siamese that ran up and down the curtains.

113

To top it all, and paradoxically, I was both a vegetarian and an animal hater.

That evolved through a number of reasons, but mainly because I missed Smoky, my own little Persian cat. It had been run down by a car and was now buried in the garden. Unlike Mad Ming, Smoky was lots of fun and amongst his repertoire of tricks was the regular theft of mum's cigarettes; she had always smoked too much and the cat knew it wasn't good for her.

He was Smoky by name, but not by nature.

Not long after the cat was killed, something else happened to reinforce my extreme attitudes towards the animals.

For years, dad had pulled a chicken from the coop, broken its neck and then set it running in circles. We couldn't stop ourselves from watching, even though the display was always terrifying. Mum would pluck the feathers and singe the pale, rubbery skin and the roasted bird seemed to bare no relation to the egg-laying machines still clucking merrily in the garden.

But one week, the white meat on my plate tasted more tender than usual – I couldn't work out why!

Dad had not killed a chicken, but the four baby rabbits, pets shared by Jane, Joey and I. I didn't finish my dinner and I didn't touch meat again for one year.

Now though, instead of having a greater fondness for the animals, I went the other way and hated them all. I seemed to spend my whole life trying to stop Ming from tearing holes in the furniture; the poodles were always yapping and the angry parrot became so obnoxious, I stopped feeding it. We all have an evil streak in us but poor old Bill paid dearly for mine. He did become quieter, but only because he was starving. One day, we found him hanging upside down from his perch; his red and grey feathers had lost their colour and Bill was dead and I was very sad and very sorry.

The char lady job did not turn out the way I had expected. It's the result of making compromises. Mum helped me with the housework, but there seemed to be a gap between us. She

114

knew when I stayed out late with Adam Faith or Richard Todd that we hadn't been holding hands in the local cinema and her regard for my morals had been low since she found me in bed with Richard O'Sullivan.

Jane had just gone through the ducking scene in *A Town Like Alice* and although nothing was contrived, I felt the odd man out, a real char lady, not dad's 'Pocket Venus'. To make matters worse, the bedrooms were arranged in such a way that I felt detached from the rest of the family.

On the top floor, mum and dad were in the big bedroom, with Jane on one side and Joey on the other. I had moved into Barry's old room on the half floor below and at night I felt excluded. Barry's room was very small, the atmosphere of boxing halls and sweaty men remaining with the heavy oak furniture and dark wallpaper. I wanted to be back upstairs with Jane. There were two single beds, pop stars on the wall and all the memories I shared with my sister. I was the eldest, I was earning my keep, but when Barry got married Jane asked for the room and mum said she could have it.

Once I left, Jane staked it out as her permanent territory by rearranging everything. Her bed now occupied the centre of the room, the pink cover piled high with the soft toys mum and Jane made together; they had a regular production line and added more and more knitted animals to the pile. Adam Faith had been removed from the pink flowery wallpaper, but Cliff Richard, Jess Conrad, Billy Fury and lots more remained. In the corner stood a kidney-shaped dressing table draped in frilly material, Jane's cosmetics all immaculate with the lids still in place. The room was so feminine that I wanted to go back, although another part of me was just as keen to return to the rats and scrap in Great Church Lane.

My little room was brown and dull, with a dark oak single wardrobe and a dressing table that was covered in talcum powder and jars with the lids left off. It was here, during the odd hours that I wasn't chasing Ming or starving Bill, that I applied my thick layers of jet black eye make-up and combed my bee-hive hair style. I had a framed photograph of me and Pinto, taken during *Circus Friends*, and the only other item that had come from the bedroom above was the candlewick bedspread. It was alive with garish colours, lime green, turquoise and orange. Like the bizarre hairstyle, it was the fashion twenty years ago.

I now had my feet planted firmly in two different worlds, the home, with its new-look vinyl furniture and a steadily growing TV set, and the misty, distant state of show business: a frightening, all-absorbing dimension where the door only opened for a fraction, but once in, no other way of life was imaginable. Dad had groomed me to think of myself as a rising star and, from that first leading role when I was ten, I always knew that I would reach the top.

My professional life was straightforward. I liked my job and I did it well. Getting up early has always been a pleasure and the self-discipline you need to be an actress came easily. It's not all champagne and witty companions, but long lonely hours learning parts and endless repetitions for zealous directors. Not that one even finds time to think about it, for it is just one aspect of the work. Film making for me wasn't so much a job, but a form of recreation; it was my private life that was now beginning to fill with confusion.

My experience was no longer that of a child. I had worked in various parts of England and on the Continent, I had acted on the same set as some of the biggest names in the industry and, if I counted the one occasion that I had sex against my will with the Frenchman, I had by now made love with five different men. My body and certainly my instincts were that of a woman, but I still hadn't left the child behind. That part of me continued to be old-fashioned and naively moralistic; I still refused to think about contraception, sex was a naughty secret to be kept from my parents, not a way of producing babies, a way of exchanging love and deep feelings with another person.

I was living with mixed feelings, my views changing from

116

one extreme to another. When I was very small, I was able to switch roles with ease, the tomboy one minute and mum's little pastry cook the next. Being sixteen and just hovering was more annoying than anything else; every pimple was as large as Mount Etna and an empty tube of eye-liner became a major catastrophe. I would lie in my bed at night, comparing my lovers and envying Jane the pink bedroom with each alternating thought.

It did no one any harm, but then, I still had to live with myself.

Six months earlier, I had decided to have nothing to do with men. Sex was dirty, a waste of time and I would only enter a relationship if it was to my advantage. Since that time, I had fallen head over heels in love with Adam Faith, only to betray that love and my own inner feelings.

Being housebound with a duster and the smell of brass polish was unbearable at first. I had gone from being a much sought after young actress to a full-time char lady, but while I thought I hated the very idea, in reality, I was glad to leave the glamour behind me. I still got up early and found my reward in seeing a draining board piled high with clean dishes, the silver ornaments sparkling in the glass bureau and the chickens clucking happily at the end of the garden.

It wasn't to last very long, of course, but I needed that time to tread water and prepare myself for a whole new way of life.

The family Christmas was over. The sale signs filled every shop window from Shepherd's Bush to Oxford Street. Everyone was wearing winkle-picker shoes, buying cars on hire purchase and saving for package deal holidays on the Costa del Sol. The backdrop of rationing, ragamuffin children and Saturday night singsongs had gone forever and when the family joined hands and sang Auld Lang Syne at midnight on 31 December, it wasn't a new year that we ushered in, but a whole new decade.

The fifties had gone.

I trembled with excitement.

I was sixteen, it was 1960 and I couldn't wait for whatever the future had in store.

Eight

1960.

It was nicely rounded and slipped easily from the tongue, like my name.

I was sure we were going to be very happy together.

Christmas and the old year slid into the past and I sighed with relief. Visiting aunts and uncles and my parents' lifelong friends from Hammersmith were all very impressed by my latest achievement. What were Peter Sellers and Richard Todd 'really' like? I tried to think of something earth-shattering and when I failed, I retreated into my filmstar pose and remained silent.

When it was over, it was back to cleaning floors and making beds. I had learned how to make light of the housework; the brassware still took ages, but dad had stopped noticing when I let it slip. The poodles continued to yap, but I ignored them; Ming's neurosis had diminished and the only reminder left of Bill the parrot was a wooden perch that stood in the conservatory like a memorial.

Conservatory?

Yes, we even had one of those, complete with potted palms, endless varieties of cacti and a giant rubber plant. In the corner was a small cupboard, where mum stored the stand-up Hoover. The kitchen had been remodelled with wash down surfaces, a double-drainer and a new washing machine that made strange noises and didn't get the clothes as clean as the old boiler, a washing board and a bit of dedication. Mum use the machine for the sheets and towels, but still washed dad's white shirts by hand.

When *Never Let Go* appeared in the cinemas in April, my

119

life really would change. I would be recognised by strangers in the street, producers would add me to their lists of potential leading ladies and other professionals would welcome me to their little private group. It was still only January and a long way off, but while I daydreamed on all the things that might happen, I was very satisfied with my daily routine.

I remained in my dressing gown all morning, wandering through the rooms like a housewife. Sometimes mum would remain in bed and I would play mother with Jane and Joey, preparing breakfast and making sure their shoes were polished before they ran off to school. I would stand at the doorstep and wave, watching their icy white breath until they disappeared through the morning mist. The conservatory would be wet with condensation and I would draw smiling faces that awaited the winter sun. Now that Jane was no longer competing with me at school, we were friends again. It wouldn't last, but it was nice while it did.

When the children were gone, I would make a fresh pot of tea for dad. He would ask me what I intended to do that day and laugh when I said it would be spent in cleaning up after everyone else.

'Don't worry, my girl, it won't be for ever. Something new's always just around the corner!'

'I know,' I would reply cheekily and dad would go off singing the same awful song:

> Shine your buttons with Brasso,
> Only three'apence a tin
> You can buy it or nick it from Woolworth's
> And it's always full up to the brim ... brim ...
>   brim ...

It would still be sounding in my ears as the front door clicked and, as if it was a magic spell that he chanted, I would now feel compelled to find the box of yellow dusters, the brass polish and the antique copper kettle standing dull and green by the fireside.

Outside the house, my social life was fun and reasonably normal. During the holiday, Adam's work schedule had been full, but now we returned to being boyfriend and girlfriend as if nothing had happened. We enjoyed being together and my period of promiscuity was forgotten; at least, that's what I thought.

We went to the cinema, restaurants, coffee bars and on long drives through Epping Forest. Adam was still looking for his first piece of property; his parents' flat was out of the question, so we made love in the back seat of the car. It was just as well that it was American, a large, pale blue convertible, with a hood that remained permanently up.

Adam did the occasional show and had a regular spot on the *6:5 Special*, the weekly dose of pop music that went out live at five past six on a Saturday evening. The BBC studios were in Shepherd's Bush, but the shows were recorded at the old cinema house in Shepherd's Bush Green. The teenage audience danced and jumped about, but I remained backstage with the entire genesis of rockers, Billy Fury, Eden Kane, Jess Conrad, P. J. Proby, Marty Wilde and the managers and musicians, all so energetic and scrumptious with their slicked-back hairstyles, snaking hips and tight leather trousers. Cliff Richard and Tommy Steele made the occasional appearance, but they were already on their way to better things. Adam wasn't far behind them. His movie debut came in the wake of a long string of hits and he was now expecting big things from 'When Johnny Comes Marching Home', the song that accompanied the titles to *Never Let Go*.

Jane was now fourteen and gorgeous. She often joined me backstage and delighted in being appraised by the stars who, before Christmas, were only names below the posters on her bedroom wall.

For now, I was with Adam Faith and Jane was just a little girl.

One year later, it was a very different situation.

Most of the rockers had the same act, a sort of he-man, seen-it-all world weariness. They would slide about in their leathers on stage, then drive their big cars home – to mum and dad. This dualism was rather odd and probably resulted from the movement lacking roots; the style was a direct import from the Untied States, particularly Elvis Presley, Jerry Lee Lewis and Chuck Berry, and the way of life in England didn't really lend itself to the angry young man image the singers projected. In England at that time, there wasn't a lot to be angry about.

Long hair, flower power and LSD were on their way and though it is true I had smoked marijuana, that was with the bohemian jazz set, which was also American-influenced.

It was all a long time ago and is open to speculation, although what I remember most about those early 6:5 *Special* stars was that they weren't trying to be innovative, they enjoyed their drink and were happy to be cruising along on the rock 'n' roll wave. Like me, they were all working class kids struggling to make names for themselves. Together, that entire generation acted as a spearhead to open the doors in music, films, literature, screenwriting, photography and all the artistic pursuits that had once been the private domain of the wealthy. Lots of the early stars faded away, but they should be remembered for setting the ball rolling, opening those doors and creating a landslide.

At the time, though, only one of those singers was special to me. I was happy that Adam and I were together and I felt no inclination to go off with Marty Wilde or Billy Fury, though both made it clear they were available. I would remain with Adam in his dressing room, a sentinel, like his brother, guarding the door against groupies and directing the girls to doors that opened with a smile.

Adam liked having fans, but he wasn't quite so sure about the groupie scene. Most of the boys were ecstatic about the endless supply of booze and birds, but Adam managed to remain unworldly and was only concerned with doing well in his career.

Dad had been worried when I was going out with Richard Todd, but with Adam, it was different. I wasn't yet seventeen, but dad hoped there was something permanent about our relationship. By now, so did I. I had been selfish in the past and I felt ashamed. It took very little to hurt Adam Faith; tears would well into his eyes if I said one unkind thing and during those weeks while we worked together on *Never Let Go*, I had gone out of my way to be unkind and deceitful.

Now, when I looked at Adam, I wondered what could have come over me. My own eyes became wide and child-like; I was only happy when we were together.

I was in love.

For the first time it was real. I had a funny feeling inside when we touched. While I worked in the house, it felt as if a cushion of air billowed at my feet, my head was filled with dreams and suddenly I would find that I had been polishing the same brass statue for one hour. I would look at the clock and hurry to finish the housework, retreating to the bathroom and fighting off angry calls from the rest of the family when they tried to get in. I used the greatest care in applying my make-up; I would iron my dress five times, then remain in my tiny room, waiting for the hall door bell to ring. We would sit close as the pale blue convertible slid over the countryside. We would find a romantic setting, play music on the radio and climb into the back seat to burrow beneath the tartan blanket.

In the beginning there were tiny gifts; a simple rose in a plastic box, French chocolates or perfume. We would go to cinemas, or sit surrounded by people in The Bell, at Hurley, but it always seemed that we were alone. All my attitudes towards men had changed. Being in love was living each day to the full, living each day as if it might be the last. I was gloriously, insanely happy and wanted it to go on forever. It went on for little more than a month, but then slowly, bit by bit, something changed.

We had been sitting in the front seat of the car, just kissing; but it was different, the fire was distant, intangible. In the pale glow of the winter moon, Adam's eyes were suddenly grey and cold, cold like the snow that lay upon the treetops around us. He still held me in his arms, but the warmth had gone.

That night I cried myself to sleep. Nothing was said, but a crack had appeared in our passion and all the love came tumbling out. One day he didn't turn up for a date. I remained in my room, my tears carrying black rivers of mascara and eye-liner down my cheeks, my world as empty as the desert. He called the next day and apologised. He had forgotten that he had to do a show. I said nothing, Adam said nothing, but both of us knew that it would never be the same.

Now it was Adam who was playing a game. He was doing to me what I had done to him. Once he knew that I loved him, he set out to hurt me. All the pain and anguish that I had created was being heaped back upon me.

My reaction wasn't to drop Adam and cut my losses. That would have been too simple. I had hurt Adam; Adam had hurt me. It was simply my turn.

We continued going out with each other and, superficially, nothing had changed. Billy and Jess and the others all fancied me, but it was too straightforward an option for revenge and might not have had the desired effect. I was seeking the right man to replace Adam and he had yet to appear.

It was a mistake that I would repeat many times. After Adam Faith, no matter what man I happened to be with, or what I thought my feelings were, consciously or unconsciously, I would be lining up the next one. If the minutest flaw appeared in our relationship, I would be out to prove that I didn't care, that I wasn't trapped; everything designed

124

to disguise the real me. I became so good at it, I even fooled myself.

I have always gone from one man to the next without pausing for breath or taking time to decide what I really wanted. I would use my replacement man to block out all thoughts of the one who had been left behind. I knew deep down that I was in love with Adam and I was sure that he felt the same way about me. I had hurt his pride; now he was paying me back. In time it probably would have blown over, but at the age we both were, time was in short supply.

Winter was coming to an end. The snow melted away into spring and April arrived with my birthday and the opening of *Never Let Go.*

I was a star!

I was a star and just as miserable as I had been when I got the part. The press was filled with good reviews, the telephone burned with calls and I moped about the house, loving Adam Faith and trying to find a way to hurt him. We still drove into the forest to make love, but the fumbling, immature fervour had changed into a calm, well practised exercise.

By making dates and not turning up, Adam managed to stay ahead in the game. I needed to do something to balance the scales and without looking too far, the opportunity arose.

The Italian rockstar Little Tony was the guest of the week on the *6:5 Special.* I took one look at him and decided: that's the one. He was from Rome, a real Latin lover, with dark hair and eyes that undressed you. Better still, his best friend in England was Adam Faith, who had introduced us.

Tony made his attraction apparent and I responded by looking shy. I flashed my eye-lashes while Adam was with us and as soon as he went onstage, Tony Ciacci rushed his telephone number into my hand. I smiled coyly and remained silent.

I went home that night feeling a lot better, although when

it came to making the call, I got cold feet. It took me two days to pluck up the courage and when Tony asked me to have dinner with him, I asked him if I could take a friend.

'Yes, yes, but for why?'

'I don't know,' I replied, feeling, and no doubt sounding, extremely stupid.

'Bring, bring, but better we are alone,' he said in his sexy, broken English.

The lunch date turned out to be at the down-at-heel Ollivelli's restaurant, in Tottenham Court Road, where most of the European rock 'n' rollers seemed to stay. The food was great, but the homely atmosphere reeked of cheapness. I had expected something different.

The girl who joined me that day was my best friend, Penny Lambeth, a Corona girl from Acton. Like my sister, Penny had the kind of figure that I wanted. She was tall, very thin, with long legs, dark hair and light brown eyes. She didn't have a great deal of success in the movies, but went into modelling and commercials. We were both dressed to kill, but I had the feeling that I was being upstaged. Penny and I were the same age, but she affected three extra ploys to add to her slender good looks: she had long, pointed finger nails, extra-long filter cigarettes that she chain-smoked, and she used the word 'dahling' to describe everything – 'what a dahling little salt pot, a dahling wine, the rain is so dahling' – all quite novel in 1960 and, up until the moment we sat down in the restaurant, one of the reasons why I liked Penny so much.

We drank wine and ate Italian food, Penny kept irritating me by saying dahling and Tony made it quite obvious that, although I remained in his orchestra, I was now playing second fiddle. Italians like blondes, it's true, but while Penny and I both pretended to be hard-to-get, it was her eyes that were suddenly locked in with Tony's. We were all a bit drunk by the time the meal was over and when the three of us climbed the stairs to Tony's room above. I was even more disappointed.

Tony was staying in digs, the same as I had done in Manchester, but the place was much worse, everything run-down and dirty. The room contained a single bed with a dark oak headboard, a rug over bare floor boards, a chest of drawers that was scratched and covered with spots of paint and everywhere, the walls, the windows and the candlewick spread, was grimy, the car fumes creeping from the street outside and spreading a film of soot over everything.

The three of us looked through the small, dingy room as if wondering what to do next and finally Penny set the mood by lying back with crossed legs upon the lumpy single bed, flicking her ash carelessly on the floor and affecting the wan look of Lauren Bacall. Little Tony was quick to respond, finding all the calm of Humphrey Bogart and adding an American accent to his broken English. I walked to the window and looked idly out at the traffic, pretending neither to notice nor care.

Tony, a cigarette still gripped between his teeth, discarded his leather jacket and started playing his guitar, gyrating across the room in skin tight Levi's and clumping his cowboy boots noisily over the bare floorboards. He looked great and he knew it, although by this time he was everything I didn't like in a young man; everything that was opposite to Adam Faith, Tony's only friend in England and the only person who had bothered to help him. Tony was still making eyes at Penny, but he was clever enough not to exclude me; I was a reserve in a game that I knew only too well. In the end, I was so fed up with being second best that I told Penny that Tony was my date and that she should go.

'You are a little "dahling" aren't you,' she replied. 'You've got one and now you want another.'

'Not any longer I haven't,' I lied. 'Adam and I are finished.'

The Italian remained cool and let us play out the drama.

'Well, are you going or aren't you?' I said.

'What a dahling,' Penny replied, looking at me down her nose and leaving the room without saying a single word to Tony.

Tony hid his disappointment and transferred his affections and jet black goo-goo eyes onto me. I hadn't finished with Adam, but my lie gave Tony licence to take advantage of the situation. He said he was glad that Penny had gone and that he had wanted to be alone with me. I didn't care if it wasn't true. We spent the rest of the afternoon kissing and I was glad when it was time for me to go home.

He called me the next day and the day after and the day after; and every day I went. We ate Italian food and drank thick red wine and I allowed Tony's kissing to go a little further each day. I still didn't like him very much, but in the back of my mind it remained important that I made Adam jealous. Tony kept saying Adam was his best friend, which made it even better.

On the fourth day, we went giggling and fumbling to Tony's room. He stretched me out on the bed and kissed me gently on the lips. He then stood back and slowly unbuttoned his bright red cowboy shirt, he removed his boots and jeans and finally stood in front of me stark naked. I could tell by his face that he thought he looked wonderful, the typical Adonis assuming the sight of his nude body would send me into raptures, although I found the thick tufts of black hair that covered his chest and arms more amusing than anything else.

He thought my amusement was eagerness, for a second later he sprang onto the bed and swiftly tore at the hooks and zips and elastic that bound my clothes to my body. His approach was nothing like Adam's and, as my first young man who was mature as well as experienced, he took me through a sequence of rituals that, until then, I had imagined took place only in India. All he kept saying was, '*Ti amo, ti amo*; I love you, I love you', and slowly, I learned that there was a lot more to lovemaking than I had thought. At first I was shocked, but it passed very quickly into excitement.

That night I telephoned Adam and told him that I didn't want to see him again. He was quiet for a long time, he went to say something, but his voice was soft and he hung up.

128

It was a victory.

I returned to my room and celebrated by weeping for two hours. The Carol White who had fallen in love with Adam almost called a dozen times, but the good-time Carol wouldn't let her. I cried myself to sleep. The next afternoon, dressed to kill and in my most sophisticated role, I was back in Little Tony's bedroom for lesson two.

I still didn't think much of Tony's personality. He lacked depth and sincerity and I found myself in the pointless situation of making comparisons. The thing I hated most was that Tony was at all times a celebrity; he did look great, but he needed a mirror to remind him at every opportunity. Most people in show business are vain, but Tony knew no limit. He acted like a star and treated me like a star, which I found boring. Unlike Tony, Adam left the rockstar image at the theatre and when we were out together, he returned to being plain Terry Nelhams from Acton. In those days, I still called him Terry, we acted like any other pair of courting teenagers and never once did I have to fight off a mob of screaming fans.

But I had burnt my bridges and now set about making the most of a new situation.

For all Tony's faults, he did know how to treat a girl; being from Rome, he really was romantic! He said 'I love you, I love you' with every second breath, treating me like a little girl and delighting in undressing me, as if I couldn't manage it myself. My lovemaking had always been mechanical and vague and, although I obviously didn't find it objectionable, it lacked the poetic mystery promised by the older girls at Corona. But it changed. Tony spent many hours lifting me to a new level of desire and passion and, that same afternoon, I discovered what I had been missing. I had my first orgasm and felt absolutely wonderful.

Now I understood what everyone had been on about. Before, when my men friends became bleary-eyed and filled with satisfaction, I thought there was no more to it than that. How wrong I had been. It was like finding an extra limb, I

129

was so pleased with myself that Tony's faults suddenly became indistinct and misty, our long afternoons of lovemaking building fires that made everything but that one second in time seem unimportant.

Tony was such a breathtaking romantic that within a couple of days Adam Faith was forgotten and, once again, I was in love. I hated having to go home at night and rushed through the housework each day, so I could get to the bus stop earlier and join Tony in his room. The bedroom no longer seemed dirty, it wasn't like the digs in Manchester, but an artist's garret; the old oak bedstead a chariot that took me higher and higher and further into new realms within myself. I could think of nothing more beautiful than the sound of the early evening traffic in the street below and the golden shafts of sunlight, piercing the curtains and dancing bright elvan silhouettes upon the wall.

We made love every day and lots of times for two weeks and when it was time for Tony to return to Rome, he cancelled his ticket and remained for another week. It went by so fast. Every second was so important, for I was afraid that if he left the spell would be broken – which is exactly what happened.

We kissed goodbye for the last time and real huge tears were rolling down his cheeks. He said *ti amo* for the ten thousandth time and, when we finally parted, I retreated back to my own private world for another long think. I had fallen in love after that first great awakening, but although I was satisfied to have found a whole new dimension in the man/woman ball game, I yearned to call Adam Faith and share that experience with him.

The first day I didn't miss Tony; the next day I did. By the third day, I was unsure. Then the telephone rang, long-distance from Rome and I became very confused.

'Come quickly, *ti amo, ti amo, ti amo,*' he said. 'You need bring nothing but yourself . . . '

I wasn't sure if that was what I wanted and, more importantly, I thought it doubtful that my parents would allow me to go. The whole Le Havre upset had eventually come out, I was hopeless at keeping secrets, and it seemed unlikely that mum and dad would want to see the incident repeated, or their daughter skulking about depressed for six months. I listened to another few dozen *ti amo*s and promised to call back. When I told my parents, their reaction floored me. They were eager for me to go; they liked Little Tony, just as they were fond of Adam Faith, and I suddenly had the sneaking suspicion that they wanted me married off before it became necessary to shine up the shotguns. It was 1960, free-love was becoming the catchword of the age, but mum and dad were still old-fashioned.

Dad spent an hour urging me to take advantage of the opportunity, as he put it, although the more dad and mum pushed, the more uncertain I became. I still wasn't convinced when I telephoned Tony an hour later, but I said I would go as the easiest solution.

'Very good, very good,' Tony said excitedly. 'The ticket is already waiting. You leave today.'

'Today?'

'Yes, isn't it wonderful?'

Wonderful? Only time would tell. I was unable to say goodbye to Jane and Joey; I packed a few things in a bag, my parents drove me to Heathrow and, true to his word, at the Alitalia desk there was a first class ticket for the 5.00 p.m. flight to Rome. It was the first time I had flown first class and I loved every minute of it.

The pink-edged clouds engulfed the plane, and as England disappeared I dismissed my doubts and became numb to everything but the present second. Drinks were free and I sat undecided, swinging like a pendulum between orange juice and Richard Todd's cure all: a double brandy. I settled for a vodka and lime, which I drank like lemonade, the hostess refilling my glass, and the clouds outside looked like waves of ice cream that seemed good enough to eat.

By the time I stepped out into a warm Rome sunset, my head was spinning. The sky was a glinting fan of pink, orange and burnt copper and the white buildings quivered like bed sheets on an English washing line. It was like a scene directed by Fellini, the flashing bulbs of an army of photographers blinding me and a great gang of reporters firing questions at me in French, English and Italian. The words were abstract and meaningless and although I smiled filmstar-like, instead of seeing the world in toyshop colours, I had that old sinking grey feeling of being a fly, trapped in a spider's web.

The feeling passed quickly, for I suddenly spotted Tony Ciacci, standing in the middle of it all and answering the questions for me.

Never Let Go had been a huge success in Italy. I was the new Lolita of the film world, not a British celebrity, but a European queen of the silver screen; I was Brigitte Bardot and Marilyn Monroe; I was an international star. I was a lot of things that I hadn't been two hours earlier at Heathrow and one of them was Little Tony's *fidanzata*. I was engaged to an Italian rockstar ... and I knew nothing about it.

To say that I was taken aback would be a masterful piece of understatement. I didn't feel swept from my feet, but more as if I had plunged deeper into that spider's web. I didn't know if the whole thing was a publicity stunt that Tony had staged, or worse still, if he was serious. Going for a holiday in Italy was one thing, but being engaged! I now stood speechless at Tony's side, the troubled thoughts that had accompanied the journey just childish nonsense, for the confusion cleared and my thoughts crystallised: I was still in love with Adam Faith.

Everything about my relationship with Tony had been physical. We hadn't partied with friends or danced in discos; every second had been spent in bed. I thought I was teaching Adam a lesson and when Tony returned to Italy I had expected us to get back together. I thought it would be the same as in the beginning, the little gifts and long drives through the quiet evening countryside. I felt that I was being manipulated; my parents urging me to go, the first class ticket on Alitalia, Tony's big smile and confident eyes as he joked with the press. I too smiled, like the actress I was, but inside I was weeping, weeping as I had done when I broke up with Adam.

With my usual aptitude for extremes, I liked being treated as a huge celebrity, but while the camera shutters immortalised us for the morning papers, all I could think of was Adam seeing Tony and me apparently so happy; I could just imagine what his mum's reaction would be as she poured the tea and gave Adam his bowl of cornflakes. For once, I was concerned with the way Adam was going to feel when he heard the story, or read about it in the English newspapers.

Tony, still sporting a big smile, finally managed to get me and my suitcase through the crowds. He set me down in a bright red Maserati sports car and we drove into the warm Italian night.

I closed my eyes and let Tony's excited string of broken English flow over me. He drove the car as if he was a grand prix racer, the highway soon passing between the ornate façades of churches and palaces as the city appeared and drew us to its heart. Above, the sky had congealed into a vast maroon blanket, lying across the rooftops and bringing me down to earth. Adam was now far, far away and before me, somewhere in that labyrinth of winding cobbled streets was the future.

Little Tony really was a huge star. His songs only made a minor impact on the British charts, but in Italy he was the European answer to Elvis Presley, with the following and I assumed the money that goes with it. As we passed through brightly lit squares and high impressive arches, I thought about our destination. I imagined a long curving drive leading to a white columned mansion, fine rooms with a weird mixture of Roman antiques and crazy London fashions, disco lights flashing inside and on the terrace, a view of the hills and the city lights below. There would be swarms of servants, all wearing zany tee-shirts and I would have a maid to spread toothpaste on my brush. The vision was so clear, I frightened myself.

The squares and the fountains drifted by, Tony slowed

and pulled the red Maserati into a side street of old buildings and, finally, we jerked to a halt. Perhaps he had a city pad, as well as the big house in the hills.

I was wrong.

The disappointment I had felt when I saw Tony's room in the Tottenham Court Road returned the second I entered the apartment. It was decorated in the style of middle-aged Italians and there in the centre of the living room were Tony's mum and dad and Tony's two brothers. Before I could get over the shock, all four of them were flapping around me with outstretched arms and garlic breath. I wondered what I had let myself in for.

Mum was short and plump with eager hands that loved making beds, washing dishes, rolling pasta and touching her three handsome sons. She took me in her arms and led me through the dimly lit room to a table laden with food. Dad disappeared and reappeared with a dark green, labelless bottle and filled half-pint wine glasses with a wine that looked, and even tasted, so much like blood that it now felt like the Last Supper as we sat before huge bowls of spaghetti. Needless to say, they were orthodox Catholics, the walls filled with sad-eyed madonnas, Italian-looking disciples and a vivid crucifixion scene, placed strategically above the table lamp.

It was all very homely, the wine, the food and the warm spring night lulling me into a strange euphoria. It didn't matter where I was for the people around the table, if nothing else, reached out their arms in friendship. The only problem was that no one, except Tony, spoke a word of English and Tony was so full of himself that he couldn't be bothered to talk to me, or translate for anyone else. I sipped my wine and listened to the lilting tones of another language. It could only get better.

I was still waiting for the right opportunity to discuss the *fidanzata* question. If it was all a publicity stunt, it certainly wouldn't do me any harm, but what if it wasn't? I assumed that Tony would talk about it when we went to bed, although that was something else I had yet to figure out. The apartment was tiny and, unless there was another floor beyond a hidden stairwell, I couldn't imagine where we were all going to sleep. I was soon to find out.

Old Mr Ciacci was draining the dregs from another bottle of wine and singing opera, throwing his small head of white hair upwards and serenading the ceiling. He kept breaking off to say something deep and solemn, holding one arm across his chest and using the other to salute his empty wine glass. I think it was me he was toasting and I tried desperately to find *fidanzata* in his speech, although before he was able to finish it, his little round wife was leading him to the adjoining room.

The adjoining room was the bedroom; *the* bedroom, not *a* bedroom. I was about to sigh with relief, that white-columned mansion house settling back in my imagination, but the three young Italians, all giggling and frantic, started attacking the G-Plan-style false book shelves, converting them into three matching single beds. I remained composed; doesn't this happen to seventeen-year-old English actresses every day? Tony kissed me on the cheek and left for the bedroom; it was a sweet gesture, he slept on the floor in his parents' room, leaving me with his bed – and his two brothers.

I didn't mind, they were nice boys; Alberto was twenty-four and Enrico was about fifteen, although both seemed very immature, just like Tony. He was twenty. The three brothers were a singing, guitar-playing trio, but they used only one name: Little Tony. He was the star and expected to be treated like one by everyone, including his family. It was obvious when we sat down for the meal. Everyone talked at the same time, as Italians tend to do, but when Tony wanted the floor he demanded it, raising his voice and fluttering his hands like a politician. *Fidanzata*, I kept saying to myself, like a mantra that carried me to sleep. I dreamed lots of strange dreams and awoke to the smell of real coffee. The sun made patterns through the wooden shutters, the brothers were creeping about like mime actors in an absurd French play, Signora Ciacci was smiling her all-loving, madonna-like smile and I felt prepared for anything.

The beds became bookshelves, we ate heavy white bread with jams and chocolate spread, drank lots of fresh coffee and soon the family were all kissing and hugging, as if the three sons were marching away to war, although it turned out to be three gruelling weeks of one night stands across the whole length and breadth of Italy.

As we set out, at least Tony and I were alone together and I could ask about the engagement.

He hedged around the question. No, it wasn't for publicity, he loved me; there wasn't a ring, but he would get one; he always had an answer, a big smile and a friendly pat, as if I was his pet dog. It was obvious that I was just an extension to his image, a macho symbol, like the bright red Maserati that he drove too fast. I was pleased with myself, because I had seen it all so quickly. In not caring a great deal about Tony, I felt that I was still the master of my own destiny.

The three weeks of constant shows was unmemorable except for the boredom. We spent hours on the road, Tony's two brothers keeping up the rear in an old van that carried the equipment. After the shows, I was barred from the dressing room; having a *fidanzata* wasn't good for Tony's image, even though it had been splashed across every newspaper and magazine in Italy. Was it anything to do with the scantily dressed lines of teenage girls that appeared at his door after the show?

'No, no, no. *Ti amo, ti amo, ti amo.*'

I didn't give a damn. Even if Tony was screwing around with the groupies, he still had the vitality of a steam train when he found his way to our hotel room at the end of it. Everything in our relationship remained detached, but in bed we found perfect harmony. I never tired of feeling Tony locked against my skin and, unlike most men that I have known in my life, Tony never tired of making love. To him, it was another extension to his ego, a part of being a rockstar.

He dressed and acted as if sex was his invention and then set out to show it to the world. In that respect, he was different to the majority of morally confused Italians, different even from most of our contemporaries, the beat generation that went through puberty in the fifties, only to reach the sixties unprepared for that mythological beast called freedom. For a woman, making love can so easily be tenuous and incomplete; men may think that they have a wonderful gift that drives women crazy, but not many know how to use it.

The constant travelling and Tony's bad driving would have been enough for me to want to fly straight back to London, but I was enjoying the greater sense of freedom. I could do whatever I wanted and not a soul would know about it. I was away from my parents' control and all the restrictions of living at home. In a way, I was more able to be myself. I'm not sure what aspect of my personality I was exploring, for I was becoming aware that a lot of different girls made up Carol White. The little Hammersmith schoolgirl with a strong sense of right and wrong was still there, somewhere, but the teenager who sat naked in her hotel bedroom had equally strong desires and passions.

So many people went through the sexual revolution with the wrong attitude. Like the Victorians, they still labelled you a whore if you enjoyed sex and went with whatever man you wanted. But then, if you did say no, you were a prude, a celibate or a selfish cock-teaser. I was beginning to loathe the double standards that so many people lived by. I had reached a new decision, a virtual landmark, I would do whatever I wanted and not care about customs, conventions or social mores. This was the sixties, after all.

After a few weeks, that extended to Tony's older brother, Alberto. Some nights, Tony would be very late, he was off with the groupies, but always blamed the press, or his guests, or his agent. It was a double standard and I didn't like it. Alberto would put Enrico to bed and join me with a bottle of wine. We fooled around, but Alberto was too loyal to betray his superstar brother. It was obvious by his tight pants that

137

he wanted me, but he was unable to cross Tony. I was too sophisticated to drag him into bed and so both of us laughed and giggled and toyed with the frustration. I thought it was very funny, but I admired Alberto's resolve and before the three weeks were up, I liked him and young Enrico a lot more than my fiancé.

Tony wasn't just selfish, everyone suffers from that problem, it was more that he thought of himself as being the centre of the universe, a sort of young Zeus who had descended from the heavens to please us earthbound maidens. He didn't think he was treating me badly. I had been 'chosen' and it was my place to serve. If I complained about anything, he acted mortally wounded; I had insulted his act, his family, Italy, his manliness; our room became a disaster area and Tony would lie upon the bed, flooding the sheets with salty tears. He then became a little boy and crawled into my arms, not to apologise, but for comfort. This was all new to me and, without thinking, I usually gave in and complied with what he wanted.

When the tour was over, we returned to the one-bedroomed apartment. Tony and his brothers performed in Rome and spent weekends away, but I was now left at home. It was an insult, another double standard, but I liked Tony's parents, I liked the ancient city and I now spoke passably good Italian. French had been my best subject at school and languages came to me easily.

I was happy enough to be on my own, walking through the little squares and enjoying the looks that followed me. A lot of girls hate those Latin lovers with their bottom-pinching fingers and dirty stares; the custom can be maddening, but so long as you have a strong right arm, which I have, a good healthy slap makes you feel good inside and wins everyone's respect. I did my hair carefully, hitched my dresses up another inch and drove them all wild. Every time I went out for a walk, I would end up at the Trevi Fountain, where I deposited all my coins and purchased another wish. I was neither satisfied nor dissatisfied with my life; I lived in a sort of daze and although I was wishing for something, even I didn't know what it was.

It took a telephone call some months later for me to find out.

At the apartment, especially when Tony was away, I was treated like a princess. Senora Ciacci had so much love for her sons that when they were away she transferred it all on to me. It was very strange at first, but soon I was lapping it up. She was so different to my own mother. She loved us all just the same, but she was a beautiful woman who enjoyed her own social life. Senora Ciacci didn't have a life outside the small apartment; her family was everything. I spent a lot of time with her in the kitchen – a woman's place, indeed – learning the secrets of Italian cooking: pasta, macaroni and sauces so carefully balanced that Senor Ciacci was driven into fits of ecstasy. I had not let a morsel of meat pass my mouth since the demise of Bill the parrot, but disguised in those delicious sauces, I left my vegetarian period behind me, for a while.

Tony's parents were aware of their son's selfishness. It showed in their faces when the six of us sat down to eat and it was even more apparent when the boys were away and mum and dad spent a good deal of time saying what a good boy he really was. But I no longer cared one way or the other. The domestic scene was fine and when Tony did take me out, the parties, dinners and receptions were something else!

Every European country has its elite set, Americans envy it and its reproduction in the Beverly Hills is a scarecrow facsimile that only fools the birds. The jet set encompasses the top of the pile in the movies, the rock business and royalty, but in Italy, the group sees itself one step further removed. That small handful of top directors, producers and stars are more than aristocrats, they are deified, they are thought of as gods and, in time, they come to act like them. This represented the other side of my life in Rome. Tony took me to the world's best couturiers and I was dressed in the most exquisite finery that existed. The parties we attended were not directed by Fellini, but a consortium of every respected film lord in Rome. Tony, always so full of himself, was now in his element, depositing me with some aged count, while he spread his charm amongst the aggravatingly perfect, black-eyed starlets, the debutante duchesses from the country and every sleek-looking woman with a title.

I was thrown into a world, not so much of power and money, that's Hollywood, but of class. I was out of my depth, but being seventeen and well-rehearsed in the skills of the femme fatale, I lisped along with my pleasingly halting Italian and Tony was given a regular taste of his own medicine. I found it much easier than I had with Adam, for I never loved Tony and even the physical infatuation was beginning to pass. Beginning to pass? On the way home from a party at the home of producer Dino de Laurentiis, it passed completely. Tony was very loving, driving his little red car at full speed and resting his hand up my dress at the same time. He had made the right people laugh at the party and now expected to find himself with a film offer.

It seemed like the right time to tell him of my own little problem. My period was three weeks late and all my instincts told me I was pregnant.

'Pregnant,' he screamed, first in English and then accompanied by a string of abuse in Italian. 'Pregnant, pregnant. If you are, I will kill you.'

Hot Latin words? Hardly.

He stopped the car and I got out to look down upon the city lights, the Via Veneto ablaze with colour and the warm summer night embracing my shoulders. Tony joined me and when he started to stamp his foot like a spoilt child, I had the sudden urge to push him from the hill. But he wasn't worth it. I remained composed and returned to the car. He continued to shout and wave his fists, my silence driving him frantic.

'It's not mine,' he wailed. 'You sleep with other men, you sleep with Alberto and Enrico and, and, and ... '

He said it all and I ignored him. Tony's parents gave me a feeling of security; they were a good Catholic family and Tony would have to marry me, whether he liked it or not. I still didn't have an engagement ring, though I had pushed the matter, just to see how far he would go. But every newspaper in Italy was proof that I was Tony's *fidanzata*. His publicity stunt had backfired.

I didn't love Tony and now I had no respect for him either, which made the idea of getting married somehow appealing. It was still only 1960, that flood wave of freedom may have started, but the thought of being pregnant and not getting married never even occurred to me. Before we arrived back that night at the small apartment, I forced myself to cry and told Tony that I would have to tell his parents.

His attitude changed.

'Please, no, anything, anything. We get married maybe.'

'You really mean it?' I said.

He was silent for a long time.

'Maybe we get married and maybe I kill you. If you say anything, I will kill you.'

I wanted to laugh, but I squeezed out a couple of extra tears instead.

The drama continued for several days and then, almost to my disappointment, my period started. The game was over. The parties, the sunny days at the beach, even the cooking lessons were no longer fun. I continued the charade by not releasing Tony from the worry, but then, after another screaming row, I told him that my period had not been late in the first place.

'I just said that to see your reaction,' I said in Italian; it was better than Tony's English.

He stamped off and the matter was closed.

Tony and his brothers were away for the rest of the week on tour. It was too hot to walk the marble-lined streets, which was just as well, for I was at home when Julian Wintle called from Beaconsfield. The studio had been paying me £20 a week since Christmas and I had to return to England to keep up my end of the contract. I was to play the lead role in another movie; my rest between roles was over and I was relieved to be going back to work.

When I replaced the telephone receiver in its cradle I discovered a smile upon my lips. I was happy and I realised what it was I had been wishing for when I emptied my coins into the Trevvi Fountain. It must have cost me thousands of lira, but it was worth it.

Tony's parents were pleased that I was to star in another film, but I knew them well enough to see a sadness in their eyes. They knew I would never return. Senora Ciacci managed to contact Tony and he instructed his parents to take me to the airport and buy me a ticket. I remained by the telephone, but after speaking to his mother, Tony hung up.

'Tony's a very unhappy boy,' she said in Italian, but I knew better.

We stood in the small lobby, unsure what to do next. I hated long fairewells and so we called Alitalia to arrange a ticket. Then we called my parents, so they could meet me at Heathrow. I packed my bags and with Senor Ciacci at the wheel of an ancient Fiat, I was soon looking upon the streets of Rome for the last time, the Via Veneto, where on boring afternoons I had allowed a few amorous Romeos to woo and win me, the beautiful old buildings and the fashionable squares where everyone went to see and be seen. The day had quickly passed and the sun was now setting in a kaleidoscope of late summer colours, as if Federico Fellini had been called upon to direct an exit that matched my arrival.

We went to Alitalia to collect my ticket. It was economy, not first class.

The suitcases, I now had two, one filled with the latest Rome fashions, disappeared along a rumbling black belt and the three of us stood there weeping in fine Italian style. I promised to write and I promised to return when the film was over.

I meant it at the time.

I looked forward to the two hour flight back to London. It

would give me some time to reassemble my thoughts. Things rarely work out the way you expect and, in show business, strange meetings, coincidence and chance are a maxim. As I sat down in the tight confines of the economy cabin, sitting by the window was Charlotte Rampling. Not travelling first class had been a relief, for I was eager to disappear amongst the crowd, but being with Charlotte was also hard work. Up until that time, I had probably had more success in films, but she was so poised and sophisticated that I found the need to emulate her.

The plane lifted from the runway, Rome became smaller and smaller and was soon gone. I yearned to see the dark rich greens of England, the narrow streets and tightly packed rows of houses, but I kept the excitement hidden. Perhaps Charlotte Rampling was doing the same. Like me, she had been in Italy with her Italian boyfriend and was overjoyed to be leaving the relationship behind her. We both nursed our private thoughts and remained silent.

The episode with Little Tony was over!

Or was it?

Nine

THE GRASS really was that lush velvet green so unique to England. The leaves on the trees were turning brown and golden and the window displays in the West End were keeping pace with the season, the coats and skirts mirroring those same rich autumn colours.

I was so happy to be home. I had learned a lot in Italy and while even the bad bits transformed into good memories, I was now impatient to catch up on all the things I had missed. Six months out of your life when you are seventeen is an eternity. I wanted to gulp down everything at once; the taste, the atmosphere, the smell of change that flowed upon the city streets. I felt that I belonged somewhere, that no matter where I travelled and what I did in my life, London would always be my home.

We were coming to the end of 1960, but the next decade still found me breathless with excitement. In another year, I would meet Mike King and really fall in love for the first and perhaps only time in my life. But before then, my social calendar was active, to say the least.

A few months after my arrival back in England, my old Corona friend Mia Karam and I compared our number of lovers. As I went through the list in my mind, I was amazed to count fifteen names, although for all my worldliness, Mia managed to upstage me by claiming, as she put it: 'At least a hundred different men!'

That year, unfortunately, I set out to catch up.

In a way, I became a sort of super-groupie, hanging out with all the *6:5 Special* stars, dropping one to go with the next, from rehearsal studios to roadie vans, night clubs and

An early portrait.

An early pose on the beach.

Carol White's mother and father, Joan and Joe.

A family of talent — (right to left) Carol, her sister Jane, and brother Joey in a seaside talent contest.

Left: Aged 15 with her sister Jane and Adam Faith, from the film *Never Let Go* (1960).

Right: An overweight Peter Sellers in *Never Let Go* (1960).

Below: With Adam Faith in *Never Let Go* (1960).

An early publicity still for *The Boys* directed by Sidney Furie.

With Terry-Thomas in *A Matter of Who* (1962).

Arriving in America with Mike King with her two sons, Stephen and Sean.

Cathy Comes Home, BBC Television 1966, directed by Ken Loach and written by Jeremy Sandford.

(l. to r.) Ken Loach, Nell Dunn, Carol White and Jeremy Sandford.

With Terence Stamp on location for *Poor Cow* (1967).

Publicity still for *Poor Cow* by Nell Dunn, directed by Ken Loach (1967).

With Oliver Reed, a publicity still for *I'll Never Forget What's'isname* directed by Michael Winner (1967).

With Alan Bates in *The Fixer* (1968).

Carol White with Paul Burke in *Daddy's Gone-A-Hunting* (1969)

With the actor John Bindon and her son Stephen.

With Jeremy Sandford.

With
John Mills
in *Dulcima*
(1971).

With Dean Martin in a scene from *Something Big* (1971).

Frank Sinatra.

With Steven Boyd in *The Squeeze* (1977).

With Stacey Keach in *The Squeeze* (1977).

With her husband Mike Arnold.

discos and on in one endless party. Who and when and where are now unimportant; my memory was lousy even before the drug-tinted years, but if my story has any value at all, it is as a chronicle of the times, the record of a cultural revolution; the breaking down of hypocrisy and false morals in readiness for the hippie, flower power, peace loving era just waiting to be born.

I wasn't aware of the changes while they occurred and I'm sure even John Lennon was more a product of the age than its progenitor; but something powerful and indefinable took place in the speedy, swinging days of the sixties and more good than bad came out of it. To claim the peace songs and protest movies at the end of the decade stopped the war in Vietnam may be too bold, but they created an air of peace and unity. It was the stars who helped influence the generation and it was the first generation to stand up and say no, we don't want to go.

Already it is history, so quickly did that feeling fade into non-existence, but while it lasted, there was change in the air and an uncanny, joy-filled freedom lit the path on which we travelled. I was a young actress, simply enjoying life, but I did so during a time that was very special and no doubt will never be repeated.

Renewing my friendship with the rock performers did not take place for several weeks and I returned from Rome to start work almost immediately on *Linda*, an unmemorable B flick made at Beaconsfield. Linda was a vulnerable, amazingly stupid girl from south of the river and, naturally, I played the title role. We spent days and days on location at Battersea Fun Fair, the icy wind like cold fingers up my dress as I went from whirlygigs to the big wheel, every shot being repeated until the director managed to film me with a dumb, exhilarated grin and my legs wide open.

Such are the trials of the silver screen, but it was a relief to be working again, Little Tony was just a memory and my friendships in London were quickly rekindled.

One lunchtime when the November rains brought the day's filming to an early end, I went with Mia to the Rose and Crown, a beautiful, dimly lit Victorian pub next to the tube station on Hammersmith Broadway. I had no real plan in mind, but I had a vague recollection that Ian Hendry used the pub when he was in London. Filming for *The Avengers* still took place in Manchester, but rehearsals were carried out in another part of the same old building, shared by the Corona seniors and a fanatical group of whist-playing pensioners.

Three years had passed since our last meeting, but Ian recognised me immediately, his eyes suddenly gleaming and almost projecting the little girl in pigtails and knee socks. I slipped back into the role, much to Mia's amazement, lisped my words and drank cider instead of vodka and lime. I became the coy, inexperienced child Ian remembered and Ian almost fell over himself with excitement. At closing time, Mia Karam left and I went with Ian to see his houseboat, a converted barge that looked very cold and desolate at its mooring near Chiswick Bridge. On board it was warm and cheerful; Ian had been talking about his wife, but needless to say, we were alone. Ian opened a bottle of something to 'warm me up' and went through the ritual of luring me to the bedroom. By the time we had managed to get our clothes off and our bodies into a narrow, swaying berth, we were both well gone on the alcohol and instead of making love, we fell fast asleep.

Ian was a great drinker, rather than a great lover, and though we continued to see each other, the ceremony of us getting high before we made it into bed was repeated virtually every time.

The following week, I invited Ian to meet my parents. Their dancing days were tapering off and instead, most weekends they had a party. Mum and dad, and particularly mum, enjoyed Ian's company and he became a regular visitor, calling in after closing time at the Rose and Crown

146

and waiting for me to get back all cold and wind-blown from Battersea. My mother was a rather well kept, attractive woman in her early forties, more Ian's age than I was, and it seemed that slowly, Ian Hendry was transferring his affections from me to my mother. I'm sure it went no further than that, but as mum had once been jealous of me, I now had a taste of that same medicine.

Ian was divorced soon after our romance came to an end and he then married Disney star Janet Munro, who nearly drowned when she returned alone one night to Ian's houseboat.

It all came back to me this week while we worked on the manuscript, for in November 1981, Natalie Wood was involved in a similar accident, and tragically, she drowned. We weren't close, but we did meet on various occasions after having dinner together during the promotion of *Poor Cow*. It happened only a matter of days after the accidental death of actor William Holden and it affected me like a warning – another cloud over my love affair with Hollywood. Suddenly, I am bored with the spotless blue skies, the spotless sidewalks, the plastic grass that lines those sidewalks and the plastic smiles that are worn like theatre masks by everyone in California. The feeling of belonging that overwhelmed me when I was seventeen and returned to England from Rome is with me again; I still have my poolside apartment off the Sunset Boulevard, but my home is once more in London.

Ian Hendry and I parted company that Christmas. It had been fun while it lasted, but when I went to a party with my sister Jane, I met all my old rock 'n' roll friends and instantly slipped into a new scene.

With a new scene came a new style. I left the high fashions of Rome in a suitcase under the bed and Jane and I dressed as twins, with wide skirts, sweaters with big numbers and bouffanted hair that required an entire can of lacquer spray to hold it in place. Jane was now fifteen and had been going out with Billy Fury for six months; it was Billy who came to pick us up that night and the party was at the home of his manager, Larry Parnes. Larry also managed Tommy Steele, but Tommy wasn't there.

When we arrived the driveway was already chock-a-block with American cars and inside everyone was dancing and drinking beer. Marty Wilde was there, Eden Kane, P.J. Proby, Jess Conrad, Lionel Bart and all the roadies, musicians, song writers and record journalists and, virtually to a man, they were all sleek in their black leathers, greased-back D.A. hairstyles and winkle-picker boots. The music was deafening, Chuck Berry, Jerry Lee Lewis and Elvis albums interrupted by new hit singles, for all the boys had a record high in the December charts. The house was a frenzy of people dancing jive and bop steps, resting only long enough to pour drinks from giant cans or to creep off to a dark corner with a new partner.

I went home that night with Eden Kane, the tall, dark, suit-wearing college boy of the group and for a few weeks we double-dated with Jane and Billy. Jane had by this time given up on her ambitions to be an actress and, with the influence of the music business all around her, she was passing through the heats of a *Search for a Star* as a singer.

The Christmas party rambled on to New Year's Eve and continued into the new year. 1961 ... I was intrigued to discover that you could stand it on its head and it still read the same: 1961. It was an invitation to turn everything upside down, the way the rock singers were doing with their songs and aggressive appearance. There was no time for doubts or introspection and my resolution for that way out, turned-about year was to be the wildest of them all.

The next day, I put my college girl clothes in another suitcase and went out to buy a pair of skin-tight black leather trousers, a leather jacket, knee-length boots, a selection of tight black tee-shirts and a whole new set of black underwear!

There was another party at the weekend and although I went with Eden Kane, he didn't seem particularly bothered when I went off with someone else. It was a very small clique, like a private members club, the girls all models, actresses and drama students and the boys always singers, musicians and roadies. The gatherings were riotous, disorderly mix-ups, the music so loud that conversation was unnecessary and impossible, the floors and carpets swimming in spilled alcohol and the bedrooms all dark and noisy with couples making it in every spare corner.

Large cars and garishly painted vans would line the pavements and block other people's driveways; inevitably, the police would arrive with a patience never known in Los Angeles, the traditional "allo, 'allo, 'allo' and a request that the vans be moved and the music volume be lowered. The records would be changed for Buddy Holly and the harmonious tones of the Everly Brothers, the rockstars would swagger in from the doorstep like heroes and rarely was anyone arrested.

I had a ball, dancing into the early hours and hopping in and out of one American station wagon to the next. Jane was the same. Her relationship with Billy Fury eventually came to an end and, one by one, she managed to go out with nearly all the stars who filled the posters on her bedroom wall. There was never a dull moment and the only sad one I remember was turning up at the *6:5 Special* studio with Jess Conrad and bumping into Adam Faith. None of the old chemistry was there, but a lump came into my throat when I thought about the closeness we once had. Adam was no longer a regular on the show and was moving away from the rock fringe to the cosier inner sanctum of show business.

Linda was still in the process of being cut and edited, and long before it was released I was back again with the Beaconsfield film crew as the leading lady on *Jailbreak*, the story appearing to carry on where *Linda* had left off, although, as the title makes clear, a jail bust was the central theme. I spent many cold hours stamping through the damp, derelict streets of Wandsworth.

The studio was still paying me £20 a week, which may have been enough to feed a family in 1961, but with me it didn't go far. There were so many parties and concerts that required my attendance that it became necessary for me to restock my wardrobe every Saturday; £3 went to mum for my keep and, if that wasn't bad enough, the taxman had the nerve to hold out his plump palm for a fiver! My finances remained desperate until the spring, when I continued my social life for the benefit of the film cameras – and got paid £500 a week into the bargain.

I was cast as a party butterfly in the American production of *All Night Long*, the story of a jazz drummer, in the shape of Patrick McGoohan, who pounds his drum kit through the long hours of an all night party, his story being told through the comments of the guests. I flitted in and out, changed partners, went for walks and reappeared in what I considered a very minor role; but I was on set for the six weeks of shooting and went home with a fat cheque for £3,000. Dad had become very liberal in his attitude towards my social life, but he still maintained control on my pocket book. He made me put most of the money away with my *Never Let Go* savings, although I kept enough back to make sure the cupboard was never at a loss for a reserve supply of make-up and tights. I had to – Jane was still a starving drama student driven by poverty into raiding my room whenever I was out.

I didn't really mind. Our parents had taught us not to be selfish and not to worry about money and possessions, an attitude that sometimes created problems. I always carried my own cash and often settled restaurant bills when my date assumed that I was still in the bathroom. It was wicked, but I found great pleasure in watching many a pair of cheeks redden before a sombre waiter as he explained that the bill had already been paid. In that respect, I wasn't really like a groupie at all. Most of the girls were hanging on for the easy ride, but I liked being with the boys because they were fun and they liked being with me for the same reason. I continued this stance through my marriages and, with one or two exceptions, through every relationship that has patterned my life.

My trick of settling bills drove my rock friends crazy. They were all very macho and acted grievously offended, conjuring great fists full of notes from their tight leather pants and waving them in front of me. I never allowed these disputes to turn into a major catastrophe, for I was in a hurry, moving on from boyfriend to boyfriend in the teeth of Mia Karam's challenge.

After Jess, I went with P.J. – 'Jim to ma fre-yuns' – Proby, the only American and certainly the wildest member of the group. If it was humanly possible for someone to wear skin-tight trousers that were tighter than skin-tight, Jim Proby was the man who tried – a style that did have its drawbacks. I was with him the night he burst out of his trousers on stage, an event that amazed the fans and made Jim the anti-hero of the morning papers. Everything about Jim Proby, including our liaison, was a bit bizarre and the memories remain vivid, even after twenty years that haven't exactly been dull, two nervous breakdowns and a drug problem. He enjoyed his booze, he liked to shock just for the hell of it and seemed happiest when everything around him was in pieces, everything including himself. He was also a great performer and if his act had anything wrong with it at all, it was only that Jim Proby was before his time. Ten years later, the Who started smashing their instruments on stage and they all became multi-millionaires.

Jim and I parted company, but with my taste buds tingling with each new risk, I moved my affections onto a mad drummer named Dave, who got his kicks by doing the ton along the North Circular Road on his Vincent motorcycle. There was no law about crash helmets in those days so, like Dave, I didn't wear one; my hair, it had grown long again, caught in the slip stream and my face was always streaked in black make-up.

We went to dirty little cafes where the tea and coffee were served in pint mugs and the sound of ringing pinball machines competed with the juke box. Dave was the only musician in the gang and the rest of the boys all seemed to be mechanics. I was introduced as 'Carol White, that chick in the movies', and found it refreshing that none of them cared. The only thing they talked about was pistons and carb adjustments and ways of tempting their bikes from 100mph into the speed of light. I was surrounded by people who weren't eaten up by ambition; or, if they were, it wasn't the lure of the lights and the smell of greasepaint that moved them. I had started my acting career just before my tenth birthday and, in the eight years that had since passed, I had spent all of my time with actors and musicians and people driven by the desire to be famous. I wondered then, as I wonder now, what force creates that need, for it is a need, a drug no different from those that come in little bottles. I knew that I was 'different' from the other girls who hung around with the bikers, although what exactly that difference was and why it came into existence was then, and still is, a question with no answer.

All I do know is that inside there is a nagging little ache, like an insect that won't go away, chewing and stinging and driving you to reach out for something that may not even be there. It's not fame and success and it certainly has nothing to do with money, for even when the cup overflows, the restless insect pushes you to work more and harder, to search for greater thrills, especially when they are spiced with danger.

Driving fast, drinking heavily and living dangerously was a sort of suicide fashion, an antithesis to the jogging, health food mania sweeping California, the bikers and the rock singers beating the last speck of energy from every second, as if their life-lines were short and time was precious. The need to do everything and see everything and feel all that there is to feel becomes an inherent part of being in the spotlight, that element of self-destruction that appears to exist in most entertainers being the very catalyst that makes the few dare to reach out for stardom. When you are working that element becomes energy, charisma, style; but when you stop, it channels irrepressibly into something negative.

I remained on the ton-up scene for about a month and managed to go out with a weird assortment of bikers with an even weirder collection of names: Flash, Ginge, Red, Foxy, Tiger and King Rex, the craziest of them all. He would drive his white and gold, hand-painted Triumph at full speed around the endless jam of trucks and motor cars on the A1 and when we were both breathless and hot from a dozen close encounters with death, we would pull onto the grass verge, strip off our damp, animal smelling leathers and make love on a bank below the traffic. Little Tony had amazing energy, the result of his super ego, but compared with Rex, he was still just one of the boys.

Rex always seemed to find the coarsest grass bank on the road north and when I pulled myself back into the tight leathers, my body would be patterned with a spider web of tiny scratches. We would end up at the Ace Cafe, drink hot sweet tea with our egg, bacon and chips and both sit there with eyes all aglow and our bodies all pins and needles, the adrenaline fired up with sex and danger. In a way, we had the perfect relationship; neither of us made any demands upon the other, we enjoyed the same things with the same intensity and while both of us realised that it wouldn't last very long, we put a lot into the time we shared.

Suddenly, it changed.

One Sunday, I waited on the corner of Goldhawk Road for an hour, but Rex didn't show up. At first I was angry, but that passed into a premonition that something out of the ordinary had happened. I ran to the tube station and took the underground to Rex's bed-sit in the Mile End. Chasing after boyfriends was a practice that did not appeal to me, but still, I returned to the station and took a taxi to the biker's usual hang-out. It was a seedy cafe that smelled of bacon grease in the heart of the East End. Inside it was quiet and gloomy, the pinball machines and juke box as silent as the leather-clad patrons. It was fashionable for the girls not to wear anything under their tight leathers and when I was with the boys, they couldn't keep their eyes off me. That dull, Sunday afternoon, it was different.

'Come and sit down, luv,' Foxy said. 'I'll get you some tea.'

I sat in a vacant chair, but none of the boys so much as looked up. They shuffled their feet and stared through the dirty windows. Finally, it was Foxy who was left to break the news. Rex had driven his white and gold Triumph head-on into a lorry; his death had been instantaneous. I didn't say anything. I sipped my tea and wondered if Rex had done it on purpose, 'for kicks', as he always said.

When it was time to go, Dave Fox offered to take me home, but I had no desire to go on the back of a motorcycle and I have never been on one since. I was shattered by Rex's death, he was only nineteen, but instead of staying at home and mourning, I sealed my grief up in a private place and I never spoke of it to anyone. I stored my leather clothes away and in the following weeks, I bought some pretty, flouncy dresses. I recoloured my hair from a sizzling yellow to a softer, more subtle shade of ash blonde.

A part of my past was buried and it was time to call a number that had been burning the pages of my address book since Christmas.

It belonged to Lionel Bart, lyricist, composer, the creator of *Oliver* and the man who became the fulcrum of my social life from that first Sunday when I called him, until he introduced me to Mike King at Christmas.

Lionel and I had hit it off immediately at Larry Parnes' party and though it had been some months since we had met, he sensed that something was wrong; something other than the usual little insect was clawing at my insides.

That night we went to a party and then, for the rest of the year, we became regular companions, attending receptions and premiers, parties with the *6:5 Special* gang and gatherings of writers, directors and all the little men whose names you can never remember. Lionel came from the same working class background as myself, but he was more practised at moving in the right circles. He introduced me to casting directors and producers, he talked enthusiastically about the films I had made at Beaconsfield and became both my patron and an older brother. It was just what I needed, for a while. I never spoke about Rex and the bikers and moved my thoughts and my life into the sphere of Lionel's influence.

It was a comfortable, secure feeling, but I started to fancy Lionel like mad and when the attraction wasn't reciprocated, I felt rejected.

It wasn't Lionel's fault. He had made it clear from the beginning that our relationship was only platonic, but even on that first date, I hoped it would go further than that. Going out with a man and not sleeping with him was a unique experience, but one I had no desire to prolong.

I returned to my search for adventure and excitement, though the lustre was beginning to dull and each new conquest was matched by a disappointment. I was too young and stupid to see that the two were linked by the same universal principle – the so-called conquests were futile and the disappointments were in fact only blows to my teenage ego. Nonetheless, I had created a man-killing monster and nothing stood in the way of me continuing to feed its massive appetite. Soon after Rex's death, Lionel introduced me to Terence Stamp; before the night was through, we were lovers. I dropped Terry for his younger brother, Chris Stamp, the one-time manager of the Who, but as if true to the law of cause and effect, when Terry met Jane, I was the one being dropped. I had given my sister cause to be jealous on numerous occasions and she made the most of her victory by going out with Terry for months.

I wasn't particularly bothered, for I was too busy being annoyed that Terry Stamp's downstairs neighbour hadn't so much as made a pass at me. Terry shared his Knightsbridge mews with a struggling young actor by the name of Michael Caine; I had made sure that Michael and I had plenty of opportunity to get to know each other better, but he never took advantage of the situation – unfortunately.

I had gone out with the rockers, the bikers, the actors I met through Lionel and, to make things all neat and tidy, while I remained Lionel's party companion, I started a more earthy relationship with the composer John Barry, my old friend from *Beat Girl* and *Never Let Go*. We had been on the verge of becoming lovers for a couple of years and now, with that all-consuming quest for great numbers, it seemed the appropriate time.

My eighteenth birthday passed with a riotous party, a night filled with passion and a sea of forgotten faces; the months drifted on as the numbers drifted through the clouds, but from out of the blue, a ring appeared on my finger and a strange new dimension was added to my lifestyle.

It all started when I went to a press reception with Eden Kane and met *Record Mirror* journalist Peter Jones. He was a charming, softly spoken man, who raved about my performance in *Never Let Go* and said all the wonderful things actresses like to hear about themselves! Poor Eden, it wasn't the first time I had gone out with him and ended up with somebody else, but that is what happened.

Peter took me home that evening and we made arrangements to meet again. Our first few dates had an air of permanence about them and I enjoyed the feeling of calm and order it created. My quick change act with boyfriends had been getting out of hand, but going out with Peter was a little different. He was about forty, more than double my age, he treated me like a queen and gave me the feeling that he would be good for me; my life, my career, I wasn't exactly sure what, but I was entering a period of reflection and Peter Jones was the right man to guide me through that time.

Reflection? I was beginning to have some doubts about

that old chestnut of a new year resolution. It was all very well when I was seventeen. It was childishly good fun, an extension of my self-discovery during the filming of *Never Let Go*, but after my birthday on 1 April, I started to think again. One thing was clear, and it still is: I didn't think of myself as being easy, or cheap. That's for the prudes, the people who went through the sixties in the shackles of their parents' moral code. I did what I wanted because that was me. I lived by my own code and I cared nothing for what other people thought. Anyone who looked down upon me did so from the lofty towers of their own jealousy. So why the doubts? I was now infamous as the good time girl; and that was it, I had a good time. The doubts I had were caused by other people. I liked Eden Kane a great deal, but I had twice made him look a fool. I had done the same with a lot of other people; dropping one boy to go with the next, or stealing a girl's boyfriend just for the hell of it.

It was time for a new wardrobe and a new way of life.

I went to demure cocktail parties where everyone was about 300 years old, plays in Shaftesbury Avenue and expensive restaurants where the men wore club ties and the ladies were seen but not heard. It was a massive contrast and dad didn't like it very much. I think he preferred it when I was out of control. His concern became mistrust; he waved his finger and said Richard Todd's name as if it was a dirty word.

'They're all the same,' he warned, but although dad remained grumpy whenever Peter called, Peter did nothing to warrant dad's perennial promise of a punch on the nose.

It was a calm, collected period, the spring days warming for summer; Joey suddenly a teenager and as tall as me; *Linda* and *Jailbreak* opening to mixed reviews; and my parents' Saturday night soirées becoming more a meeting place for people in show business than a Cockney singsong with old friends from the Royal Napier. Dad was now very successful. A small team of men worked under Barry's management in the scrapyard and dad turned over fortunes in paintings, jewellery and real antiques. The derelict house in Hammersmith, with Snowy the cart horse and Nell, the rat-catching Alsatian, had long since passed into memory, but now, even the memory was fading from our lives.

Jane left school that summer. She had won the *Search for a Star* contest, but nothing had happened with her singing career. Since I was still 'between roles', we spent the days together, shopping, sunbathing in the back garden and learning how very similar we were to each other. Jane at sixteen was going through the same scenes as I had done. She talked about Terence Stamp and the other boys she met and, suddenly, the joy of putting on a formal evening dress dulled into sheer boredom and I almost yearned for the smell of leather.

I had a natural intolerance for order and while I carried on with Peter Jones' circle of receptions and quiet dinner parties, I secretly returned to being a raver, each tranquil evening at Peter's flat matched by a wild session with an actor or musician more my own age. Nothing stood in the way of my relationship with Lionel Bart and although I still got no further than holding his arm, while I was with him, I did get to meet a steady supply of exciting people.

Now, I was enjoying the best of both worlds: while I was able to do whatever I wanted, Peter remained in the background, patient and philosophical, loving me the way I was and finding no need to mould me into what he considered the perfect woman. It was a trap that most men tumbled into, seeing their partner as an extension of themselves, instead of a whole and separate entity. In that respect, he was different and I respected him for it. I respected him, but I wasn't in love and I had no intention of giving up my freedom.

Peter, though, took it much more seriously and when he produced an engagement ring, I didn't know what to say. He wasn't a sixties' person and he thought that just because I went to bed with him, it must be love.

My silence on the night of the proposal was probably

shock, but Peter took it as my consent and, once again, I was betrothed. It made absolutely no difference to my life and, except for the ring, it was the same as being Tony Ciacci's *fidanzata*. So strong were the parallels inside me, that later that same night I found myself whispering '*ti amo, ti amo, ti amo*,' but the words were spirited from my subconscious and Peter didn't notice the irony that flavoured them.

One of the things I did like about Peter was the fact that he wasn't a performer; I was always the centre of attention when we went out, Peter standing on the sidelines with his praise and support. I hated sycophants and hangers-on, but Peter wasn't like that. He meant everything he said and while I had no great need for regular pats on the back, Peter's supply of compliments made a nice contrast to my young singing and acting boyfriends, who were all so full of themselves.

The weeks wilted into months, autumn became winter and all the time Peter made no more than the occasional hint that we should be 'looking towards the future'. I was happy to avoid anything more permanent than the ring on my finger. To me, it wasn't so much an engagement ring, as a very nice present.

That was my attitude the night we attended an EMI Christmas party and Lionel, with his usual fizzing enthusiasm, rushed me over to meet 'three of the most talented young men in the business today'. We left Peter with Lionel's traditional parting words: 'You don't mind if I borrow her for a few seconds . . . ' and suddenly I was shaking hands with Mike, Denis and Tony: the King Brothers. They had been voted the nation's number one vocal group, their latest release was leaping up the charts and when Mike King asked me to dance, I knew immediately that I had met the right man for me.

I had shaken the habit of changing partners halfway through a party, but when Peter took me home that night, I knew it would be the last time. I didn't say as much. It was late, I was tired and I had other things on my mind . . .

Ten

THE RISE and Fall of Carol White.

The days sparkled like an endless vat of champagne. I didn't have the slightest desire to spend my time or give my attention to anyone but Mike King. I was in love. Peter Jones called, but I was not at home. He was the last victim of Mia Karam's challenge and my own compulsive, yet intrinsic need to be promiscuous. Life had been wonderful, a constant party, a paper chase through the assault course of a hundred different bedrooms, a spiral staircase with broken hearts and broken promises left at every corner.

Had I been a naughty girl?

The heavy hand of fate was biding its time and waiting to crash down with all the awesome inevitability of predestination.

I was pregnant.

And that wasn't the worst of it. A new girl by the name of Julie Christie had been signed by Beaconsfield Studios and she had been cast as the leading lady in *Crooks Anonymous*. There had been some crosswires with my agent, Hazel Malone, and I had not been put up for the part.

After making *All Night Long*, I had only made one more picture, *The Boys*, with my rock 'n' roll ex-lover Jess Conrad, the handsome and still charming Richard Todd, who played the part of a judge and appeared before me like the Ghost of Christmas Past, funny men Roy Kinnear and Robert Morley, and Tony Garnett, who would play an important part in my career in the future. It wasn't that important that I wasn't cast in *Crooks Anonymous*, but the

160

only cure I had for any dilemma, including pregnancy, was being out at work.

It was one of Julie's first films and I was already an established leading lady. During the next three years, I went into a state of withdrawal and semi-retirement, while Julie made a whole host of films, including *Billy Liar* and *Dr Zhivago*. After my comeback in *Cathy* and *Poor Cow*, I was hailed as the new Julie Christie, but if one bothers to look back to 1962, there was a time when Julie was called the new Carol White.

Julie and I had never met and I had no way of knowing that our lives was to embroider the same fabric over and over again. Not that it would have mattered on that December morning after the EMI party. I remained in my room, the words of all the King Brothers' songs in my mind like Christmas carols and the vision of Mike King's round, friendly face bringing a breath of fresh air into my life.

We had parted without exchanging telephone numbers, but Mike called Lionel Bart, and before I had finished eating breakfast, he was calling me.

There were parties and receptions every evening, but it all felt new and exciting, the way I felt, the things we did, even the way I looked. I started to wear my hair down, instead of lacquered in a bee-hive; I looked younger, prettier, innocent. The face that stared at me from the bathroom mirror was glowing and radiant, my eyes were filled with laughter and the indiscriminate little flirt who had found momentary prominence had disappeared. If I had been suffering from an evil dose of nymphomania, it had well and truly passed. The laughter lines that marked my cheeks came from the feeling of being settled, although Mike's circle of friends were partly responsible. During the Christmas week, I met Ronnie Corbett, Bruce Forsyth, Tommy Cooper and Tony Hancock, who was even more funny offstage than he was on, his troubled face disguising one of the quickest comic brains of all time.

All were established performers and, as a group, they

161

made a nice change from the rough and ready rockers still trying to prove themselves. There was some rivalry between the comedians, naturally, but I felt as if I had entered a circle where the people were aware of their talents and had no need to flaunt them at every possible opportunity. I may have been seeing this world through rose-tinted glasses, but even if everyone wasn't quite so self-effacing as I imagined, Mike King certainly was. He was one of those rare individuals who knew how to listen – and not just listen with a fixed smile and glazed, far away eyes. He was concerned when someone had a problem and if he was able to do something to help them, he did so. Like my dad, as soon as Mike had a spare fiver in his pocket, he gave it away.

The young singers and actors, even the roadies and bikers, were only interested in themselves, or the image they tried to portray – I was guilty of the same thing – but suddenly, here was a man who was different. He enjoyed the spotlight, the same as everyone else, but he didn't mind sharing it with others.

The last in the series of parties was at the home of Mike's parents, an impressive country house in Essex. The funny men all made it, there were several dancers from the London Palladium, Ronnie Carroll, Millicent Martin, Johnny and Marion Spence, who were to become close friends in the future, and Lionel Bart, who was thrilled that Mike and I were together, as if a weight had been removed from his shoulders. Finally, there were Mr and Mrs King's county friends, who made an interesting contrast with their sensible tweeds and expressions that permanently seemed to be reflecting a state of shock.

That may have been due to the antics of Tommy Cooper, the red fez now a regular fixture and his jokes as mind boggling as his magic. His favourite gag at the time was to empty ice cubes into his trousers, then open the zip and say: 'My impression of an Eskimo peeing . . .' A few people were shocked, but most of the audience would be falling about in hysterics. Tommy only had to say: 'Would you like a drink,

Carol?' for me to clutch my stomach and bend over double with laughter.

The party came to an end, Christmas was over and the topsy-turvy year slipped into the past. The King Brothers were booked for a long tour of the north and when Mike asked me to join him, not only did dad readily give his consent, he seemed just as pleased as I was. Dad had grown to tolerate my 'engagement' to Peter Jones, but he was relieved when he discovered that I was serious about Mike. The King Brothers had particular appeal with my parents' generation; clean cut 'good family entertainment', as it said in their billing – the very things that would go against them in the coming years. It was 1962 and the Mersey sound had been born.

Peter Jones still called, but I remained 'out' until it was time to pack my bags and join the entourage on the long safari from Birmingham, to Bolton, Leeds, Liverpool, Manchester, from lodging houses to cheap hotels. The tour was like an expedition into foreign soil, the girls in our group all very glamorous and feminine, our London fashions about twenty years ahead of everything north of the Tottenham Hotspurs football ground. The club circuit was new to me, everyone shouting, drinking and joining in with the songs, the clubs warm and filled with life, while the streets outside were shabby and depressing, the houses reminiscent of the slums that had long since disappeared from Hammersmith. It was like stepping into a time warp, the clothes, the severe pride in the men's faces and the cart horses that punctuated the city traffic.

The nights were bitterly cold, the coal-blackened houses beneath caps of grey snow and the sheets in each boarding house needing a blow torch to melt their icy feel. Mike was very considerate. I made sure he got into bed before I so much as removed my fur-collared leather coat and he never complained when I eased myself into the spot he had already warmed up. Most important of all, I was happy, I mean really happy; happy for the first time since I had parted company with Adam Faith. Mike and I loved each other a little more each day and even the sombre telephone calls that followed our journey became more an amusement than a problem. The calls?

They came from Peter Jones, the love-lost record journalist, who wanted his present back. The trouble was, I had sold the ring and Mike didn't have the heart to tell him. Peter had given up trying to reach me, but when he asked Mike to pass on a message, Mike became evasive and said he would do his best, or try to find out, anything but reveal that I had sold the ring to my dad for £75 and he had since resold it. Peter found out in the end and, although he went to see my father, I never did learn what happened. Dad, in his new role as an antique dealer, had stopped rolling up his sleeves every time there was a minor contention and although it came late in life, he now practised the canny art of compromise.

By the time we arrived back in London, I would have been delirious with joy, but my period, always as regular as clockwork, was three weeks late and this time, it wasn't a phantom pregnancy. My tummy started to swell, I was sick every morning and my taste buds were crying out for the most ridiculous things.

I took to moping listlessly around the house. Last time, mum had told dad that I was 'only growing up'. Now she said gaily: 'Leave her alone, Joe, can't you see she's in love ...'

It was true, but she didn't know the whole story.

My mind went round in circles and I couldn't reach any definite conclusions. It suddenly seemed that each fleeting moment of happiness had to be paid for – and many times over. I was afraid to tell Mike, in case it ruined everything, and I was afraid to tell mum and dad, in case they threw me out.

Confused?

I certainly was!

I always thought: it could never happen to me – and then it did. I had no idea what to do and I didn't know how my own body functioned. Biology wasn't a big deal at Corona and mum's words of advice had been limited to: 'You'll get yourself into trouble one of these days, Carol', said when I was fourteen and she found me in bed with Richard O'Sullivan.

Strange as it may seem in these enlightened times, I was still under the ill-informed delusion that only when you fell in love was it possible to become pregnant; being pregnant was at least proof that I was in love, but I still felt that I had made a mess of things somewhere along the line. Through all my sorties between the sheets, I had remained childishly naive. I knew nothing about birth control. I had approached mum a few times on the subject, but she ignored me; mothers never spoke to their daughters about such things. Sex was a dirty word.

So I didn't know how my body worked, or how to protect myself.

It seemed ironic that I had slept with all those men without anything going wrong and now, the first thing I did after waking each morning, was rush to the bathroom and throw up. It wasn't long before mum noticed and with that maternal mixture of instinct and knowing the obvious, she guessed the cause of my malady.

'Did you have too much to drink last night, Carol?'

'No, mum, I didn't,' I groaned.

'What's wrong then?' Her voice was very patient. Dad had gone to work, Joey had gone to school and Jane was still in bed.

'I don't know,' I replied, a tear coming into my voice.

'Don't you think you ought to tell me? It will make things easier, Carol.'

'I'm going to have a baby.'

'You are a stupid girl,' mum said. 'Why weren't you more careful?'

'I don't know. I didn't think it would happen to me.'

'What are we going to do with you,' she said to herself. 'I suppose it's Mike's?'

'That's a horrible thing to say,' I cried. 'Of course it is.'

'Well, have you told him?'

'No. He might not like it.'

'So what are you going to do, Carol? You've got to do something.'

I did do something! I broke down and cried my heart out. Mum put her arms around me and we both remained in the bathroom, sobbing together and somehow enjoying a rare moment of being mother and daughter. I had been very grown up for a long time, but in that second, I was a little girl again.

The days fogged into a weary, half-hearted panic. Mike was away and mum was rushing in and out of the house every five minutes. I had a craving for chocolate and each time she returned, she had a fresh supply, heaping the sixpenny Cadbury's bars into my lap and admonishing me at the same time: 'You'll get as fat as lard if you don't watch yourself, Carol.' Not that I cared. When I was deprived of having sweets to munch on, I chewed my fingernails down to the quick.

I didn't say anything to Jane, but like mums, younger sisters have an evil awareness of older sisters' problems.

'Has Mike dropped you or something?' she demanded.

'No he hasn't.'

'So what's wrong with you then? Why aren't you going out?'

'Mind your own business.'

Jane would leave for the pretty pink bedroom, a knowing look in her eyes and the bounce in her step a cruel reminder that I was now having difficulty in just getting up from the chair.

Three or four days passed with the morbid lethargy of three or four years and finally, when the house was conveniently empty, mum joined me with a steaming cup of tea, the English way of dealing with everything unpleasant and I braced myself for whatever plan she had worked out.

'Have you decided what you're going to do?' I shrugged

and mum continued, 'There's a lady, she's a fully qualified nurse ...'

It wasn't fashionable to have babies out of wedlock; abortion wasn't legal and the old ladies with their magic potions and size 5 knitting needles, they were always a 'fully qualified nurse', thrived in secret basements and grimy, far away backstreets.

A big salty tear plopped into my blue-ringed tea cup and mum came quickly to my side.

'It will be for the best, Carol, really it will,' she said, weeping now, the same as me. 'You're just a little girl, what will you do with a child?'

'I don't know,' I sobbed. 'I thought it might be nice to have a baby.'

'If you're sure that's what you really want ...'

'Course I'm not sure, mum,' I replied. 'I'm so confused, I don't know what I want.'

We cried and hugged each other until, with English dignity, we dried our eyes and drank another cup of tea.

An hour later, we were standing at the bus stop, the rain beating down and soaking our clothes and the sky above as dark and foreboding as the way I felt. We went to Battersea, leaving the High Street to follow a pencil-drawn map through a winding maze of neglected houses, like those I had looked upon with scorn in Manchester. Tall chimneys beat out black palls of smoke and the smell of the famous dogs' home seemed to hang in the air like an omen. Way in the distance was the merry tinkle of the funfair organ, but *Linda*, the movie I had made there, now belonged to another lifetime.

The number 163 was painted roughly on a brick façade; mum stopped and looked at me, her expression saying: well, it's up to you. However, the die had been cast and I had retreated to the now familiar pose of viewing the events of my life with the detachment of an outsider. As if it had been a premonition, something else that was becoming habitual, I now followed mum down a narrow brick stairwell into the basement. Mum beat the heavy iron knocker and we stood there in a puddle until the door opened.

The woman peered at us through a narrow crack for several seconds, then closed the door to release the safety chain.

'Come in dears,' she said. 'You look perished.'

Inside it was warm and musty, the living room only lit by the glow of a coal fire. Large, decaying armchairs, a couch, a dining table and four dining chairs filled the small area; a black cat stood watchful in the corner and a dreadful smell crept steadily from the adjoining room. I closed my eyes and the opening scene from *Macbeth* entered my mind like shadows appearing through mist ...

> When shall we three meet again
> In thunder, lightning or in rain?
> When the hurlyburly's done
> When the battle's lost and won ...
> ... Fair is foul, and foul is fair;
> Hover through the fog and filthy air.

Mum and the woman were speaking quietly, the couch between them like a counter and when mum finally produced a brown £10 note from her purse, the woman became all matronly and benevolent.

'Now, don't you worry about a thing, dear,' she said to me. 'I won't be a minute, the kettle's on.'

I was thankful that it wasn't for more tea, although I changed my mind when mum escorted me into the kitchen. The woman was now grating a bar of carbolic soap into a saucepan; she added the water and after stirring the mixture over another flame, she poured it into a thick rubber bottle.

'Slip your things off, there's a good girl,' the woman said.

I removed my tights and knickers, while the woman attached a black tube to the bottle. When she had finished

168

her task, she motioned me to stand with my legs apart. Below me, she placed a metal bucket.

'It won't hurt, dear,' she said. 'Just pop it between your legs and push it up as far as it will go.'

Up until then, I had been very brave, but now I cried like I had never cried before, the woman coaxing the vile black tube into me, while I stood there helplessly with my legs apart. Along with my tears, I started to retch, but each time I relaxed, the woman forced the tube another few inches into my body.

When the tube was in far enough, the woman started to pump the black rubber bottle, the thick, soapy mixture flooding my stomach and running down the insides of my legs. The woman, she seemed to be grinning, although I'm sure she wasn't, said something to mum, but the words were lost. I was gasping for breath, but suddenly she started to punch me in the stomach. At the same time, the lost words materialised and mum and the woman were chanting: 'Push, Push, Push,' their faces seen through my tears like stretched plastic masks. Once again I felt lost in a scene from stage school ... When shall we three meet again, In thunder, lightning or in rain ...?

I squatted down further, mum held my shoulders and the fully qualified nurse pummelled me with both fists, her actions making the black tube coil like an angry serpent. I suddenly felt that my soul was being sacrificed in some gruesome black magic rite. The carbolic soap had all gone, flushed through my stomach to spill into the bucket and flow across the floor. As I closed my eyes, I felt a warm, almost pleasant sensation of water trickling down my legs. It wasn't the little being we had tried to draw out. I had peed myself.

'Don't worry dear, we'll try again,' the woman said.

'No, I can't, I can't,' I cried. 'I don't want to.'

'But sometimes it takes five or six goes.'

'I won't do it.'

'But the money ...'

'It's not important,' mum interrupted. She put her arms around me. 'Come on baby, I'll take you home.'

There was no bathroom in the small basement, not that I was in a fit enough state to be embarrassed. I washed my face and the urine from my legs; I climbed back into my knickers and tights and we returned to the rainy cold streets of Battersea.

I went to bed as soon as I got home and I cried all night. In a way I was glad that the abortion had failed, for deep down, I wanted to have the baby. Sex and motherhood have nothing to do with age. I had all the feelings of being a woman when I returned from making *Doctor at Sea* with Brigitte Bardot. Now, with the love I felt for Mike King, it was a natural, maternal instinct. I cried and felt sorry for myself, but then, in the next breath, I wondered if it would be a boy or a girl.

Dad didn't go to work the following morning. He sat at the breakfast table, sad and stern, and before he even spoke I knew that mum had told him.

'You can't just have a baby, just like that,' he said. 'It's not done.'

I didn't know what to say, so I just stood there and cried.

'Don't cry, Carol, we'll look after you,' he continued. 'But you can't have a baby. What will it do to your life, your career?'

'I don't know, but I'm not going back to that woman again.'

'No, of course not,' he said, putting his arms out to hold me. 'You can go to Switzerland like the toffee-noses, have the baby in a clinic and leave it for adoption. Nobody ever need know.'

I stood there in silence, tears rolling down my cheeks, my father's large hands patting me. He wasn't a man to argue with once his mind was made up. I was lucky that my parents were both so supportive, although at the time it seemed that they were against me. I shrunk from dad's touch and

170

returned to my bedroom to think. Everything went round in circles and finally, in a state of hysteria, I telephoned Mike and told him.

He was thrilled.

'And it doesn't matter that I'm pregnant?'

'Matter? Of course it doesn't matter. I love you.'

'But what shall we do about the baby?'

'All the things that people usually do, I suppose,' he said.

'But we're not married,' I said. I was secretly so old-fashioned.

'So, we'll get married ...'

It wasn't much of a proposal, but I was overjoyed. Mike was my saviour, my hero. Gone now was the fear of a depressing, lonely journey to Switzerland or another confrontation with the Battersea abortionist. I told Mike I loved him about a million times and then ran into the kitchen, mum and dad still surly-faced, like Scottish accountants, and the two poodles pacing in circles by the door, angry that they were being ignored.

'I'm getting married,' I said. 'Isn't it wonderful?'

'Not to Peter Jones you're not,' dad said. 'He's too old for you. You're throwing your life away.'

'Of course not, silly, I'm in love with Mike.'

Mum and dad both stood up and the three of us did a sort of ring-around-the-roses dance, the poodles yapping bitterly and the spring sunshine lifting above the trees outside and flooding the kitchen in yellow light. It was the end of March and there was a lot to do. Mrs King wasn't that happy, but when she learned that I was pregnant, she was proud that her son was 'doing the right thing by me'.

I floated through the house in a dream – maybe it was a bubble! I started to blow out like a balloon, a bar of Cadbury's chocolate always close at hand, like a medicine that had to be taken four times an hour. Jane, now a party to the secret, did my share of the housework and became a confidante for all my private hopes for the future. Mike

171

called several times each day with news of his mother's additions to the festivities, things like the choice of hymns and the colour of the best man's socks.

Dad, a slave to tradition, was paying for everything and to avoid a dispute, the Whites and Kings agreed to have the reception at a restaurant in Leyton. Dad's major concern was ensuring that enough beer was ordered, spending every waking hour whispering mathematics to himself . . . 'Now if there's a hundred men . . . we'll need ten pints for each . . . so with twenty-four halves to a crate . . .' and so it went on, dad's computations related to his capacity, no one else's.

1 April arrived with a mysterious telephone call and a muffled voice saying: 'It's all over, my heart belongs to the Foreign Legion . . .' It was one of the King brothers speaking through a handkerchief, but even when I caught on to my birthday/April Fool surprise, the owner of the voice wouldn't identify himself.

Wow! I thought. Nineteen and soon to be a bride. I was growing up   and still growing out, a fact that was quite evident when Mike took me to see the local priest in Leyton. Mrs King had insisted on the sanctity of the church, although I'm sure there was a lot of string pulling before they accepted me. I had to go to six 'indoctrination' lessons, where I was taught the precepts of Catholicism. I didn't become a Catholic   not that they wanted me   but I had to be made aware of my place to marry one.

The poor priest, he was only a young man, had to explain the facts of life and the Catholic stand on birth control. It all seemed rather silly, the priest a celibate and me already pregnant, but he was very understanding; he absolved all my sins and ended the last lesson by saying: 'The Lord in his wisdom is forgiving and compassionate, but stick to the rules from now on.'

I went away with a little white prayer book and the priest's words like a cloud that only dispersed when I snapped my way through the four fingers of a Kit Kat bar.

The days passed in trauma and catastrophe, those

inevitable April showers lashed Ravenscourt Park like a monsoon, no cars were available, the order for the cake was lost, the heel came off one of my shoes and to top it all, the honeymoon we planned had to be cancelled because the King Brothers had a late booking that couldn't be turned down. 'Someone is trying to tell me something,' I kept saying to myself, but the morning of 29 April arrived without a cloud in sight, striped sunlight fell in patterns through the conservatory glass and the whole world, well, my world at least, seemed bathed in a new optimism. The order for the cake had been found, my shoes were replaced and three black Humbers that reflected the sun from their shining chrome arrived at the appointed time.

The chauffeurs, with peaked caps tucked beneath their arms, waited patiently with their steeds while a clutch of press photographers gathered about me with their clicking cameras; golden coins of light filtered through the apple trees, my sister drawn in to overshadow me with her radiant peaches and cream beauty and, for a second, I felt like a little dumpling beside her. It was fleeting, a moment's panic, a sudden fear and lack of self-confidence – although Jane, who had now developed a figure, was stunning, her cowl-necked yellow chiffon gown clinging to her slender limbs and making me feel even fatter than I was. No one would have blamed me had I hated her presence, but I didn't. For the first time in our lives, we were really close; as close as two sisters can be.

Dad was busying himself with bottles of beer, ably assisted by an expert, his brother Jim, the publican at the White Horse, in Southall. Little Joey, all grown-up and wearing a three-piece suit, stood with his hands in his pockets, at home in the men's private gathering. The ladies stood together on the lawn, a flight of graceful flamingos that had descended from the heavens, mum at the centre in a pale grey, wild silk suit with a matching hat, more of a show stealer than Jane; there was Barry's wife, Rona, Auntie Cath and her daughters, Valerie, June and Sandra, all in various pastel shades of chiffon and silk. Jane fluttered nervously from the circle to stand at my side; her photograph was taken and she lifted on invisible wings back to the lawn.

I was wearing a shapeless pink tent dress, blue underwear; something old, something borrowed, everything prepared according to custom, the ladies whispering things like: 'The sun always shines on a happy bride', the press photographers still shooting and, unbeknown to us all, Ming, the insane Siamese, creeping stealthily through the branches of the tree under which I stood. Its prey was my carefully coiled and bouffanted hair and, with the cameras all clicking their staccato beat, the crazy animal leapt at my head and made a bird's nest of my tresses.

It was that picture that made the Sunday morning papers.

The cat was kicked, the damage was repaired and with my pride all pieced carefully back together, I led the family to the waiting cars; dad and I alone in the first; Jane, the only bridesmaid, with mum and Joey, and Barry bringing up the rear with Jim and their exotic charges.

We were a fashionable five minutes late in arriving at the old brick church. Mike and his brother Tony, the best man, were waiting in the arched porch; more photographs were taken and as the organist felt his way into 'Here Comes the Bride', I held Mike's arm and we walked slowly along the red-carpeted aisle.

The church could not have been more beautiful: the stained glass windows were like lanterns, the coloured specks of sunshine lighting the polished wooden pews, the grey arches and columns, Mrs King's tiers of spring flowers and the people as they rose to their feet and watched our progression towards the priest. It was serious, yet gay, the organ music very subtle in the background and Jane's sudden attack of nervous giggles echoing into the high vaulted ceiling. Dad was saying 'shush, shush,' Tony was checking his pockets, making sure the ring was still there and Mike was grinning like a Cheshire cat. I had an awful job getting through the vows, Jane's condition both worsening and becoming contagious, but in next to no time, the priest was closing his large book and saying, 'You may now kiss the bride ...'

It was over.

Lots of people had gathered on the pavement outside, the press, fans of the King Brothers and Saturday morning shoppers with their bags and curious faces. We left the porch to enter a snowstorm of confetti. I had never been so happy and I had the feeling of being inside a plastic dome, Mike and I glued together, toy people in a seaside toy, with smiles that last forever. The photo call lasted for hours, but finally, the crowds on the curbside all waving, Mike and I led a convoy of limousines and American cars to part one of the reception, a silver service luncheon with champagne and the comedians having to work overtime to stay ahead of dad and his friends, all ex-market traders, taxi drivers, publicans and vaudeville performers from Hammersmith.

All went very smoothly until it was time to leave the restaurant and continue the reception at the Kings' country house. Dad, who was prone to exaggeration at the best of times, was talking to a young girl named Anne, whose marriage was in the near future and whose reception was to be held in the same restaurant. Dad told the girl that the charge was five times what he had really paid and she went immediately to the owner and cancelled the booking.

Mrs King was outraged. Anne was her maid and confidante and the owner of the restaurant was a family friend.

'Really, Mr White,' she said. 'If I had of thought you were going to cause such a fuss over the bill, I would have paid it myself.'

Dad just laughed and called her 'Lady Muck', but when Mrs King retorted with a stage whispered: 'Just what I would have expected from your type', Mr King sensed that it was all getting out of hand and stepped between them with a conciliatory smile and led his wife away.

It had all blown over by the time we arrived at the house.

The doors were open, the sun was shining and Tommy Cooper soon started one of his routines. He did a series of tricks that didn't work and for a finalé, he put a silk scarf into a hat and set it on fire. I wasn't quite sure of the point, but it was very funny. Tommy was hilarious even when he wasn't trying to be so, his absurd jokes and bizarre tricks somehow an extension of his very being. Everywhere was suddenly a jamboree of comedians, clusters of people all laughing, getting drunk and enjoying themselves.

My faithful friend Lionel Bart arrived with the singer Alma Cogan. Lionel seemed so pleased that I had married Mike that an outsider would have guessed that he was my father. He stood there, talking with mum, praising my abilities as an actress and finally declaring: 'She has got to get back to work as soon as possible, she's got too much talent to waste it!' I noticed Alma squirm, but I just looked on with a smile as big as my waist line.

There were several toasts, endless speeches, champagne corks rained through the air like missiles and when the celebration reached its noisiest, Denis King's golf partner turned up to perform a Highland Fling. It was Sean Connery, not in the suave pose of James Bond, but in full Highland costume. He spotted little Ronnie Corbett, a fellow Scot, and when Ronnie joined the dance, it became an invitation for all the guests to do likewise.

The prolonged fling became something a little more sedate and as everyone paired off for a waltz, I found myself in Sean Connery's powerful arms. Wih his party piece over and done with, a very solemn face had replaced his high spirits.

'Now look after that boy of yours, Carol,' he said. 'He's one of the best.'

'I know he is,' I replied, Sean guiding me in a circle that ended with a new partner – Mike King, my husband.

We danced away the late hours, the day's minor dramas becoming material that the comedians were already moulding into subtle one liners. Nearly everyone had managed to get drunk and no one appeared eager to go home. I was nearing midnight and before our car turned into a pumpkin, I changed into a white suit, kissed lots of cheeks and listened to a good supply of highly inappropriate wedding night quips. Suddenly, it was time to go. Everyone was waving and shouting, but as mum came forward to say goodbye, her shoulders sagged and she burst into tears.

'What are we going to do without you?' she said. 'The house will be so quiet.'

Jane, always a sucker for a good cry, started to weep even louder and when I joined in, we must have looked more like mourners at a wake than a bride and her family on a day so wonderful that it remains one of the best memories of my life. Mum and Jane kept lamenting my departure from home – not that they had a lot of time in which to miss me! Mike and I did have a honeymoon: three days alone together and then the King Brothers were back on tour. Did we go somewhere exciting, half-way across the world? No, we stayed at the Kensington Palace Hotel, three miles from Goldhawk Road. The tour lasted for two weeks and I returned home again to my tiny bedroom.

The days were long and slow. May sunshine filled the park and the sound of children's voices gave me feelings that were new and strange. I was looking forward to having a baby, but I also wanted to return to my own childhood, to the days when I watched Richard O'Sullivan kicking through the drifts of autumn leaves. I had been the leading lady in three films, an actress, but not the star that dad had hoped for. As I sat and watched from the window, it felt as if the distant clouds contained all my dreams; dreams that were floating away in search of other horizons.

Jane had a new boyfriend; Joey had one of his rare film parts and mum and dad were fussing over him all the time. Mike called every evening and I remained in my room, eating and eating and eating.

Eleven

THE HAZY mirror of the past had captured my imagination ever since I was a small girl. I liked things to remain how they had always been; I remembered my mistrust of a world where cart horses were no longer necessary, the advent of television and the bulldozers that lay waste houses and memories and streets that were once filled with friends. I was always the first to wear the latest fashions, but privately I was very conservative.

During the three years that had taken me to my nineteenth birthday, I had continued with my habit of looking back, only the reflective moments usually came when I was feeling insecure. Some mismatched wires had fused together when I was raped in France and everything that had happened since was part of the same confused pattern – my own personal vendetta against order. The seduction scene in Mayfair, my engagement to the energetic, yet misogynist Latin lover and my unrivalled performance as London's best known good time girl, all were moves in a pointless, destructive game. Those years had been lived in a long, dark tunnel, a complicated maze where each crossroad represented a trial that I had to undergo; the conquests had been steps on a treadmill, a ladder that went neither up nor down, but round and round in circles. Suddenly, I was free from that treadmill; the past had slipped away, as unimportant now as yesterday's news.

The future was all that mattered. For once, I was satisfied with simply being me. I had reached the end of the tunnel and found real happiness in the daylight. Mike King filled

178

my every dream and I felt like the luckiest newlywed in the world.

The girls at school had always called me lucky, the word on their lips sounding a bit like 'leper', but I suppose it was true, if luck played an important part in our lives, I did have my fair share. Everyone said: 'You always land on your feet, Carol', as if we lived life in bitter competition with each other and I had found some way in which to cheat. What the moaners and complainers couldn't see was that opportunity poked its head in everyone's door and it took more than just luck to grab hold of it. Sometimes, you needed guts.

Now I was plump, pregnant and pleased with myself; I was matronly and mummyish, as if my condition was the result of some clever trick, which in a way it was! Men thought they could do everything better than women, but when it came to having babies, we really had the market cornered.

I mused away my solitary honeymoon and when the tour came to an end, Mike returned with his brothers to start work in a regular television variety show, with the singer Marion Ryan. We found a flat in South Kensington and with dad directing removals like a grumpy sergeant major, I left Barry's small bedroom with my grand collection of wedding presents, my suitcases, all jammed full with last year's fashions, and my changing moods. Under my arm, I carried the framed photograph of a chubby ten-year-old in a scene from *Circus Friends*.

Mum and Jane stood on the doorstep, crying again when it was finally time to wave goodbye, although when Mike went off to rehearsals the following day, they presented themselves at the flat, all dressed up and ready to take me out to lunch. My taste buds needed a rest from chocolate bars and with the Star of India just around the corner, I developed a liking for hot spicy curry. From then on, rarely did a day go by when I didn't eat at the restaurant, the waiters becoming as familiar to me as the wild-eyed and multi-armed images that lined the walls.

I went out for quiet lunches with my old friend Mia Karam

179

and school friends from the Corona academy only to return to the Star of India with Mike and his brothers the same evening. The waiters would smile, but never once did they give the game away. The King Brothers had become tremendously popular and, whenever we went out to eat, people would appear at the table between courses to ask the boys for their autographs. They were on top of the world and their television shows were receiving great reviews, but while the public still wasn't aware of the sounds that left the Cavern Club in Liverpool, everyone in the industry itself was sitting on the edge of their seats and waiting for the explosion.

Mike, Denis and Tony were too busy working to worry about the future; they had been booked for a twelve-week season with Lonnie Donegan in Great Yarmouth and just before we packed our bags and left for the summer, they were asked to appear with Frank Sinatra at the Royal Festival Hall. I sat in the box above the stage, my stomach filled with butterflies, instead of mutton curry, and watched Mr Frank Sinatra woo and charm his audience. His eyes flashed messages and intrigue, as powerful as the light beams that lit the stage, and his presence created an energy that took my breath away. He was obviously the sort of man who could reach out and take whatever he wanted, although little did I know that a time would come when I was one of the things he would reach for.

That night, as I looked down from the heights, I thought: That's one hell of a sexy man, even though the top of his head was shining rather strangely. It was before the time when Frank started his hair transplants and, in the spotlights, the dark make-up he had used on his scalp had become as bright as polished leather. I joined the King Brothers backstage during Frank's encore, but we didn't get a chance to speak. The curtain fell and he left the theatre almost immediately.

He said in passing, 'Great show fellas, thanks a lot.' That was the last I saw of Frank Sinatra for nearly ten years.

When we finally managed to get the flat straight, it was time to leave for Great Yarmouth. I had been going regularly to see a gynaecologist in Harley Street and I had to continue with the examinations, taking the train to London once a week and returning with the news that all was fine, which wasn't exactly true. I had developed toxaemia, blood poisoning and high blood pressure, and the doctor called Mike to warn him that I would become gravely ill if I didn't stop over-eating. I had gone from seven and a half, to almost thirteen stone; or, for the benefit of my American friends, from 105 to 180lb.

But it did no good, I simply couldn't stop. Mike watched me like a hawk, but when he was onstage, I rushed to the foyer and filled up on boxes of Maltesers. On top of that I had an accomplice in the expanding shape of singer Jackie Trent, who was appearing in the show with Tony Hatch, although it was before they got married. Tony and Mike were both vigilant, but no matter how many spies they had to help them, Jackie and I managed to creep off and gorge ourselves among the hot dog stands along the sea front. Two pregnant ladies are more canny than one.

With my tendency to be excessive, I would have eaten myself into a coma, but something happened that summer in 1962 and not only did I stop eating, by my eternal feeling of bliss sagged into a deep and dreadful depression. On the night of 4 August, Marilyn Monroe died at her Hollywood home. I felt as if a piece of myself had died with her.

I had been living in limbo, as if marriage had been my means of escaping destiny. My life had been and would always be a jumble of heartaches and surprises, soaring moments of success and deep troughs of despondency. I had been living a false dream and I awoke to a future that was dark, dangerous and where the odds against survival would grow slimmer with each passing year. Poor Mike, I kept thinking, what has he let himself in for?

I had felt a special bond with my childhood idol since I won the *Sunday Mirror* lookalike competitions. It seemed as if our lives were in some way connected, that no matter what I did, Marilyn's fate would eventually be my own. I thought there was something special about me and Marilyn Monroe thought the same of herself:

> Yes, there was something special about me, and I knew what it was. I was the kind of girl they found dead in a hall bedroom with an empty bottle of sleeping pills in her hand.

I didn't consider that I had been taken seriously as an actress and I knew that, like Marilyn Monroe, I would have to fight and struggle and claw my way along every inch of the road that leads to stardom. Again, I quote Marilyn's own words:

> I want to be an artist . . . not an erotic freak. I don't want to be sold to the public as a celluloid aphrodisical.
> I realised that just as I had once fought to get into the movies and become an actress, I would have to fight to be able to become myself and to use my talents. If I didn't fight I would become a piece of merchandise to be sold off the movie pushcart.*

In the three films I had made at Beaconsfield, I had been cast as a dumb blonde, my legs and my tits being more important than the fact that I could act. As a child, I had played in even more films than I cared to remember, parts that I got because of my ability and nothing else. I didn't give a damn about the past, but I did decide that far from my movie-making days being over, they had yet to begin. I didn't care how long it took, but I would return with every ounce of power I possessed.

The come back would be a long hard climb and there would be plenty of times when a casting couch would not only have made things easier, but would have meant that I

* *My Story*. New York: Stein & Day. 1974.

walked out with a six figure film contract. The chances were there, but even through the hungry days – and there's not many people in the movie business who don't have them – I have slammed the door on such chances. Lots of girls don't and I can't say that I blame them. It's a tough world and everyone has to hustle with whatever means they have; using your body to get what you want is one of the ways, but it has never been my way. My path has been the long way round, going for parts with a score of girls, jostling in the cattle market where every casting director takes on the status of God, bit parts on television and film offers that come when you have finally proved yourself. Then comes the glamour, the acclaim, the money, but more important is the sheer joy of working, of reading a type-written film script, of pouring your soul into the part until a piece of your very being goes home with the cinema audience.

Acting is art and any work of art subtracts something from the artist; that something, whatever it is, can never be replaced and the substitute comes in dark glass bottles and pills and packets of white powder. It is no coincidence that so many performers use drugs and die young; choosing a life as an actor, a painter, a writer is in itself living a life in pursuit of death.

Marilyn Monroe was thirty-six when she died. I was nineteen and I hadn't even heard of barbiturates, but far from her death being a warning, it appeared as an invitation to walk the same road. Up until this time, I had never bothered to stop and think about what I was aiming at in life. Dad had pushed me through stage school and the film work just followed as if it was meant to be. I didn't know what it was like to be without money, or to want a part so badly that it made you ill. I had lived by my instincts, eating, sleeping and making love whenever I felt like it; appearing in the movies was simply an extension to my social life. Suddenly, it all changed. I looked out at the grey troubled ocean, I was five stone overweight and six months pregnant and a new element had entered my view of life: ambition, the precursor of all problems.

With my new demon and Marilyn's death went the last of my childhood dreams. I had always hoped that we would meet, or even work together. That was no longer possible, but more than that, I stopped having idols, I stopped looking upon the superstars as being anything other than mortal. When I arrived in Hollywood, Irv Levin arranged for me to take the children to a tea party with Elvis Presley. I was excited at first, but when the car appeared I sent the nanny with Sean and Stephen and remained at home. Had I known that Elvis was rushing headlong towards an early grave, I probably would have gone.

The summer months passed with me grown a little older and my life didn't cross again with the legend of Marilyn Monroe for many years, not until I moved into a new apartment in North Doheny Drive, the borderland between Beverly Hills and West Hollywood. The building is next door to the house where Marilyn once lived and where she is said to have entertained, among others, President John F. Kennedy. Three months before she died, she had flown to New York to sing 'Happy Birthday' to the President at Madison Square Garden, when Peter Lawford announced her appearance onstage as 'the late Marilyn Monroe'.

The pleasure I had found in sneaking off to eat hot dogs had come to an end. I was fed up with being so fat, but I still had a few more months of pregnancy ahead of me. We returned to London at the end of September, but within a matter of days, we were back on the road again. The doctor advised me to stay home, but the Kings were playing at the Liverpool Empire, right in the heartland of the 'new' sound and I wanted to see what all the fuss was about.

Two months later, I met the Beatles at EMI's Abbey Road studios, but during our brief excursion I was under the impression that it was Rory Storm and the Hurricanes who were going to rocket to stardom. Tony King was going out with Rory's sister, Iris, whom he had met in summer season, and according to her, the Hurricanes were on their way. As it turned out, only their drummer hit the big time. His name was Richard Starkey, who was soon to become Ringo Starr.

Mike, Denis and Tony talked excitedly about 'going electric', but I was now too preoccupied to take much interest. October seemed endless. I found walking almost impossible, but when it got to the stage when I didn't think I could go on for even one more day, I was rushed into hospital. It was 4 November and Sean was born three weeks premature. We chose the name Sean from a long list I had made with Jackie during the summer, I think the connection was a certain Highland dancer; though had the baby been a girl, the choice would have been much easier. She would have been named Marilyn.

I finally met John Lennon, Paul McCartney, George Harrison and Ringo Starr in December, while the King Brothers were recording 'Peculiar' and 'My Mother's Eyes'. Johnny Spence was the arranger and the Kings' session drummer, Andy White, was rushing from one studio to the next. Ringo had just replaced Pete Best on drums, but although his drumming was suitable for the dance hall circuit, it was considered too raw for recording. It was a temporary embarrassment, for this very rawness would eventually set the pace for a new sort of music.

So this was the Beatles! I thought it was a very silly name and I told them so.

'Why not the Ants, or the Bugs?'

'Why not?' one of them replied and they all laughed.

'What sort of music do you play, anyway?'

'Rock and roll,' Paul replied. I thought he was really cute.

'Beatles music,' John added and the other three looked at him in awe. He was obviously their spokesman.

We chatted away. They all had a great sense of humour, funny hair styles and accents that seemed out of place in London. They were four nice likely lads from Liverpool, but I thought their music was far too loud and I couldn't see why everyone was so excited. They had already released 'Love

Me Do' and 'PS, I Love You' without making much impression on the Top 20 and, while we talked that day between recording sessions, even the Beatles didn't know that history was in the making. They were recording 'Please, Please Me', which was released in January 1963. It went straight to Number One in the charts and the Beatles became the hottest band of all time.

What happened to the two songs the King Brothers recorded that day, nobody knows.

We went home to the flat in Kensington, Christmas passed and the King Brothers' career started its downward curve. The next time I met the Beatles, they were huge stars, the Kings rarely worked and I was on my way up. What happened in between was my housebound period. Almost as soon as it was possible for me to get pregnant again, I did so. I still hadn't learnt anything about birth control and Mike was a good Catholic boy.

We moved from South Kensington to Wellesley Road, Chiswick. The new flat was just as nice, but money was getting tight and it felt as if I was slipping away from the centre of things. Dudley Moore and Ronnie Corbett called in and I cooked them beans on toast, but my taste buds were hard to please and I yearned to make a pilgrimage to the Star of India. I felt like a foreigner cast into a web of suburban monotony, even the great balloon of a body that filled my clothes to bursting point seemed like an April Fool's joke that had gone too far. I remember one of the biggest thrills during that time was going with Mike to a furniture showroom, signing lots of forms and buying a dining table and four chairs on hire purchase. Money had always come to me easily, but it went just as easily. My £20 a week Beaconsfield contract came to an end as soon as they knew I was pregnant and my savings had disappeared on little necessities, like a pink leather coat that I wore only twice. I picked up restaurant bills and bought rounds of drinks, there were weekends at the coast and there was Jane, of course, who didn't have a penny, but did like to have a good time.

Mike had been at the top of his profession for years, but that was in the Dark Ages when singing groups took home no more than a.1yone else. Some weeks on tour, the amount the boys paid out in hotel and restaurant bills was more than they earned. I suppose Mike could have economised by booking the band into single rooms and sleeping three to a bed, but that wasn't show business and it certainly wasn't Mike King. 'Genius is born, not paid ...' I had learned at school; we may not have been in the same class as Oscar Wilde, but as artists, we weren't paid either.

I took Sean to the clinic, I walked in the park with mum and Jane and the months filtered through my own private hourglass. The King Brothers still talked about going electric, but in the wake of the Beatles' success, hundreds of imitators had been spawned and the bandwagon wasn't an exciting prospect. Mike earned enough to pay the rent and buy the food and I waited for Mr Opportunity to come knocking at my door.

The year passed with nothing more exciting than my parents moving into a superb apartment in Hammersmith Broadway. They said the house in Goldhawk Road was too large for them, but it was more that dad missed the good old days. I rarely left my bed during the first weeks of the new year, nursing my swollen legs until 20 January, when Stephen was born. Again, I was pleased to get pregnancy over and done with, although I really had my hands full. Sean was now a toddler, forever getting into mischief, and the baby took up so much time that I couldn't give him the attention he needed. Being a mum and a housewife may well have its own rewards, but I just found it a lot of hard work. I was also worried about my career. A lot of things were happening. The Swinging Sixties had finally arrived and I was desperate to get back in front of the cameras. The frustration became boredom and the boredom gave birth to the worst period of depression ever. I had never been very happy in Chiswick, but when Mike found us somewhere new to live, it felt as if I'd gone from the frying pan into the fire.

187

The move was to a tiny beamed cottage in far-flung Essex. It would have made a great summer house, or a weekend retreat, but I had never lived out in the sticks before and I hated it. The rooms were narrow, there was no central heating and I was convinced it was haunted. When Mike was away working, I remained awake, a dull grey presence sucking at my will to go on. I became even more depressed and the weather matched my mood. It snowed in March, Stephen went down with measles, he became deaf in one ear and nearly died. It made my own depression seem very selfish, but while I was unhappy, it was difficult to be a good wife and a good mother to my children.

Mrs King, my mother and my sister were all very helpful, but while I was nursing poor little Stephen, I became sick myself. The small cottage, with its white walls and low ceilings, became my own personal version of hell and only when we moved out did I start to get better. The basement flat below my parents had become vacant and we moved in at the end of the month.

It all happened quickly, but with wonderful timing.

The icy winds disappeared from the city streets, the grey sky gave way to a pale blue wash and on 1 April 1964, the sun was shining once again. It was my twenty-first birthday, my depression had melted with the snow and I was back with my family in Hammersmith.

Stephen sensed that everything was how it should be, but although he was soon out of danger, it was some months before his hearing was back to normal – something that in recent years, he has been fervently trying to reverse. He plays drums in a band with his brother Sean and two Malibu school friends, Ronnie Russell and Tony Rugalo. They play, as Stephen puts it 'post punk, new romantic', but it took me a long time to soften my conservatism and the name of the band is graphic enough to describe its volume. They call themselves The Grand Manor.

*   *   *

With our second wedding anniversary on the horizon, it was time for a change. Mike was determined to remain the family breadwinner, but with mum and Jane upstairs and my figure back to normal, the ingredients for my comeback were perfect. Mike started the ball rolling by talking to his agent, Sydney Grace, and Syd recommended me to Jean Diamond. Only the sky was the limit and, with a new agent, I had my foot on the ladder's first rung.

At the risk of being repetitious, in the past it had all been so easy, but now, fired with ambition, the going was tough. I wanted a lead role in a film, but all Jean put me up for were television parts. It started with *Emergency Ward 10*, the twice weekly dose of hospital soap, in a role that I found undemanding and slightly absurd. I had been playing a bosomy, all-woman leading lady since I was sixteen; now, with two small boys and the right to vote, I was cast as a runaway teenager.

It was a start.

I remained impatient to get back into the movies, but Jean Diamond wanted to ease my career along a gentle incline and, as events turned out, that was the right move. *Emergency Ward 10* was followed by guest leads in *Dixon of Dock Green* and *The Saint*, parts that I again didn't really want, although I was pleased to be working. What was more important, I was getting to know a circle of writers and directors, with new ideas for TV drama and the BBC as their base. Its central figures were Tony Garnett, whom I had met on *The Boys*, Ken Loach and the writers Nell Dunn and Jeremy Sandford.

Tony Garnett brought me into the circle during the casting of Nell Dunn's *Up the Junction*, a unique documentary film that found many raised eye brows in the morning press. It was about the exploits of three young women in South London, with free love as the underlying theme and an abortion scene used for the first time ever on television. It was very controversial and it placed me another rung up the ladder. I shared the billing with Geraldine Sherman and

Vickery Turner and found myself with a new label; one of the critics described me as the 'Battersea Bardot', which was nice enough, although it came too late to make any difference to my career. It would have been more helpful when I was sixteen and went for a screen test with Roger Vadim, the French director who created the myth of Brigitte Bardot and who was then searching for another sex symbol to enliven the new decade. I had just returned from France and, in spite of my ordeal there, I was at ease with my schoolgirl French and had managed to acquire a little chic. I almost wet myself in excitement when the interview day arrived, but then, everything went wrong. I got caught up in the crowds in Berwick Street market, it poured with rain and by the time I reached the studio, I was a mess.

I hated being tested for parts and not getting them, but that's one of the trials of being an actress. I usually gritted my teeth, smiled sweetly and went home to punch holes in the wall though I did react somewhat differently when I was rejected for a part shortly before the casting of *Up the Junction*. The fat, stuffy producer looked at me down his nose and said my hair needed a good comb and my nail polish was all chipped.

'I beg your pardon?' I said.

'You really should be more careful with your appearance ...'

The fat man didn't know what hit him.

'I'm not a bloody model,' I screamed. 'I've got two small children who take up all of my time when I'm at home and when I go out to work, I happen to be a damned good actress.'

'But, I, I, I ...'

I left the producer stuttering to himself and slammed the door so hard that I could still hear the echoing woodwork when I stormed out of the building.

I met that same producer at a party years later, but he avoided me like the plague.

My chipped nail polish and mess of streaky blonde hair

worked to my advantage when I was cast as the fair-skinned leader of a tribe of Neanderthals in a low budget follow up to *One Million Years BC*, Raquel Welch's first movie. Hammer had bought the costumes cheaply from 20th Century-Fox and they had been hanging about in storage while someone came up with a script. The result was *Slave Girls*, the only film I made during this period. The story was little different from *One Million Years BC*: it had all the vision and expanse of an Ice Age – and it was made entirely in the studio. The fur fabric costumes were smelly and uncomfortable, but I had plenty of fun leaping about with cave man grunts and leading my tribe against our olive-skinned adversaries.

Their leader was Martine Beswicke, whom I didn't see again until I walked into Roy's Restaurant, off the Sunset Boulevard ten years later to find Martine working as a waitress. She was another good actress going through hard times, although she was back in make-up soon after in a forgettable farce called *The Happy Hooker Comes to Hollywood, Part 2*.

We all make films we prefer not to remember!

After *Slave Girls* and *Up the Junction*, more demanding roles and greater recognition seemed only a matter of time. I was feeling good about myself and I was happy with the way it was all working out. The King Brothers had weathered the early storm and Mike continued to earn enough money to pay the bills. I wasn't earning great fortunes, but mum and dad fed us most days and there was enough spare cash to make another all-important come back, the return to a social life where the strings are pulled and a chance meeting can make the difference between holes in your shoes and an Academy Award. Just as many film parts are cast across night club tables as they are in the studios; the whole business is incestuous and who you know often plays a bigger role in the movies than what you can do. Who you have slept with, or more to the point, who you haven't slept with, can be another key factor in building a career.

Evidence of the who-you-know syndrome was clear in that tight clique of documentary makers. I was desperate for something big. Julie Christie had just made *Dr Zhivago*, new names like Marianne Faithfull and Judy Geeson were surfacing, but another TV special was on its way from the BBC planners and, when I was offered the female lead, I could hardly refuse. It was *The Coming Out Party*, written by former prison inmate Jimmy O'Connor and directed by Ken Loach. With a story containing all the underlying social import that was now expected, I added another notch to my curriculum vitae and went home with a neatly typed cheque from the Beeb.

The months had wandered into the depths of 1965 without a major role appearing, but when Jean Diamond put me up for the part of Bianca, in *The Taming of the Shrew*, I was sure it was meant for me. I would receive third billing to the legendary team of Richard Burton and Elizabeth Taylor; I had the right sort of training for cinema Shakespeare and, as the film was being shot in Rome, I felt I had a nostalgic right to return there in triumph.

It was some weeks before casting was completed and I got the news while I was visiting Nell Dunn at her home in Putney. The colour drained from my face and I had to stop myself throwing a tantrum. I didn't get the part and I felt sorely cheated.

'You didn't get it?' Jeremy Sandford said. He sounded pleased. He was Nell's husband, another writer, who was soon to play a very important part in my career.

'No, I didn't get it, so what's the big deal?'

Jeremy, softly spoken and public school, was taken aback and said defensively, 'I'm terribly sorry, Carol, of course, it's just that I have been working on a play and I was rather hoping that you would do it.'

Jeremy Sandford had just finished writing *Cathy Come Home*.

I wasn't that excited, although when it went into production early in 1966, I realised that we had something special. Its success put me in the public eye and when Ken Loach directed me in *Poor Cow* the following year, my future was assured. We had become a team and while Ken's direction was always there, subtle and sensitive, we had got to the stage where we communicated by telepathy; if something was going wrong with a scene, we both knew what it was before we stopped to discuss it. I excelled because the scripts had something to say and Ken Loach's finished product was always a work of art. The three BBC films we had done together were each made in short periods and on low budgets and much of their success was due to the fact that the cast and crew worked in close harmony. We created a homely, folksy atmosphere, which we took with us to the big screen when we came to make *Poor Cow*. It had a great sixties feel to it, Donovan's songs were perfect and I received nine separate awards for my performance.

Everything had worked out the way I had hoped when I looked out at the dark ocean waves at Great Yarmouth in 1962, but five years is a long time for any relationship to last and although Mike and I still loved each other, our parting was inevitable. I was moving away from my old life and the final push came when I started work on Michael Winner's *I'll Never Forget What's His Name*.

Gone were the days of drinking tea with the crew between takes. I was supplied with a sumptuous dressing room, a maid, caviare with my digestive biscuits and champagne everywhere but in the faucet. Michael Winner treated his top-billing cast like royalty, like rare porcelain figures, and when you are treated as someone special you start to believe it.

It was a memorable year and everything I touched seemed to turn to gold. When I wasn't filming, it was fun, fun, fun in the best night spots and, with bank account now overflowing, I found time to become the Lux Girl. I spent two days with their photographers and camera crew and went home with a new wardrobe, two years' supply of soap and a cheque for £20,000.

Carol White was rich and famous, but everyone has to pay their dues. Mike and I had both had our secret flings, but during the filming of *I'll Never Forget What's His Name*, my affair with Oliver Reed became public property and my marriage to Mike King suddenly appeared to belong to a changing era. We came back together when it was time for me to make *The Fixer*, but though we both tried, it was never the same again.

I had climbed the ladder up and up and into the clouds, losing sight of the real me and losing sight of the things that really mattered. That vintage year of 1967 passed into 1968, when Irv Levin appeared with his massive film offer, a hidden cache of dollar bills and a navy blue sports car. I was still in the clouds, a Pan Am jet winging me to Los Angeles and Shakespeare's *The Rape of Lucrece* spanning the gap between the past and the future:

> What win I if I gain the thing I seek?
> A dream, a breath, a froth of fleeting joy;
> Who buys a minute's mirth to wail a week;
> Or sells eternity to get a toy?

Twelve

'IF YOU don't go to Hollywood, you're not a star.'

These were the words that Irv Levin left me with at the end of our hideaway week in Italy during the spring of 1968. His wife had tried to kill herself, which left me to return to London with the future undecided and my feelings in a state of confusion. Irv Levin was a man of many surprises and great generosity. With his parting words came a weighty chunk of gold, a hand-painted bracelet that cost a king's ransom and formed yet another link between us.

I was wearing it when I flew to Los Angeles to star in *Daddy's Gone a Hunting*, although it disappeared mysteriously years later, shortly after my mother died.

Six months and three lovers had intruded upon my romance with Irv and I stepped out into the California sunshine with few expectations. With Irv and his wife, Lenny, 'trying again', I was about ready for a new man to enter my life.

The only expectation I did have was that I would receive full-star treatment and I wasn't disappointed. National General Pictures was paying for everything and dear Irv was as generous as ever. My main concern was somewhere to live, which wasn't as easy as it sounds. With Sean and Stephen being non-swimmers, I demanded a house with *no* swimming pool, almost unheard of in Beverly Hills, although within a few frantic, hair-pulling days, we were all settled in a mock Tudor mansion on Oakhurst Drive. The house had white picket fences, black shutters, a large garden of palms and luxuriant plants and was placed among the most valuable pieces of real estate in the world.

With the children running riot and Mary, their nanny, left in charge, I was taken to the MGM studios at Culver City, where I was found a lavish suite of dressing rooms in a bungalow that was larger than the house I had bought in Putney during the summer. A gang of props men arrived with wallpaper patterns and carpet designs and when the whole place was redecorated with a royal blue carpet, pale blue and white Regency striped wallpaper and a fresh coat of paint, I left to start work – in San Francisco.

It was typical.

Everything was money, money, money, but I was getting used to it. I went to Max Factor to chose make-up and as many hair pieces as I could carry. At the Travilla fashion house, I was praised, measured and supplied with enough new clothes to fill a Lear jet.

There were cocktail parties, luncheons and meetings and I found it a relief when it was time to take up residence at the Mark Hopkins Hotel in San Francisco and start filming. My co-star arrived some days later, when our first scene was an all-white wedding, with me as the bride. Director Mark Robson put his head around my dressing room door and said: 'Couple of minutes Carol – and I'll introduce you to your new husband.'

He was almost immorally good looking, tailored to a T, poised and very sure of himself. His name was Paul Burke, star of television's *Twelve O'clock High* and the leading man in the *Valley of the Dolls*. My heart fluttered merrily and my palms were all wet by the time the minister said: 'I now pronounce you man and wife.' It felt like the real thing, me an innocent bride and Paul Burke the man who would love me and cherish me and fill the future with joy.

But that's not how it happened.

'That's it for today folks,' Mark sang cheerfully and Paul Burke disappeared.

It was Paul's favourite trick. Sometimes when he rushed off, he went to Las Vegas, just for the night. He was a real-life playboy and I was impressed; impressed, but unwanted. I was used to having men falling at my feet and Paul Burke's indifference made me furious. It was all an elaborate game that continued for nearly two weeks and only came to an end when I got the message from London that my father had suddenly collapsed and had been rushed to hospital for immediate brain surgery. I wanted to return home straight away, but I had signed a forty-page contract and that was one of the things I couldn't do. Everything I wasn't supposed to do would fill a book by itself.

I was angry and upset and when I needed a shoulder to cry on, Paul was there. My father did survive and, while he was recuperating, the film continued. I knew now that it was only a matter of time before Paul and I became lovers, although before we did so, he first found a way to make me green with envy.

In one of the film's most dramatic sequences, I had to hang over the side of the roof, fourteen floors up on the Mark Hopkins Hotel. I was being paid $150,000, but I suffered from vertigo on high pavements and so a stuntwoman had to stand in as my double. The scene was shot with Scott Hylands and when he appeared in the hotel lobby with the girl, Paul put his arm around her waist and led her to the bar. It was the last scene of the day and the director was shouting, 'Okay, it's a wrap, we've got it', the crew were filtering off in all directions and there was me, dressed the same as my double and looking a complete idiot.

It was the final straw. I hated Paul Burke, but he was a man who knew his way around women and the next day he came to my room and looked at me with pure, crystal clear eyes and said: 'Carol, I've been a fool.' I swooned into his arms and we made love there and then.

It was the beginning of a relationship that was to last for four years during which I was to learn about the seamy side of stardom; the drugs, the booze, the lethal, mind-twisting games and the love scenes that required me to share my bed with another woman.

Like most Americans, Paul could only do everything in a big way. He was addicted to the gaming tables at Las Vegas, but he didn't have the earning power of the rich circle in which he moved. He walked a continual razor's edge between debt and total ruin, a playboy who could not imagine any life but the good life. He was a great myriad of faults and contradictions and I loved him madly. With the love came a new set of problems and by the time I arrived back in Hollywood to start work in the studio, I was as depressed as hell.

Strangely, it was Irv Levin who was soon there at my side. He was aware of Paul's irresistible charm and while he was still patching up the breach in his relationship with Lenny, he found time to comfort me. He was like a godfather, protecting me from afar, while closer attention was directed in the gloomy person of Jean Diamond, who arrived with a long, stern face and a forefinger that she waved at me like a gun.

'You've got to behave yourself, Carol,' she said. 'You can't keep running about with married men.'

My old school friend Vicky, married to actor Mike Anderson, agreed with her and between them they scoured Hollywood for an eligible and unattached male. The candidate turned out to be James Caan. I was at least willing to give it a try. We were companions at a quiet cocktail party and I allowed him to drive me home that night. I kissed him on the cheek, agreed to have dinner the next day and ran into the house. The dinner date was at the La Scala restaurant, where we talked about the movies and the people we both knew, what else, and by the time we were ready to leave, I was aching with boredom. Again, he drove me back to the house and again I left him with a peck on the cheek. Mr Caan sat there, dumbfounded, for several seconds and then chased after me to bang on the door.

'Let me in, let me in,' he shouted, but I kept the door bolted and although in the weeks that followed he trailed me all over Los Angeles, I managed to stay one step ahead.

Jean and Vicky couldn't understand why I had rejected James Caan, or why I had such a fatal fascination for married men; but I did and I couldn't do anything about it. The end of my no-go relationship with James came when he turned up at my door in the middle of the night and didn't stop pleading with me to let him in, until Mike Anderson appeared and took him away.

I was still secretly seeing Paul, but that was most unsatisfactory, which I made very clear to him the night of a big party at Paul's city home in Hollywood. He acted as if we were strangers and when I became tearful, he asked agent Abby Greshler to take me home.

'He's not taking me home, you are,' I said and as Paul's wife, Peggy, came through the door, I slapped Paul across the face.

The room went silent.

'Why don't you tell her what's going on between us?' I cried and ran off into the hills.

I kept running until I was lost and then I hid in a garden, where I spent the night. I was cold and tired by morning, but I had made sure that everyone knew I was upset. It was Patty Duke who found me and took me back to Paul's house. While Paul was still out looking for me, I told Peggy everything. I was young, vulnerable and an award winning actress. I broke down and cried my heart out and when Paul returned, Peggy told him to pack his bags.

And where did he go?

To my house on Oakhurst Drive. That was really the beginning and from that day on, we went back and forth in a contest of wills that aged Paul and led me to a nervous breakdown. At first it was wonderful. Paul was loving and considerate and I felt secure enough to go home for Christmas and see my dad. The surgery had been to remove a tumour in an operation that few men would have survived, but dad was as tough as the old iron he had once collected and, though he was confined to a wheelchair, he was aggressively cheerful throughout my stay in London.

It was a relief that my family were still there, my sanctuary in a world that was going crazy and where the tentacled arms of the movie business were able to reach home before I did. Irv Levin was still with his wife, but Hollywood insiders knew about our affair and my scenes with Paul Burke and James Caan had made him appear foolish. The blue Merc turned out to be the property of National General and the accounts department wanted it back. I could have refused, but instead, I went with my own money to the show room in Park Lane and bought the same model car, this time in silver.

The car wasn't all I lost. I had spent a lot of time with writers Jerry Belson and Gary Marshall, reading over and adding my own ideas on the script for *The Grasshopper*, National General's next picture and one that I was expected to do. It would have been the second in the proposed three-picture contract, but I had managed to contravene something in that forty-page agreement and Jacqueline Bisset was signed to replace me. When I met Jackie in Canada years later, we spent a lot of time together and became good friends; we talked of many things, but carefully avoided the film that launched her career.

After receiving so many awards and so much acclaim for *Poor Cow*, I imagined that success would simply follow success in an endless chain, a fool's paradise that I took with me to San Francisco. My face peered down from countless larger-than-life-sized posters, I decorated displays filled with sunglasses, car lots, toy shop windows and every newspaper on the coast. *Daddy's Gone a Hunting* was going to be the biggest thing since sliced bread and *Gone with the Wind*. All the chemicals were right; it was a fast moving drama, jam-packed with thrills, romance, danger and children; there were songs by Dory Previn, the direction was faultless and a fortune had been spent on advertising. But something was wrong, the timing, the release date, Mars in opposition to Mercury? Something, at least, that nobody had foreseen. The film received little attention and mediocre returns.

Hollywood doesn't like failure and although my performance wasn't criticised, I was in everyone's bad books because of my affair with Paul Burke because by Hollywood standards he was a happily married man. Talk about double standards. As somebody said at the time, you can play any instrument in the orchestra, but nobody messes with the star. I didn't care. My feelings were so bound up with Paul that as soon as Christmas was over, I dashed straight back to join him at the house he had built himself in Palm Springs. It was a strange relationship. We constantly argued and we made love with a passion I hadn't known since I was a teenager. He was a womaniser, a heavy drinker, he was twenty years older than me and I worried myself into exhaustion when he wasn't there. He still did his disappearing act, usually to pass money across the roulette tables and sometimes to call on one of his many lady friends. Paul had a passion for prostitutes and, on the nights when he didn't return home, that was where he spent his time. It didn't really matter and at least it was cheaper than gambling.

I could put up with Paul's games while we relaxed in Palm Springs, but when I worked, I didn't have any spare energy. At the beginning of the year, I was signed to do *Something Big*, with Dean Martin and Honor Blackman. I wanted to be on my own for a while, but when it was time to start filming there was Paul, beside me on the plane.

Spaghetti Westerns were all the rage and *Something Big* was a sort of chili-bean version, filmed in the middle of the Mexican desert. We all stayed at a sleazy motel, with warm beer, sand in the beds and dreadful food. Everyone had bad stomachs, there was nothing to do when we weren't working and it turned out to be a lot of fun. Dean Martin was nothing like I had imagined. He seemed a quiet and solitary man, so relaxed on set he was almost asleep and, contrary to his reputation as a heavyweight drinker, he did no more than tackle a few warm beers with the rest of us. We picked carefully at the poisonous food and with us all nursing each other's ailments, the film was completed on schedule.

We now faced a long drive across the desert to a tiny, sun-baked air strip at Durango and a dubious flight in a propeller plane to Mexico City.

I was thinking about another superstar I had met before Christmas and whom I would meet again in the coming months. His name was Frank Sinatra.

I returned to Palm Springs to live the good life. It should have been a happy time, but it wasn't. A sadness had stolen into me like cancer, something was changing in the world and that change was eating again at my insides. The Swinging Sixties would soon be over and I would leave those psychedelic, sunny days with another shadow upon my dreams. The castles we had built were collapsing into dust; mini-skirts had gone, long hair was old-fashioned, the Beatles were splitting up and in July 1969, Rolling Stones' guitarist Brian Jones drowned in the swimming pool at his home in Hertfordshire. We had been friends during the special years, we had talked and danced within the glow of a million fairy lights, in a fleeting glimpse of paradise that was London in the sixties. That same dreadful emptiness that had filled me when Marilyn Monroe died came to me again, although this time, it only made me stronger. Brian Jones was one of the first to go and I suddenly felt older – not wiser, but a survivor.

It was just before Brian's death that I arrived once again at the vinyl ice hall of Heathrow Airport. I had returned to star in Joseph E. Levine's *The Man Who Had Power Over Women*. I had been offered the film as the first in another three picture deal that, to me, would have been worth one million dollars. In their wisdom, my American management said I didn't need to be tied to another contract and to this day I still don't know why I took their advice. When you turn down a big offer, you don't get another chance and the film I did turned out to be the only one with Avco-Embassy.

Throughout the whole of my life I have listened to the advice of those people who call themselves experts; agents, managers, publicity men, writers and lawyers, everyone from fellow actors to Uncle Tom Cobleigh; husbands, girlfriends, lovers and liftmen. They all know the movie business inside out and with blind, careless naivete, I have thrown away more chances than most people even dream of getting.

Still enjoying my own glorious delusion and allowing others to manage my life, I stepped from the first class cabin into the welcoming crisp winds of a bright but chilly day. Pan Am officials had taken control of my hand-luggage, the press photographers were busy jostling each other and, from the background, three starched customs men appeared with red English faces and the traditional almost comical request:

'Anything to declare?'

It sounded like a parody, or a line from a script.

'No,' I said. 'Not a thing.'

'We would just like to have a look,' the man with the grimmest and reddest face said.

'Of course.'

Amongst my hand luggage I carried three fur coats, a leopard, a white mink and a ranch mink. I didn't declare them and I didn't know I was supposed to.

'What are these?' the custom's man said.

'They're my coats.'

'And why didn't you declare them?'

'Why should I?'

It was the wrong thing to say.

'I'm afraid not even filmstars receive special treatment with the customs,' the man said. 'Come this way.'

203

The photographers were having a field day, the Pan Am porters and officials were all milky-faced and unsure what to do, Sean and Stephen thought it was wildly amusing and I couldn't understand why they had picked on me! In the past, my luggage had passed through customs with no more than a cursory glance and a chalky scribble. Something was happening and it went from bad to worse.

In a small room where I imagined men with rubber hoses beat confessions from dope runners and gem smugglers, a team of uniformed men and women picked through my nests of suitcases, while the man with the most gold braid on his shoulders cut the lining from the fur coats. I couldn't believe my eyes.

Sean suffered from asthma and the doctor who had given him a shot before we left Los Angeles had presented each of the boys with an unwanted syringe, for them to use as water pistols. Incredible as it now seems, the customs men even searched Sean and Stephen and, when they found the plastic syringes, they hoped it would lead to something even more exciting. It didn't, of course, but when the head man realised that I wasn't smuggling drugs, he decided to throw the book at me anyway. I thought that as the full amount had been paid for the coats, there wouldn't be any duty, but ignorance is no excuse in the eyes of the law and I was only allowed to go home when bail of £5,000 had been arranged. I felt like a criminal.

I learned later that British customs had been alerted about the coats by a jealous lady who assumed that her husband had bought them, which wasn't the case. I had bought them myself in a moment of extravagant self-indulgence and I imagined the crisis was the product of all those animal spirits beaming their disapproval through the universe.

I went off to start filming, the story filled the newspapers for several days and I left the whole thing in the hands of my lawyer, Mr David Napley, the then head of the Bar Association. I didn't have to attend court, but I did have to pay the bill.

I paid: £5,000 in fines
£2,000 in legal fees, and
£3,000 for the return of one of the coats.

I was amazed. The three coats were confiscated, but with Britain's quaint tradition for fair play, the final and mere sum of £3,000 allowed me the right to get one of my coats back again – enabling me to face the English summer, wrapped in a fur. The saga had a similar sequel to the last one. Two years later, I was back to being a vegetarian. I sold the coat to Mike King for £750 and he gave it to another girlfriend.

There was only one more occasion when I bought myself a fur coat and that one, I threw out of a hotel window, never to see it again.

Working with Rod Taylor and James Booth on *The Man Who Had Power Over Women* was like a vacation and with Paul Burke still doing his own thing in New York, or Las Vegas, my tumultuous social life ground to a halt. I recoiled into my little nest, Sean and Stephen went to a private school for American children, mum was nearby, as strong and solid as ever and my dad was trying hard to be his old self, though it was sad to see him all small and weak and still in a wheelchair. The silver Mercedes stood rain-splattered and rusting in the square, the summer days were deliciously English and I was happy to spend my evenings alone with a glass of red wine and the BBC. I had grown to loathe American television, with its constant commercials and programmes sponsored by toothpaste and tampon manufacturers.

It was a short respite and ended when Paul turned up in London. My house in Putney was far too small and ordinary for my pleasure-seeking lover and while Paul stayed at the Dorchester, I set about finding something more suitable. Paul was used to the space and luxury of his home in Palm Springs; I felt obliged to provide something as nice and by this time, I, too, only expected the best. My search came to an end the evening we had dinner with director John Boorman and his German wife, Crystal. They lived in a Georgian mansion in Montague Square and a four-storey house was available in the same block. It was so close to the West End night clubs and casinos that, when we all moved in a week later, Paul felt very much at home.

I paid twelve months' rent on the house and while I went off to the studios at Twickenham each day, Paul toured the best stores in London, furnishing our palatial residence with the most exquisite trappings that money could buy. Paul had a great eye for the costly and I developed writers' cramp from signing cheques. By the time the task was completed, the house had become the party scene for itinerants and show business gypsies and, with most of the draperies coming from Harrods, I felt that I had become the living embodiment of the store's famous motto: *Omnia, omnibus, ubique* – everyone, everything, everywhere.

My shelter from the chaos was the film set.

More parties followed and when Paul suggested we went to Paris for a weekend, I thought it would be a relief.

We were joined by New York lawyer Israel Katz, his girlfriend, Anna, and George, Paul's masseur from Palm Springs, who flew in just for the party. We stayed at the George V Hotel, near the Champs Elysées, we went to Maxim's for dinner and after going to The Lido to see a show, Israel and Anna decided to call it a night. But not Paul and his musclebound companion.

With me tagging along as the interpreter we toured the red light district and went to see shows where people did things that I wouldn't have believed possible. Pornography, debauchery, abnormal, the terms are all too mild, but Paul considered it an important part of my education and, being a sophisticated lady, I wandered from one seedy backstreet dive to the next.

The shows were all very well, but Paul and George were now rather eager to get in on the act. I was suitably drunk, but it was still with some reluctance that I was urged on with my halting, schoolgirl French to ask directions to a brothel where, for the right price, the Madame could indeed supply us with three girls, a blonde, a brunette and a redhead.

Paul liked everything in sets.

The girls must have thought I was very kinky, but they were French and game, it seemed, for anything. By this time, so was I. The six of us made our way to a dust-coated bedroom, Paul went off to acquire more champagne and with the willowy trio of whores stripped naked, George was chasing about the room, without achieving the same results we had seen onstage around the corner. The chase went on for some time, but I just sat back, as if it happened every day. It was all one of Paul's complex games. I was being tested, being pushed as far as Paul could push me, but I had seen through the ploy and only acted bored. Paul thought of me as being very inexperienced. I had never told him of my teenage adventures and now that I had proved that I wasn't shocked by the evening's entertainment, Paul lost interest and we all went back to the hotel. The whole insane exercise had cost more than £1,000 and the blonde, the brunette and the redhead were left untouched amidst the dust and unopened bottles of champagne.

The next day, Paul was more loving than usual and I rounded the weekend off by buying him a Cartier watch and myself a diamond and ruby ring. I was hinting that Paul ought to divorce his wife and marry me, not that he got the message. He may have done so in time, but before that time arrived, Peggy followed Lenny Levin's example and tried to commit suicide. Paul wasn't exactly sure what to do, but when he decided to fly back to Los Angeles, I took the boys out of school and went with him.

There was one small matter that had to be cleared up before we left.

My long fight to get a divorce from Mike King was finally completed by David Napley. Mike had wanted custody of Sean and Stephen and it had taken seven lawyers, twelve months of constant wrangling and ten court hearings before

I won the case. It also cost a lot of money: the final bill came to more than £20,000.

In three years, I had earned nearly one million dollars, money that was running through my hands like water.

Thirteen

WHEN WE met the first time at Jilly's Restaurant in Palm Springs, Frank Sinatra acted as if the long private table had emptied of everyone but me. The other voices became distant and indistinct and it felt as if I had been carried away to a dimension where everything was new and special. I was mesmerised by Frank's amazing technicolor-charisma, the world on a string and a power that was envied by every politician in the land.

In the beginning, I was only trying to get one over on Paul, and Frank was simply lining up another lady. But it didn't remain that way for very long. I looked into those famous blue eyes and suddenly, I was seeing the man, not the legend.

It happened very quickly, as if a magician had chanted a spell. Something rare and hard to define had taken place between us; it became vital that we hang on to that brief moment, for the future was cloudy, as far away as the people all around us. I wanted to leave, to be really alone, to take Frank by the hand and run through the warm desert night. I wanted to look up at the sky and make love amidst the stars.

The hours slipped by and all too soon it was time to go.

Frank put his hand on mine and said, 'Hope I'm going to see you again soon.'

'I hope so,' I replied.

He got up from the table and went to leave. Everyone went quiet, as if Frank was a member of the Royal Family, but then he turned back to me and said, 'I forgot to tell you, Carol, I really loved *Poor Cow.*'

I thought to myself, Oh no! Not again ... but Frank

209

Sinatra had a wide grin on his lips and the next day, I found out why!

Paul had amused himself all evening with a young starlet whose dress was like an ad for indecent exposure, but on the way home he swore and cursed and drove his white Lincoln at full speed. I smiled to myself and looked out at the night; the blood in my veins was boiling and for once I felt truly happy. I complied with Paul's rage and argued for hours; we drank half a bottle of vodka each and made love as if there was no tomorrow. I held Paul Burke in my arms, but that night I was thinking of Frank Sinatra.

There was another dinner party the following evening at the home of Danny and Natalie Schwartz. Frank was in high spirits and, with everyone engulfed by his energy, we went with Lucille Ball and Gary Morton to see a late night movie at Frank's house in Rancho Mirage. It was all a big surprise, although I was the most surprised when the private screening turned out to be none other than – you guessed it – *Poor Cow*.

Frank again flooded me with attention and although Paul acted as if he didn't care, on the drive home we argued once again. Frank wanted to be with me, but I couldn't let go of Paul. We were soul twins and each time we parted, we were desperate to be together, addicts forever in need of one more fix and lovers who found harmony the moment we touched. It was and had always been a complicated game, a game that was destroying us both, but one in which I felt a long way behind. I needed a grand coup to break even, but even while we argued that night, I had no intention of using Frank Sinatra for that purpose.

The happiness I had felt the previous day was already collapsing; I drank more, I couldn't sleep at night and the future looked more cloudy than ever before.

I would have liked to have spent more time with Frank, but my life was now a whirlwind of jet-setting and movie-making; I was a celebrity on both sides of the Atlantic and I wasn't able to see Frank again until the following year.

When I had paid up my divorce bills, Paul and I returned to Los Angeles to rent Hermione Baddeley's English-style house in Coldwater Canyon.

Paul regularly went to see Peggy and his children and everything went smoothly until the night a gunman appeared and blasted holes in the boys' bedroom windows. I almost had a fit and wanted to fly straight back to England, but Paul refused to go with me and I didn't want to be on my own. The police never managed to find the gunman, even though Peggy freely admitted that it was her son, Brian, who had done the shooting, trying to wreck my life, to avenge my having wrecked his mother's. I wasn't that sure of the logic and, although the shooting wasn't repeated, I employed an armed, twenty-four hour guard, just in case.

It was dull and claustrophobic in the city smog and we decided to escape to Palm Springs where, to be discreet and considerate towards Peggy, we didn't move into Paul's house, but rented yet another piece of luxury real estate nearby.

I owned my own house in Putney, I was paying for the mansion in Montague Square, Hermione's house on Coldwater Canyon and, in Palm Springs, I was still signing the cheques. Paul never had any money. He was an unlucky gambler, an incurable ladies' man and he wasn't doing anything towards getting a divorce from Peggy. We lived like millionaires, but money can't buy happiness and I began to sink deeper and deeper into a private and gloomy place.

From the outside, it may have looked as if I was on top of the world. We lived in splendid, sun-draped surroundings and there were plenty of diversions to fill the time. We went fishing for trout at White Water, Sean and Stephen learned to swim, I drove Paul's Lincoln Continental over the hills and I spent hours alone upon the stone and cactus-strewn desert.

There were parties whenever we wanted them, a steady stream of new faces and, most nights, we dined at Perrina's Restaurant, where I could impress one and all by conversing in Italian. It was a special place and the big stars liked to go there because the elderly proprietor, Larry Perrina, created a homely atmosphere and treated no one like a big star. Larry became one of my few really close friends in the United States and still is today.

I constantly fought the little insect that roamed the passageways of my mind, but all the optimism that had filled me when the decade began had gone. The seventies were on their way and I could only think of the future with dread. In ten years I had become a star, I had spent fortunes and I had slept with every man I desired. I looked into the past and felt sad about so many things. I knew that if I brooded for too long I would become really psychotic and, for relief, I returned to arguing with Paul. We both drank too much and when I couldn't sleep at night, I used the old film star remedy and dosed myself up on sleeping pills. I knew I was heading for a breakdown, but suddenly Frank Sinatra reappeared in Palm Springs and the world became a little brighter.

Only now, after the passing of several busy, but strangely empty months, did I recognise what had drawn me to him. He was the biggest name in the business, but he hadn't forgotten the long climb up the ladder, nor all the little people who had helped him reach the top. Those people he cherished, while he hated the hangers-on with equal intensity – the parasites who wanted the cream, but didn't want to work.

Frank invited me to the last night of his show at Caesar's Palace, in Las Vegas. He made it obvious that it was me he wanted to see, but when the private jet turned up to take me, Paul decided to go along for the ride. A limousine was waiting in the gambling city's small airport and when I reached my suite at the Sands Hotel, I found the bedroom filled with flowers and iced champagne. On each bouquet was a card that read: For Carol – Love Frank.

That night when I watched Frank in his show, every woman in the audience may have been dreaming a special dream, but he was singing his songs for me.

After the show, we all had dinner at an Italian restaurant

212

and later at a night club, a complete stranger directed some wisecracks at Frank and Frank responded by throwing ice cubes at him. Frank was unhappy because Paul was there and I could see the tension building into one of those scenes the press sharpened their hatchets on. The wise guy became louder and when Frank went for a fresh bucket of ice, I stopped him and said, 'Let it go, they're not worth it.'

He looked at me for a long time and then, slowly, his lips turned into a smile, 'You're right,' he said. 'Let's get out of here.'

It wasn't an easy thing for him to do. People sometimes shouted insults just because of who he was. Frank may have been the uncrowned king of show business, but it was a role that had been thrust on him by others and he found it as much a burden as he did an honour. The incident at the club had destroyed the atmosphere and, when we got outside, the party broke up and everyone went home. Paul had fumed silently all evening, but when he arrived back at the Sands, he stamped around the bedroom, he shouted abuse at the flowers and finally, he stormed out.

And hour later, the telephone rang and much to my surprise, it wasn't Paul, but Marion Spence, who was taking a late drink with Johnny and Tom Jones. They were in the main bar at the Sands – and so was Paul, with a girl. I called the bar and when Paul came onto the line, he just laughed.

'I'm with a hooker,' he said. 'She's very pretty, you may like her.'

'What's that supposed to mean?'

'We're just finishing our drink, then we'll be up.'

'You're what ...?'

'You heard, darling, see you in a couple of minutes.'

The line went dead and, true to his word, Paul appeared a few minutes later with a magnum of champagne – and his lady friend.

'What the hell's going on?' I said. I didn't lose my temper, for that was what Paul wanted. Instead, I drank some champagne, talked with the girl and made sure I was just as

213

sophisticated as everyone else. One thing led to another and before the red fiery sun lifted into the desert sky, the three of us were lying naked together in the suite's king-sized bed. It was the ultimate insult, Paul making love with me and another woman at the same time, but in complying, I felt that I had shown that even if he thought so little of me, I thought just as little of him. It was a crazy thing to do, an extension of our weekend trip to Paris, and the next morning all the anger that had built up in me during the night burst into the most awful row we had ever had.

'What are you trying to do to me?' I shouted. 'I'm a mother and a star and you treat me like dirt.'

'This is America, baby,' he replied. 'We do things differently here.'

'That's a load of crap, Paul. If things don't straighten out between us, I'm about ready to call it a day.'

The last thing Paul wanted was to have his ego knocked by my going off with Frank Sinatra, but while he did his best to turn on the charm, I knew the old act and our soul-entwined relationship lost the first of its ties.

We went out again that evening with Frank, his bodyguard, Jilly Rizzo, the lawyer, F. Lee Bailey, and a couple of girls. We finished up in one of the casinos, where I tossed my money away with great abandon until Frank took control of my chips and changed the losses into a $5,000 windfall. It rounded off the weekend nicely and we left for Los Angeles the next day. I had told Frank about the shooting incident, so instead of going back to Hermione Baddeley's house, we accepted Frank's offer and moved into his hillside retreat off Cherokee Lane.

On the flight to LA, Paul and I were happy enough to be alone again, but the mood changed the second we entered Frank's house. Standing in the white-carpeted lounge was a case of Crystal champagne and three cartons of Rothmans cigarettes, my favourite brand and one that isn't easily available in Las Vegas. Paul became angry, we argued and, strip by strip, we pulled away the ties that held us together.

Our moments of sparkle had become rarer, our love affair was just another ritual and ritual breeds boredom. Paul and I both had business to attend to in Hollywood, but as soon as it was completed, I returned to Palm Springs and telephoned Frank. He wasn't there, so I packed my bags and moved with Sean and Stephen and their nanny into an hotel. I was unsure what to do, but then the telephone rang and it was Frank Sinatra, returning my call.

'Look, if you're unhappy, you can come and stay here while you sort yourself out.'

I didn't need to be asked twice.

I left nanny in charge of the children, Frank sent a car and that same evening I rode to meet the future head-on. Black palms, bent and twisted from the desert winds, stood silhouetted against a crimson sunset, my pulse was going clickety-click, clickety-click, like a train going over sleepers and the juices in my body were burning with desire.

The night was warm and silent. The servants had gone and for the first time, we were alone. My heart was pounding and my breasts were swelling out, as if trying to escape from my half-buttoned shirt.

Frank remained motionless for a long time, his eyes glowing in the candlelight and, as he moved towards me, I felt strangely, wonderfully ashamed of wanting him so much. I was still a young woman and I was with a man who, I assumed, was used to taking whatever he wanted.

I couldn't have been more wrong.

Frank Sinatra wanted to make love to me, for sure, but he still wasn't over his relationship with Mia Farrow and, while he was aware that Paul Burke and I were going through a bad time, he considered Paul as one of his friends, and he wanted to keep it that way.

We held each other tightly, but we did no more than that.

'Let's eat, Carol,' he said at last. 'Let's eat and talk about the world.'

And that's what we did. We talked about all the people we knew, the zany, crazy world of show business, the paths that had led us to both be sitting there in Rancho Mirage. In a way, it was no surprise that our backgrounds had many similarities and before the evening was through, the desire we each had to be lovers had moved into another dimension. We had become friends, and that was much more important.

There was a baby grand in the lounge. Frank played a simple melody and sang a love song.

'Love makes the world go round,' he said. 'But you have to work as well.'

With that, he shut the piano lid and escorted me to one of the guest bungalows.

Frank left the next morning with his pilot for a business meeting in Los Angeles and I spent the day alone. I wandered through the grounds, a high wire fence and electric gates protecting me from the outside world. I felt uncomfortable, an intruder in another woman's home. Frank and Mia had only just parted, her photographs filled the house and her memory was everywhere. I knew that what had developed between Frank and I could be special, but still I saw myself as being a replacement.

I lived in a vacuum. I was happy enough, but I wasn't contented. Frank had given me the use of his home so that I could work out where I was going, what I was doing with my life. I spoke to no one but Frank and his housekeeper, a big, black Southern lady, who cooked fried chicken nearly every night, it was Frank's favourite dish, and treated us both like her children.

'Now you get in here before this dinner gets cold,' she'd call and obediently, we would both rush for the dining room.

It may have drifted on that way for weeks and weeks, but when I spoke to Sean and Stephen on the telephone each day, they seemed upset and they wanted to be with Paul. I knew I was selfish, but I did try to be a good mother and it was time I put them first. I contacted Paul and, the following day, we all moved back once more to the rented house in Palm Springs.

Everything that could have happened between Frank and

216

me was left in the air. People naturally assumed that we had become lovers, but everyone underestimated the depth of our feelings. Neither of us were interested in a casual fling and it wasn't the right time for us to commit ourselves to something more lasting. We had become as close as two people can become without actually being lovers ... which created a bond that will never be broken.

At least with Paul, everything was straightforward. We picked up the pieces of our cracked and tarnished relationship, although we knew that it wouldn't last very long. That seemed even more obvious when Paul promised to divorce Peggy and marry me. I was depressed. I had started to use tranquillisers. Every day I changed my mind about everything. I loved Paul, I hated him; I wanted to return to London, to Hollywood, to anywhere but where I was. I wanted to be anyone but who I was. I started to lose grip on things; the sun was baking my skull and, by October, I thought I would go insane if I didn't do something.

What I did was pack the children and their nanny off to London, while I went with Paul to see Israel Katz, his lawyer in New York. I was relieved to say goodbye to the boiling sun and the constant blue skies and the excitement of the city sent a feeling of well-being coursing through me. The trees in Central Park were turning gold and every time it rained, I wanted to run out in the street and start dancing.

We saw some new plays on Broadway and we dined closeby at Sardi's, the restaurant where ideas are born, shows are conceived and from where I had fond memories of 1968. Endless numbers of great writers and performers had been faithful customers in Sardi's long history and with all that artistic energy seeping from the walls, I didn't really like to go anywhere else. Paul considered variety the spice of life and the night he insisted we went to Jilly's New York restaurant was the night I saw Frank Sinatra for the last time.

Paul and I were sitting at a quiet corner table when Jilly appeared and said: 'Did you know Frank was here?'

217

'Say hello for us,' Paul finally said. 'Perhaps we'll have a drink together later.'

Jilly left and Paul glared at me, his eyes filled with anguish and hurt pride and, suddenly, I realised that I was ahead in our dreadful game. Just as suddenly, Frank turned up at the table, his blue eyes like chip of ice and his face as unhappy as Paul's.

Frank looked straight at me and said, 'This is your last chance, Carol, I want you to chose him or me.'

I wanted to shout, 'It's you, it's you, Frank; I love you', but the silence was long and decisive; I was afraid of my own feelings and, still without saying anything, I leaned over and kissed Paul on the cheek.

Frank walked out of the restaurant and out of my life forever.

My relationship with Paul was everything but over. We had wasted a small fortune, we had lived a fast, dangerous and careless life and I suddenly felt that I was slipping on a glass bottomed helter-skelter, racing in disordered circles and getting absolutely nowhere.

Fourteen

WE ALL have a line inside us, a point that divides normality from madness.

Since my move to Hollywood, everything that had happened only served to drive me closer to that line.

My private life was constantly in a mess and it was only working that kept me from going over the edge. *Something Big* had opened to good reviews and the film critic in the *Daily Mirror* described *The Man Who Had Power Over Women* as having captured the essence of the age more than any other film of its kind.

'Carol White's unique blend of sensuality and subtlety is always a pleasure to watch,' he wrote, but the words no longer made me happy. Life had become one long test that I had to endure.

There was something wrong with the way we lived. Tinsel Town, with all its baubles and green dollar bills, was where I rested my body, but a part of me remained far away in the working class streets of my childhood. I could never completely disappear behind the high walls of stardom, walls that screened us from a world where a lot of people didn't even get enough to eat. John Lennon had said, 'Why us? What makes us special?' I still didn't have the answer. I squandered my money and I lived a fast life because I couldn't see the point in doing anything else.

As soon as Frank Sinatra walked out of Jilly's Restaurant, I knew I had made a huge mistake. I loved the man, but I was afraid of my own feelings; I was overwhelmed by Frank's reputation, his stature and his power. Had he been a bar tender, we would probably have got married and lived happily ever after.

Paul and I left Jilly's soon after Frank, and back at our hotel we clashed yet again in battle. I hated Paul as much as I loved him, although when it was time for me to leave alone for London, my instincts told me to stay where I was. I wanted to spend Christmas with my children, but when we reached the airport I was suddenly frightened of being alone. I didn't want to lose Paul, the way I had just lost Frank. I locked myself in the bathroom and missed three flights, but in the end I allowed Paul to persuade me to go.

'I'll call you as soon as I get back to LA,' he said.

'Promise?'

'Promise.'

Paul said he was going to spend Christmas with his own children and then join me at the mansion he had so carefully furnished in Montague Square. I waited for his call but, needless to say, it never came. I contacted Israel Katz, but he didn't know where Paul was. I called Palm Springs, Las Vegas, Paul's friends in Hollywood and as a last resort, I even telephoned Peggy Burke. She had stopped hating me; I think she even felt sorry for me.

'Don't worry, Carol, he'll turn up,' she said. 'He always does.'

Christmas passed without a call, my depressions mounted one on top of another, I was drinking more and I started taking pills: pills to sleep, pills to wake up, pills to eat, pills to lose weight, until it felt as if my body was a machine that no longer worked in the normal, ordinary way. I never functioned that well without a man in my life. I hated the long, lonely days and most of all I wanted to turn back the clock, I wanted to be at Rancho Mirage, waiting to hear the sound of a car racing across the desert. My mind was a tangle of confused, half-formed thoughts and, although they may have resolved themselves, I was suddenly preoccupied by the sinister atmosphere that prevailed in the Georgian house. I was susceptible to the dark forces, to anything supernatural;

I thought back to that eerie little cottage in Essex and I felt as if I was going out of my mind.

There was a story that the original owner of the house had left his wife and children to go to war, only to return with a beautiful young French woman. The wife was so distressed, she threw herself from the balcony and died upon the cobblestoned courtyard. Her cold presence remained in the bedroom, and at night she still screamed that last long and mournful scream. I would awake with it echoing in my brain, a cold dusty glow filtering from the narrow light shaft, snowy white shapes moving upon the walls. I was walking on a tightrope, that line that crosses the wasteland into delirium. When Paul did call, his words gave me the final push. It was an icy, colourless day in January 1970.

'Happy new year.'

'What's that supposed to mean? Why haven't you called before?' I said.

'I haven't had a lot of time, Carol, I've been busy.'

'What are you doing now?'

'What, right now?'

'Yes, right now?'

'I'm in bed with two hookers.'

I dropped the telephone receiver and threw the first thing I could get hold of across the room.

'You bastard,' I shouted to no one in particular. I carried on throwing things until, in a state of exhaustion, I swallowed a bottle of pills and the best part of a quart of vodka.

I woke up in a nursing home in St John's Wood. It was very clean and the smell of disinfectant made me think I was in heaven. My mind was fuzzy and everything that had led me to the breakdown was momentarily forgotten. There was a dull, throbbing pain in my stomach and it was only months later that I learned that I had been unconscious for two weeks. My stomach had been pumped, I was fed intravenously and I had undergone six electric shock treatments to bring me back to 'normalcy'.

The shock therapy was replaced with hallucinogenics, which carried me far, far away into new and dangerous extremes. I would lie there for hours, fishes swimming on the covers, little pink men dancing elvan dances, flames of Greek fire leaping from the walls, my whole body tingling and wet with sweat. I plunged into the depths of my own secret universe, white creamy thought waves, phantoms from the past in grotesque parodies of real life. Rainbows formed in my mind, California blue, the yellow hair from Donovan's song, lightning strikes of insect red, the greenest green of England.

My body became weightless, gravity had departed. I floated in a bubble, the colours of a spinning top flashed by and through the confusion, my father appeared with a large bouquet of man-eating orchids; they terrified me and I threw them across the room. On other days it was bottles of Lucozade, magazines and oranges that concealed black hairy spiders.

In moments of clarity I found the telephone and made calls all over the United States. I was searching for Paul, but in the haze I just called any number that came into my mind, and the bill when I left the nursing home would have made Howard Hughes demand a recount. On some days, the telephone would be under the bed or in a cupboard and, search though I may, the small private room was suddenly a black and lightless cathedral where my thoughts froze into the ikons that decorated the high walls.

It took two months for Paul Burke to find out where I was and what had happened and, in that time, I slowly surfaced into the real world. I wasn't completely cured, but the pink dancing men had left to dance elsewhere and, in a world where everyone was a little crazy, I was no worse than anyone else. The doctors advised Paul to stay away, but when he turned up at the nursing home I decided to leave with him. I suddenly realised that I was only punishing myself and perhaps more important, like the fishes that swam on my bed covers, there were plenty more fishes in the sea.

Life outside the clinic was overshadowed by the stormy dark clouds; the pavements were wet and the wrappings from countless bags of fish and chips rushed by like tumbleweed. The trees on Hampstead Heath were drab and forlorn, like the people all bundled up in their cheap winter coats. If this was reality, I preferred the acid-tinted realm back inside the nursing home gate. We had dinner somewhere in Kensington and I felt as if I was sitting with a long lost brother. Paul looked so much older.

While I had been recovering from the breakdown, mum had got rid of the haunted house and had sold my own house in Putney. I needed new surroundings and my search led me to Neville Terrace, in Fulham, a cosy little hideaway I rented from Ursula Andress and finally bought a year later. Paul moved in with me, but the old sparkle had gone. Our love was strongest when we were at each other's throats; now, there was no point. The game was over and so was our relationship; not with a bang, but with a whimper.

I devoted my time to Sean and Stephen and on the days when Mike King turned up to visit, it was just like old times. My memory remained tender and I lived in a sort of halfway station; I continued to be neither happy nor unhappy until a voice from the past appeared on my telephone and made the world seem bright again. It was Jean Diamond, as stern and as affectionate as ever and with the news that I was wanted for another movie.

'Are you sure you're up to it?' she said. 'It's a very demanding role.'

'Up to it, Jean,' I replied. 'It's just what I need.'

'What about Paul, what's he doing?'

'Paul has gone back to Los Angeles and we won't be seeing each other again. It's all over between us, Jean, and I'm getting on fine by myself,' I said. 'I really am better and I really want to work.'

'I'm sure you do, darling, I'm sure you do,' Jean

continued. 'We'll have lunch together and I'll show you the script.'

Jean's voice was a tonic in itself. She was like a second mother and I loved her for it. I still had severe head pains and, with most of my memory banks burnt out, I wasn't even sure if I would be able to learn the part. The overdose of pills had been a mild attempt at suicide, but I wasn't so much trying to destroy myself, as put myself back together again. Jean had a shrewd eye and our lunch date would be the test.

We met at a small bistro in Chelsea a few days later and I felt like a teenager on a first date.

'You look mah-vellous, absolutely mah-vellous,' she said. 'But tell me, how are you feeling?'

'Mah-vellous,' I repeated and Jean laughed. That afternoon, I signed to make the award-winning *Dulcima*, a story adapted and directed by Frank Nesbitt and co-starring John Mills, one of my all-time favourite actors. Jean, at least, had confidence in me and I didn't want to let her, or myself down. I spent hours each day going over my part and I even studied the scenes that I wasn't in. It was a heavy going romantic drama and, with a script steeped in the Cotswolds' dialect, it wasn't an easy part. But by the time filming commenced, I had found my way into the heart of the character; the lines all filed into place and I had started to feel whole again.

The balmy June days warmed away my melancholia. Short skirts had gone, but in an emancipated frenzy of Women's Lib, the girls were all wearing hot pants and burning their bras. Elton John's string of releases were playing every time I turned on the radio; *Monty Python's Flying Circus* was the best thing on television; Paul McCartney had formed a pop group called 'Wings' and, fresh back from a long sojourn in India, George Harrison was singing 'All Things Must Pass' sentiments I agreed with completely. England was comfortable and secure and the only thing I missed was my little silver car. In a mad moment, I had shipped it to New York; a driver had taken it across the States to Palm Springs and there it still stood, basking in the sunshine.

I met John Mills for the first time in the middle of June, when we started work on the film. He was dressed as a ragged yokel, a straw in his mouth, his hair all over the place and his dark, inquisitive eyes roaming the quilt-patterned landscape. It was wonderful to be out in the country, a hint of mist on the distant hills, the tree-lined fields and England at its best. Working was the real cure. The crew and cast clicked immediately and the only time I felt a bit down was when the weekend came and we all packed up and went home.

John sensed this and at the end of the second week, he took me with him back to Richmond, so that he and his wife, Mary, could play mum and dad. I slept in Hayley's four-poster bed, I was served breakfast on a silver tray and for a few days we all lived our own little fantasy.

The harmony was too good, almost too boring, to last and while *Dulcima* slowly progressed, I took one step back into the past and allowed a moment of disorder to spice-up my social life. The ingredient was Bekim Femu, who smiled at me across a crowded reception hall before he joined me with two glasses of champagne and an expression that said: 'Let's go back to my place and talk about old times'.

'No thank you to both,' I said before he had a chance to speak. 'I'm on orange juice tonight and I start work early in the morning.'

'But Carol, it's been so long, we have so much to talk about,' he said. 'You'll never believe how much I have missed you.'

'Missed me?' I replied. 'Surely you're not still in need of English lessons?'

He smiled and looked more handsomely rakish than ever. I was tempted to take his arm and say an early goodnight to the cocktail party, but I thought it unwise to give in to my instincts too easily.

'Perhaps another night?'

'Perhaps.'

We exchanged telephone numbers. Later in the week we had dinner and I was still at Bekim's side as a taxi carried us through the summer night to an apartment that looked out upon Hyde Park. It was romantic, in an odd sort of way, but I was under no illusions.

It was just as well.

We arrived at the apartment to find Leigh Taylor Young, Bekim's co-star in *The Adventurers*, hugging her knees unhappily upon the sofa. I was surprised to see her, but the look on Leigh's face was more one of horror. Her mouth fell open and she looked very hurt when Bekim ushered me into the next room. It turned out to be the bedroom. He held me in his arms and tried to kiss me, but I struggled free and walked out. Leigh was in tears and I knew just how she must have felt. When I first met Bekim, he engineered a similar meeting between Suzy Coe and myself.

Bekim was a passionate lover, but I wasn't able to understand his Slavic sense of humour.

I left the apartment and took a taxi home to Fulham. Game playing belonged to the past.

And so did Bekim Femu.

Now that Paul and I had made the final break, he called frequently from Los Angeles. I missed him, naturally, and it was tempting to ask him to join me in the Cotswolds, not that I gave into the temptation. I was cocooned in the tiny village of Tetbury, in a beautiful, sixteenth-century inn, the English countryside and my work on *Dulcima* combining to make me enjoy my life once again. I enjoyed Frank Nesbitt's zany wit, as well as the company of Sir John and his lovely wife Mary, although sometimes, only sometimes, I missed the mad, mad world of Hollywood.

I still didn't relish the idea of having no man in my life and it took my old schoolfriend Mia Karam to come up with the remedy.

One weekend when I was back in London, she asked me to go out on a blind date and make up a foursome for dinner at a French restaurant. I trembled at the very thought of it, but I didn't want Mia to think I had lost my spirit and so I agreed to go.

Mia was now married to golfer Ivor Dixon and the date turned out to be with one of his friends, the young amateur golfer John Davis. We met at the restaurant, where I tried to conceal myself in a quiet corner. Waiters with bristling moustaches hurried by like ballet dancers, red candles were wedged in old sherry bottles and the people at the next table were speaking in such loud, theatrical voices, that it seemed unnecessary for us to start talking.

We were quiet for a long time, but when the menus arrived, Mia asked me about the film and I plunged into a long, detailed account of *Dulcima*. Suddenly, it was turning out to be a nice evening and I realised that John was good fun to be with. He was tall and blond, with clear blue eyes and an innocence that made me feel great. He was twenty-one, just six years my junior, but I had spent so much time with older men that I felt old myself.

It was time for a change.

From that day on, John Davis and I became regular companions. He taught me how to play golf, he was one of the top amateurs in the country, and the long walks over the greens and fairways brought a healthy pink glow to my cheeks. John was different from any man I had known in the past and I found it very easy to fall in love with him.

We met in July, while I was completing work on *Dulcima* and, six weeks later, we were engaged. I thought it would be third time lucky. John bought me a diamond ring and was in the process of buying a house for us in Twickenham. He was independently wealthy, clean cut and he wanted to give me the world, and I was in love.

Everything seemed right for us, but one temptation stood in the way.

Fifteen

HIS NAME was Warren Beatty.

We met at a dinner party, but as soon as we were alone he said he wanted to make love to me. I had the same immediate desire, but as I looked into Warren's eyes, I saw a vague, hesitant reflection and realised I was seeing myself.

Warren cupped my cheeks in his palms, but as our lips met, I became afraid, the brief moment of harmony that had entered my life was now at an end.

'I must go,' I said.

'Can I call you?'

I nodded.

'Soon?'

'Yes, Warren, very soon.'

I fled Warren's arms and stepped into my dark-windowed Mini. My thoughts were in turmoil and I drove the new car at full speed, the grey, deserted streets flooding behind me, along with the many resolutions I had made. Nothing was ever going to be simple for me, a point that was emphasised just a few seconds later. A blue flashing light appeared in my rear mirror and as the siren became louder and louder, I suddenly wished that Warren Beatty was there at my side.

There were tears in my eyes when I stopped and wound down the window. 'I'm really sorry,' I said. 'I didn't mean to drive so fast.'

The policeman was silent for several seconds and when he spoke, I felt thankful that I wasn't in Los Angeles. 'Any trouble, Miss?'

'No, not really, I just had an argument with the boyfriend, I

228

replied, trying to ooze charm and avoid getting a ticket.

The policeman went silent again, but then he said, 'You're the one in the films and on the telly, Carol White, if I'm not mistaken?'

'Guilty,' I said, smiling now, then adding, 'I don't usually drive so fast.'

'You'd better not. There'd be hell to pay at home if I nicked Carol White,' he said. 'You're the wife's favourite.'

I knew I was saved and I waited for the usual request.

'I'll just give you a warning this time and,' he paused. 'Don't suppose you'd mind giving me your autograph, for the wife, of course.'

I signed the policeman's little black book and drove slowly home, thankful that I was a movie star, but confused, nonetheless.

The dinner party had been at the home of producer and matchmaker Michael Winner, who claims me as his protégé and was the first person to suggest that I compile my memoirs. 'Biography shapes life into art,' he once said, and although at the time I was unsure what he meant, I now feel that the critics must be left with the final judgement. Like David Copperfield, I have always wondered if I would be the hero of my own tale.

I arrived home feeling awful and didn't start to feel better until Warren called. It was two days later and we arranged to have a meal together in Mayfair. I thought it was going to be a private affair and was shocked to meet Peter Sellers and the writer Robert Towne at the restaurant. Peter was very warm and acted as if our relationship had never come to an end which, in a way, I suppose it hadn't.

'Darling, it's wonderful to see you. Where have you been hiding?' Peter said, still jovial and goonish, although I knew the smile concealed many disappointments and Peter was no longer the happy man he showed the cameras. I kissed him on the cheek and sat down.

It turned out to be a business lunch, the script for a new film being the main item under discussion. I found it all rather boring and made little headway with the large steak that was ordered on my behalf.

When lunch was over, we all went to a flat nearby, but although the scriptwriter seemed anxious to continue the conversation, the thread had been lost with the last bottle of wine – not that Warren had any. He didn't smoke or drink. Peter Sellers had discreetly let me know that he was available, should I wish to renew our ancient affair, but was sensitive enough to see that I wanted to be with Warren. He tapped the walls and spoke as if he were a Chinese landlord renting out the room, but while everyone was still laughing, he took Bob Towne's arm and led him to the door.

Warren's mind was still filled with the new project and, as he talked away the daylight hours, it felt as if I had known him all my life.

'Sometimes it feels like a miracle, just being alive,' he said at last, his eyes dancing wildly. He pulled me into his arms and kissed me properly for the first time. He held me close and I felt like clay in the hands of the sculptor; primeval woman, not Eve the eternal temptress, but the willing novitiate in a pursuit where Warren was the master.

We had both experienced a multitude of lovers, but Warren made me feel like the only woman he had ever loved. The expression on his boyish face made the slightest movement into something passionate, those movements drawing upon countless sexual urges I didn't know were in me. His actions stripped everything bare of all but pure feeling and I followed willingly, no matter where each action led.

Warren was a man of many contradictions, but only when we made love did I enter the heart of the paradox.

In his dealings with businessmen and studio executives, he was aggressive and forceful, but as a lover, he gave everything he had. His potency was rare, almost unrivalled, and his ability to be so single-pointed was the source of his power.

While he held me close, I imagined I possessed all but his

230

soul, but while he was tantalisingly within reach, a part of him remained elusively remote. Warren's many exploits were well-known and well-documented, yet he remained a very private person, the secrecy creating a myth that I felt compelled to unravel. He was a cocktail of vanity and self-consciousness that made him reluctant to speak to the media; he would spend hours looking at himself in the bedroom mirror, but run a mile to avoid a photographer.

'I don't want to explain myself to anyone,' he would say, which served to endorse the legend.

I was swept off my feet and, although I was well-aware of Warren's long-standing relationship with Julie Christie, he never mentioned her; in fact he tried to give the impression that they were then no more than good friends. Instead he talked of his romance with Leslie Caron and said how much he missed seeing her children.

'When you return to Los Angeles,' he said, assuming that I would return, 'I'll help you find a good school for the boys.'

He was so loving and charming that I imagined that I was the only woman in his life, that even if he did have a girlfriend in every capital, he would drop them all for me.

It was a very confusing time. Paul was still calling almost daily and John was growing excited with the prospect of us getting married. I knew while I had a choice, John was the right one, but with Warren Beatty so close I didn't want to rush into anything as restrictive as marriage.

Just how close Warren was I discovered one morning a few weeks later. I had just got out of bed when the phone rang.

'Can I come over?' Warren said cheerfully.

'Yes, of course, how long will you be?'

'I dunno, about ten seconds.'

'What? Where are you?'

'If you look out of your window, I'll wave to you . . .'

And there he was, in the house opposite. It turned out to be the home of Julie Christie, although that small detail remained one of Warren's well-kept secrets.

From that day on, he turned up almost every morning. We would make love, or just talk; he had so many ideas and wanted to do so many things. If we went out to eat, it would be late at night, so that no one would see him. He was almost paranoid concerning any form of attention, yet it was obvious by the way he talked that when he worked he liked to dominate every aspect that goes into the making of a film. It's hardly surprising that after the success of *Reds*, which he produced, directed and co-scripted, his next project is a biographical movie of the billionaire recluse Howard Hughes.

In a way, sex was what came first between Warren and I, yet we had some other kind of affinity and I thought that, given the right set of circumstances, it could go further than that. We talked about the world and its problems, but we avoided talking about ourselves. I was never able to press Warren about the other women in his life, for although, as it turned out, he had an assortment of bedmates, I remained engaged to John Davis and made a point of wearing his diamond ring.

Perhaps our relationship was doomed before it even got off the ground. It is said that opposites attract, but Warren and I were in fact very similar. Our birthdays were only a few weeks apart and I'm sure that many matched planets patterned our horoscopes.

I am an Aries, a fire sign, and Warren Beatty knew how to light the fuse. We made love for hours, the windows open in defiance of the creeping afternoon chill and Warren's unearthly energy lifting me to another dimension. I didn't know how long it was going to last, but I liked it while it did. Sometimes I felt as if I was moving on the edge of a whirlpool ... I see a red door and I want to paint it black humming timelessly from the stereo, the same symphony, the same dreams flickering in the candlelight. We talked of an alternative society and World War Three, living on a commune or a desert island, but still each moment was rich in gaiety; we laughed so much I sometimes wondered if the very air we breathed was charged with nitrous oxide.

While I was with Warren, the rest of the world ceased to exist. The rest of my life was a dream, not a nightmare with its acid overtones, but a pointless journey as a somnambulist. I almost yearned for the sight of a pterodactyl gnawing at my leg, or a band of little pink men dancing across the bedsheets. It was all a strange dream – but to dream, you must still be asleep.

I awoke from the dream when I discovered just who it was who owned the house opposite me in Neville Terrace. One Sunday morning, it wasn't Warren, but John Davis, who stood looking out from my kitchen window.

'Do you know who your neighbour is across the street?' he said.

'No, who is it?'

'It's Julie Christie!'

I stood beside John, speechless. It was hard to believe that it was Julie out there, weeding her garden, oblivious to the eyes that watched her and unaware of her lover's duplicity. I felt strangely sad and had to stop myself from running out, to comfort her somehow because Warren was such a complex man to fall in love with.

Julie had been in London filming and Warren had waited for her to go out to work each day before he crossed the street and joined me. It was another aspect of the paradox. Warren needed the love of many women, yet for all the love and affection that followed him, he remained a lonely man. He was concerned with the plight of the starving, with all social inequality, yet he was a millionaire many times over. Perhaps that was why he didn't buy his own home, but moved nomadically from one hotel room to the next. When he did finally buy a house in the Beverly Hills, he didn't move into it.

It was inevitable that I now despised Warren Beatty, while I loved him with all my heart.

I remained in the same position for many minutes. John sensed that I was upset and wasn't too disappointed when I decided to stay home. He was playing in a golf tournament and would be away for the rest of the week. He left and I sat in the kitchen, nursing endless cups of coffee and turning the pages of the Sunday papers; politics, unemployment, inflation; the jargon of the newsreaders belonging on a parallel, but disconnected universe. Sean and Stephen were with my parents and I was happy to be on my own.

When I went out for a walk it was raining, the autumn day breathing the air of change, although I suddenly felt free, bound by nothing but the beating of my own heart and the sound of my shoes sucking at the pavements. I turned right at the corner, past the graffiti-sprayed tributes to Fulham Football Club, past the cemetery gate and into the park, an oasis between the vast thundering highways that converged on the city.

Lots of things were going through my mind, not least of all my family. I was tempted to go and see my sister, but I didn't think I would be made welcome. She thought of my life as being filled with adventure, but she didn't know that the pleasure was balanced with an equal measure of pain.

It was important to me that my parents remained so supportive.

I kept walking, as if the rain and the solitude were the elements that would meld into a new direction. I had been thinking about going back to Los Angeles, but now I wasn't so sure. Warren and I had a half-hearted plan to get together, but I knew it could never work. Over the months, I had dropped John every time Warren came onto the scene, yet John had stood by me, knowing that my feelings for Warren were probably no more than infatuation. But John Davis was no fool; he wouldn't wait forever.

By the time I arrived home, I was soaked to the skin.

I saw Warren again later that week. I made it clear that I was angry with him, but he persisted with the story that he and Julie Christie were 'just good friends' and I remained hopeful that something existed for us in the future.

It was the last time that we were to see each other in

234

London that year. The next day, Warren left for sunny California.

It felt as if I had been abandoned. I went out with John. I loved him and I knew we could be happy, but something was missing. It wasn't John's fault, it was my fault. I needed the thrill of disloyalty, my own as well as Warren's, to add lustre to our relationship.

In my heart, I had already decided to pull up my roots and take my career back to Hollywood, but it wasn't Warren's presence at the Beverly Wilshire that prompted me to go.

In the end, it was a telephone call from Paul Burke.

When I was settled with the boys in the first class compartment of a familiar Pan Am jet, I looked out at the grey drizzle and wondered what the future had in store.

I also wondered if Pan Am had a club for its most faithful customers, for I should surely have been made an honorary member!

Sixteen

PAUL BURKE was ill with hepatitis and his call had come from a private ward at the Century City Hospital. By the time I arrived, he was out of danger, but it would be many months before his recovery was complete.

I went with the boys to a suite at the Beverly Hills Hotel, one mile across town from the Beverly Wilshire. I wanted to be close, but not too close to Warren Beatty, although as soon as we met, our romance continued with the flames burning just as brightly. Julie Christie was in and out of Warren's life, Paul was in and out of mine, but still I found some lonely moments when I missed John Davis and the air of security his love had given. The engagement was over, but John said we would always be friends.

That was more than ten years ago and his words still hold true to this day.

With Warren now aware that his relationship with Julie didn't bother me, he spoke more openly about his feelings for her and for the other women in his life. Julie was the only woman he really loved, but he was afraid of the ultimate commitment and never walked her down the aisle. In this new era of honesty and frankness, it became apparent that Warren's main attraction to me was in the bedroom, but if he had been using me in the past, it was now my turn to do the using.

Paul was again foremost in my mind. I wanted to find the happiness that had always eluded us, but even while he lay stricken and yellow-eyed in his bed, he managed to draw me into one of his tiresome games.

Permanently hovering there at his bedside was an English

woman named Anna, whom Paul described as his 'most faithful friend'. I was growing tired of everyone's 'friends', not that I felt in the least bit threatened. Anna was much older than me, a sort of Mary Poppins character and one of those women who make up the numbers at all Hollywood gatherings. She was probably a wardrobe mistress, or a fifth assistant director, not that anyone ever claimed as much.

When I wasn't sitting with Paul and his 'most faithful friend', I was able to re-enter the stage of the party circuit and, inevitably, into the thirsty columns of the gossip writers. The phone rang every day, but like Warren, I decided to be mysterious and kept a low profile.

Sean and Stephen were settled in a new school and we soon moved from the hotel into a pleasant, two-storey house on Wanda Park Drive. My life was the usual fine balance between a fragile contentment and a mass of uncertain needs, but I still wasn't ready for the bold and persevering advances of James Caan. We were both signed to the William Morris agency, where fate deigned for us to meet face to face and it was hardly possible for me to refuse having lunch with him. He drove me back to Beverly Hills and acted very upset when I didn't invite him in. He called several times that week, but much to my relief he didn't return to the house.

Paul's strength had slowly returned and at Christmas he was able to leave hospital. We all went with an air of déjà vu to his house in Palm Springs. The boys were thrilled to be back, as if this was their real home and Paul their father. It was just like old times, Paul fussing over me while I cooked Italian meals, the boys in and out of the swimming pool and the sunset painting the sky in a fan of pastel colours. The only major change was that the refrigerator shelves were now stocked with gallons of healthy orange juice. Paul was on the wagon for two years and, to avoid temptation, no alcohol was allowed in the house.

My memory had been hazy all year, but the familiar surroundings served to fill in many of the blank spaces. One thing I remembered was the location of my silver Mercedes and it should have been easy to find. It was one of the few right hand drive cars in Nevada, but though we searched through every car lot and compound in the state, it had disappeared from the face of the earth.

We went to Perrina's, where Larry welcomed me back as if I were a long lost daughter, and during one brief excursion to a casino I played my own chips and won nearly $1,000 – about the same amount as Paul lost. Nothing, in some ways, ever changes, although I did feel that I had moved on. It was good for me to spend that time with Paul, for I was able to see how stupid I had been in trying to kill myself. No man was worth that. I realised, too, that what had always been missing from our relationship was still missing and that no amount of time or effort could create what wasn't there. Paul had the emotions of a prima donna and expected to have everything his own way. Warren Beatty was the same and so, unfortunately, was I. Each of us drew our energy from the spotlight and suffered power failures when that light had to be shared.

Most of what we did that Christmas was retracing our steps over the potholes of the past, though we never mentioned nor revisited one of those ancient sites, a monument to what might have been. I didn't see Frank Sinatra and, in a way, I was glad.

Paul had invited us for a short holiday and I intended to keep it at that, not that I could have stayed longer than we did. When I first arrived in Los Angeles, my new American agent, Barry Pearlman, had signed me to make *Ground Star Conspiracy* for Universal. The movie was being shot in Vancouver and with Barry as my companion, that is where I went that winter.

After Palm Springs, Canada was a bit of a let down, although my feelings may have been exaggerated by the weather.

It didn't just rain, it monsooned, day after day, endless sheets of icy water that lashed the streets and crept into my bones. When it didn't rain, there was a blizzard, or a hail storm and at those times I didn't feel like a star acting in a movie, but a political prisoner suffering the wrath of the Russian steppes.

The only relief was work, but we lost many days to the rain and we usually found ourselves huddled in a group with cups of hot chocolate and endless plates of doughnuts. The boredom created the perfect atmosphere for intrigue, though as it turned out I rejected the advances of that wonderful actor George Peppard for the young and dashing Cliff Potts. He was just what I needed through those cold Vancouver nights, even though my relationship with Barry Pearlman was becoming somewhat less of a business arrangement.

Michael Sarrazin made up the film's all-star cast, not that I got much chance to speak to him!

He was completely preoccupied with Jackie Bisset, all fresh and enthusiastic after her performance in *The Grasshopper*. They were like two kids in love for the first time, the way they held hands and looked at each other making me think back to the early days of my marriage to Mike King. It now felt as if that period belonged to another lifetime, almost another person.

My little fling with Cliff Potts had taken place while Barry was away briefly in Los Angeles and we had in fact committed ourselves to what we both assumed was going to be a lasting liaison. Waking up on subsequent mornings with different lovers may seem exciting, but I was obviously searching for something.

That 'something' had been missing from my life for a long time and I had five more years of mental anguish and another broken marriage to look forward to before I found it.

* * *

239

I liked Barry Pearlman. He was gentle, giving and considerate. But when I awoke one morning to hear the telephone buzzing with a demanding and enigmatic roar, I was relieved to leave both him and the cold Canadian climes behind me.

'Hi! That you?'

'What? Who is this?' I replied.

'That you, Carol ... it's Carol White I want?'

'Look, who is this?'

'That's you, isn't it?'

'Yes, damn it, it's me, Carol White,' I yelled. 'And who are you?'

'It's me, Jo. Jo Janni.'

I think he was a man who loathed telephones. It took some time for him to relay his message, but when he had finished, I realised I was wide awake and smiling cheerfully.

'It's wonderful to hear your voice, Jo,' I said. 'Where are you? How did you get this number?'

'I want you, Carol, and it's got to be quick,' he replied cryptically and without answering my questions. 'You've got to get back to London as soon as possible. There is so much for you to do.'

'Lots for me to do, Jo? What do you mean?'

'We're shooting a film and you're in the lead.'

'But I can't just walk out on Universal,' I replied. 'I'm in the middle of making a film here.'

'They're over time, and I need you back in London,' he said. 'Don't worry, my lawyer's on his way over to make all the arrangements.'

It was all rather complicated, not that I have a great head for contracts. However, I was still bound to the independent producer Jo Janni and while I had been released for *Ground Star Conspiracy*, the film was way over schedule and Jo had the right to demand my return.

Later that same day, Jo Janni's executives arrived with their duelling pistols at the ready, but the men of Universal could find nothing in the small print that could force me to

240

remain in Canada. It was a costly business. The rain had prevented the last of my scenes being shot and the studio now had to recast the part and make half the film again.

I sat on the sideline, a pawn in the game; I was quietly excited at the prospects of doing another film with Jo Janni, but I didn't want to fall foul of Universal. It was nice to be in such great demand – and it did no harm to my bank account. I had already been paid for *Ground Star Conspiracy* and I would find another five figure deal waiting for me in London.

Barry drove me to the airport. We kissed and made all sorts of promises, but our affair ended the second we parted. The winds blew icily across the Pacific and, as the Air Canada jet lifted into a pale and colourless sky, I warmed to the thoughts of an English springtime. Twelve hours later, I stepped out into a crisp, but sunny day and I knew everything was going to be fine: even those red-faced men of British customs gave me a pleasant welcome.

In the following days, I read through a bulky, blue-covered script and while my pulse raced faster and faster, I understood why Jo Janni was so excited. He had produced the award-winning and financially lucrative *Poor Cow* and could see a repeat of that success with what was abstrusely entitled *Made*. Since we had last worked together, I had starred in six feature movies and turned down untold television shows and pilots. I knew what I did best and none of the roles I had played stretched me enough as an actress.

Dulcima was probably the exception. It was now opening to a steady stream of good reviews and, later that same year, it won a best picture award at the Berlin Film Festival. Praise indeed for Frank Nesbitt. It was his debut as a screenwriter and director. It was a good film, like many good films, but it still lacked the magic ingredient that made those reels of celluloid into cinema history.

I sat up through the early hours pouring over every line of dialogue in *Made* but I couldn't fault it. It was the role I had been waiting for, although when I saw that the dice had come up a winner, a cold and eerie feeling went tingling up my spine. I liked the part because I identified so readily with the character. In the story, the young mother is caught in the crossfire of time and change and when, on the closing pages, she takes her own life, it felt as if I was lying there, reading my own autobiography. In an earlier scene, her baby son had died and the anguish I felt just reading the script made me want to rush into the next room and take Sean and Stephen in my arms. I had always been split between the love of my children and my need to be an actress; no miracle bridge suddenly appeared to span that chasm, but I did find myself with a clearer picture of where my career should be going. I decided not to take just any part that came along, I would be more selective in the films I did make and, like Jane Fonda, I intended to become more involved with the production end of the movie business.

Jo Janni had promised me a busy schedule and the first of my tasks was to choose my co-star from a very short list consisting of two names. I didn't know the English rock star Roy Harper, or the American, Tony Joe White, but I rejected the American in a flash. One White was enough for any billing.

As soon as I met Roy Harper, I thought I had made the wrong choice. He was obnoxious, self-opinionated and he seemed to be trying too hard to be eccentric. He acted like an overgrown hippie still longing for Woodstock, and though he preached a philosophy of universal tolerance, he didn't extend that to the people within immediate reach of his tongue.

It was just what I didn't need. I was fast approaching my twenty-eighth birthday, when the passing of four generations of seven years was taking me into another age of development. I was sure it was going to be the April Fool's joke to top all others, but by the time 1 April arrived, Roy had metamorphosed into a completely different person. He didn't so much ask me out, as insist that we had a meal together to celebrate my birthday. I dressed in my furs and finery, Roy appeared in his Levi's and old sheepskin coat, and we dined on bean specials at a vegetarian restaurant. The clientele were all draped in beads and wheatgerm-coloured clothes, the tropical fruit cocktails were delicious and Roy Harper unveiled another side of his personality.

His past displays were a stand against what he called the 'uncreative philistines' who manipulated the performers, particularly in the recording industry, but in the real world of ordinary people he ceased to be an enemy of the philosophy he preached.

Dinner that night led us back to Neville Terrace, where Roy played old Led Zeppelin albums.

I don't think either of us had any intention of becoming lovers, but drawn together by the movie and, to our mutual surprise, many shared views on life, it was completely natural.

Roy smoked vast quantities of hash and still liked to drop acid. I hadn't done so for a number of years, but on the odd occasion when I did join Roy, we both ended on the same intellectual tangents, hovering somewhere between the spirit of the sixties and over the dust bowls of a strange and doubtful tomorrow. It could have been dangerous for me to dip even briefly back in the ocean of LSD, but I was careful and controlled and saw solutions to my problems, rather than new problems to heap upon the old.

I still felt the need to share my life with a man. We are pair-motivated creatures and a permanent bond is natural. That need for me had always been a weakness, but for once I felt strong enough to overcome it. I knew the right man would come along, but I suddenly felt less inclined to spend my life searching.

Roy was perfect, for there was no pretence. He had a child and a wife he called Mocky, but lived in a small, furniture-free flat in Hampstead. He shared it with a girlfriend, but they made no demands on each other's time. Roy would always go off somewhere when the day's filming was done, his multi-coloured woolly hat like a beacon in the twilight. He hated the cold weather, his nose was always bright red and when he wasn't talking, he spent all of his time blowing into his cupped hands. He never listened to anyone, but while he was working he was able to play out his role instinctively. He played the part of a rockstar, so I suppose it wasn't so difficult.

For me it was all very easy. I loved the character and, with the scenes taking place either in London or Brighton, it began to feel as if I really was acting out episodes from my own life. Most of the crew were old faces from the BBC and I had been friends with director John Mackenzie since the days of the Ark. He was Ken Loach's floor manager during the making of both *Cathy Come Home* and *Up the Junction*.

The guitar-strumming sequences in *Made* brought back fond memories of Terry Stamp singing a song that Donovan had written for me in *Poor Cow*. With Sean and Stephen back at the American school and my brother Joey turning up at Neville Terrace with a new girlfriend, it seemed as if my path would always be through a landscape of circles leading to more circles, a feeling made more pronounced by the men who reappeared in my life.

Warren Beatty was a regular visitor, as he commuted on business between London and Los Angeles, but two other brief encounters served to take me back ten whole years.

The first came about after a chance meeting at the White Elephant. I was having lunch with Roy, when I bumped into Michael Sloman, an executive on Decca Records, who had worked for a while with Mike King.

'You'll never guess who's in town, Carol?' he said.

I replied with a puzzled look.

'Tony. Your old flame from . . .' he paused, '. . . way back when.'

I still didn't know who he was talking about, which I made clear by remaining silent.

'Little Tony,' Michael said, his hands emphasising the point. 'Italy's answer to Elvis, surely you haven't forgotten?'

244

'Little Tony,' I replied. 'That's going back a few years.'

'I'll give you his number, case you want to give him a call.'

Michael scribbled a number on a paper napkin and we said goodbye.

I had lots of nice thoughts, but to return is so often disappointing that I decided to leave that part of the past where it belonged: in the past.

It would have stayed there, but for a series of coincidences. Roy Harper was spending the weekend with his wife in Hertfordshire; Warren was away somewhere – and no doubt with someone – and my children were with mum and dad.

It was a Friday night and when I went to get something from my bag, the paper napkin fell out. I looked at the number and it seemed stupid not to at least call and say hello.

'Carol, my dearest, my darling,' Tony whispered down the telephone. 'I have waited all these years for you to call. I have been so lonely without you.'

Tony Ciacci was a hopeless romantic, as well as a terrible liar. Still, it was nice to hear his voice, his broken strings of English reminding me of a funny, old-fashioned room in the Tottenham Court Road, the expression on his face as he danced upon the floorboards, the feeling of wonder that entered me when he taught me all the things I still didn't know about sex.

'I must see you tomorrow, or I go crazy,' he continued. 'We have lunch, yes?'

'Yes, Tony, of course.'

'*Ti amo, ti amo, ti amo ...*'

It sounded like a mantra and I still had the words on my own lips while we sat together at a fish restaurant the following day. Tony was no different. He talked incessantly, mainly about himself, but he had a Peter Pan enthusiasm that made those ten long years seem just the briefest of moments.

The illusion lasted through lunch and went with us back to

245

Little Tony's apartment in Mayfair. We spent the rest of the day in bed and there we remained through Saturday night and all day Sunday and lazily talking about old times.

For me the weekend was over. I had to collect the boys from the home of my parents and with Tony leaving Monday for a concert tour in Israel, I expected that to be the end of it. But Tony was more of a romantic than I imagined. The very next day, I received a message from El Al, the Israeli airline, that a first class ticket from London to Tel Aviv was awaiting my collection. Tony wanted me to drop everything, the way I had done once before, not that it was possible. I was still working on *Made*, the boys were back at home and, though our weekend together had been fun, a very wide gap existed between us. Tony hadn't grown up, but I had.

At least a little bit.

A similar set of circumstances conspired to find me alone on a memorable evening later in the summer.

It started with a heavy bang on the door and it was almost without surprise that I opened it to find a red-eyed and somewhat plumper Oliver Reed standing there with his traditional calling card: a bottle of Dom Pérignon champagne.

'Coming out?' he said, as if we had been together the previous day.

'How did you know where I lived?'

'Connections,' he replied. 'Come on, get your coat on.'

'What about the champagne?'

'That's for later,' he grinned.

Oliver drove his Rolls Royce recklessly through the city and we ended at a country pub.

From there we went back to Oliver's rambling old mansion in Wimbledon, where I had to go through a bizarre initiation ceremony before I was allowed to enter.

Oliver went in the front door and directed me to a

246

tumbling-down extension on the side of the building. Inside it was a bar, built to mirror a public house. There was the usual array of ornaments and horse brasses, glasses on hooks, a row of optics and a wooden bar, where Oliver stood stern and military-like, his hands on the counter, as if he was ready for trouble.

'Can I help you?' he said.

'Yes,' I replied, improvising my part and ordering a drink, which I even had to pay for.

'Anything else? Crisps? Nuts?' He spoke with great emphasis.

'I was hoping to find a room?' I said. 'For the night.'

'All night?' he replied, his eyes blazing.

'All night.'

Oliver jumped over the bar and carried me into the house. His antics were outlandish and, with me a willing stooge, we always had a good time. It didn't matter how many years separated us, our friendship remained the same.

We were still together the following evening, when Oliver's brother, David, turned up with a demure, mousy girl who spoke with a very posh accent and was in fact a lady-in-waiting to Princess Margaret. Oliver, himself a former public schoolboy, responded with the most vulgar, working class tones he could manage and with the girl almost in tears, he complained bitterly of class privilege, the role of the monarchy and a list of issues that sounded like the agenda for a meeting of the Red Brigade.

The girl looked very sorry for herself, but Oliver suddenly rediscovered his own impeccable accent and she sighed with relief. She assumed the charade was over, but she now had to go through the public bar ritual in order to enter the house. She played along with Oliver's game, but she made one fatal mistake: she ordered orange juice.

'Orange juice,' Oliver screamed. 'What sort of drink do you call that?'

I've never seen anyone look quite so frightened. She ran through the pub door, complaining about actors and demanding to be taken home. David Reed remained silent; as Oliver's manager, he was in a tricky situation.

'Take me home. Please take me home,' she sobbed and, seconds later, David's car was leaving the drive.

We stood there, listening while the motor disappeared in the distance, the silence returning like a layer of unsettled dust. A full moon was high above, bathing the house in a milky glow and lighting Oliver's impish blue eyes.

'Good job they've gone,' he said; he sounded almost embarrassed. 'Come on, let's have a drink.'

The night was warm. We drank champagne and, though Oliver was unusually sweet and loving, a part of him remained distant, far away and in communion with the night. His words were filled with whimsy and as I fell beneath their spell, I had the feeling of being a guest in Oliver's private dream. The previous year, he had appeared with Vanessa Redgrave in *The Devils* and it had obviously left a lasting impression.

The hours passed with the bottles of Dom Pérignon and the fantasy crumbled into reality. Oliver talked about the pixie at the end of his garden in such sure and familiar terms that I had no doubt that a pixie was there.

'The whole world is full of strange things, but people are too blind to see them,' he said. 'You have to believe, or you never see anything.'

'I believe, Oliver, I believe in pixies and devils and especially ghosts,' I replied, the house in Montague Square still vivid in my memory.

'If you really do believe in my pixie, I'll introduce you,' Oliver continued. 'But you have to be very quiet and you mustn't say anything to upset him.'

'Of course not,' I countered. 'I wouldn't be so nasty.'

I was ready to go, but it wasn't as simple as that. Pixies, Oliver assured me, didn't like the clothes that us big people wore and he insisted that we stripped and even took a shower together before we set out. And so, naked, as well as freshly scrubbed, we ventured on tiptoes into the night, the air outside much cooler and the sky rich with countless silver stars. We searched through slumbering shrubs, in a forest of uncut grass and deep among the rose bushes, their thorns all eager and dreaming evil thoughts.

We moved through the darkness, our search taking us over the high fence that separated Oliver's garden from the golf course and on to the green velvet fairways, Oliver transforming into a pixie, all plump and strong and unimpressed with the creeping chill of morning. Everything appeared so still and much larger than it did during the day, not that it worried me. I gripped Oliver's hand and felt in tune with the moment, free from the doubts that haunted my life. Oliver kept spotting his little friend, but each time we drew closer, he vanished in the shadows. I think I spotted him, too, but I was so busy laughing that I couldn't be sure. Oliver always managed to bring out the best in me. His smile filled the night and it makes me happy even now, just to remember it.

We wandered aimlessly towards the trees, a cloud forming to obscure the light, which in turn made me think of the Dylan songs I was again playing constantly on my stereo deck at home.

It remained dark, the moon departing to await the dawn. I suddenly realised we were lost and a moment's panic made me sure that someone would see us. I imagined the fun Fleet Street would have with the headlines:

WHAT WERE OLIVER REED AND CAROL WHITE DOING NAKED ON THE GOLF COURSE?

Searching for pixies? A likely tale!

'Oliver, we're lost,' I said at last. 'What are we going to do?'

'Have no fear, Tinkerbell will come and lead us home.'

Tinkerbell was Oliver's black cat; he attributed it with great powers, but I was beginning to have my doubts. The

249

pixie, after all, had failed to make an appearance.

'Tinkerbell, Tinkerbell,' he sang, the first hint of daylight seeping over the horizon. 'Tinkerbell, Tinkerbell.'

I stood close to Oliver, as if trying to hide myself behind his bulk; the night was deathly silent, but then, in the distance, I could just make out the gentle tinkle of a bell. Seconds later, the little black cat was there at our feet, restoring my faith in Oliver's dream world. It led us out from the trees, across the green on hole nine and back to the fence at the end of Oliver's garden. The stars were fading, the first milk train hooted across faraway fields and the sky was splashed with daybreak.

Oliver and I parted company later that same day and we didn't see each other again for another five years.

That journey into Oliver Reed's jingle jangle morning had been brief and my life now reverted to the old pattern of revolving doors. The filming of *Made* had come to an end, Roy Harper was tripped out on acid and when the autumn leaves began to fall, my mind filled up with blue skies and palm trees.

I didn't know if I was running away from something, or chasing something that didn't exist. I wasn't completely over the nervous breakdown and each decision I made was at least partly inspired by the invincible little insect that lived in my brain. It was time to go; simply to go ...

Seventeen

IT WAS an unfamiliar room.

The words of Bob Dylan's songs hummed faintly in my mind, but they faded when I noticed the snowy shafts of light that fell through the blinds. A shadow formed and with the sun fanning out in the background, I now looked into the steady brown eyes of a young doctor. He had long curly hair and a smile that made me see my life once more as a precious gift.

That smile belonged to Stuart Lerner, a man who in later years became many things I disliked, but when I first saw him in that ring of morning light, I fell deeply in love.

Stuart was the resident psychiatrist at the UCLA hospital. I was there after another unsuccessful attempt to end it all, but though there can be no justification for my act, this time, it wasn't the same old story.

I had left London hoping to find something different in Los Angeles, but nothing had changed. Warren Beatty still had a place for me at the Beverly Wilshire, but it was Julie Christie who filled his thoughts. The situation with Paul Burke was in a time warp. He welcomed me back into the maze of his unsettled life, yet his faithful friend Anna was always there, more faithful than ever. I slotted back into the usual routine, but I was quickly disenchanted. I wanted to be with a man who would cherish me every hour of the day and my resolve to avoid that need withered and reshaped into the seed of discontent. I became depressed and nervous and then the ultimate calamity drove me to the medicine cabinet.

I was pregnant.

A great number of changes had taken place since I last faced that particular dilemma and though a solution was both straightforward, as well as legal, it wasn't as simple as that. I had all the instincts that made me want to have a baby and all the doubts that face a woman who is alone. I also had enough common sense to know that the father would find his role hard to accept.

The father?

Yes, I knew who it was. It is true that I had been sleeping with two different men, but it could only have been one of them!

The days had grown longer and the Christmas that passed was the worst I had ever known. I missed my family and while Sean and Stephen were like little rays of light, all around me there was darkness. I was lonely, confused and the future was such an uncertain place.

I sat down and wrote three letters: to Paul Burke, John Davis and to Mike King, the father of my two sons and the one man I had never stopped loving. Sean and Stephen, safely with their nanny, were so young, but I hoped that one day they would understand and forgive me. I watered the plants, I drew the curtains and, carefully, I swallowed a handful of sleeping pills.

It was typical of how irrational and dualistic I had become. As soon as I felt myself drifting into sleep, I thought about all the things I still wanted to do: there were films to be made, places to see, a world of ideas to explore. I tried to make myself sick and, when that didn't work, I called an English girlfriend and told her what I had done. I tried to call Warren Beatty, but I collapsed before I reached him.

I was in a coma for three days and the next thing I remember is waking up in that unfamiliar room.

It was a bit of a cliché to fall for your doctor, but with the light creating an optical illusion and the warmth in his first words, it felt completely natural.

'I've been waiting for you to wake up,' he said. 'Just so I could say hello.'

'Thank you,' I replied, I'm not sure why.

'How are you feeling?'

'Okay,' I mumbled.

'I hope you're never going to be so silly again, a beautiful woman like you should never want to destroy herself.'

I nodded and closed my eyes.

'Do you want to talk about it?'

It may have seemed premature, but he had assessed my mood correctly. He helped me sit up, I sipped some lemon juice and while Dr Lerner sat in the striped bars of sunlight, I started at the beginning and rambled on until I had told him the story of my life, ending with the vague conclusion that I was in love with two men at the same time.

'Even if you are, you still have everything to live for,' he said.

'Yes, I know, that's why I telephoned my girlfriend.'

'There, you see, you're feeling better already,' he laughed. It was true, I was relaxed, even cheerful, and I suddenly felt hungry. I told the doctor and when some food arrived, I ate and it was his turn to start talking. He talked of love and death and human relationships and I was astonished to find so much wisdom in one so young – and he was young. Stuart Lerner had qualified as a doctor at the age of twenty-two, one of the youngest men in the United States ever to have done so. He was now just twenty-three and a psychiatrist.

'And now you love two men at the same time,' he said at last. He paused for a long time and then added, 'I think what we must do is see if either of them want to commit themselves to you.'

I was a bit perplexed, so I just nodded and let Stuart continue.

He produced a telephone and a list of numbers; he called Warren Beatty and he called Paul Burke. He told them my story and he asked them if they were willing to pick me up from the hospital. They both refused.

'Do you really want to give up your life for those two?' he said and, sadly, I could only shake my head.

The doctor's Solomon-like calls found me wiser, but there was now a space in my life that only he could fill. We started to see each other as soon as I left the university hospital. Stuart moved in with me at the end of January and three months later, we were married.

Paul Burke and I remained friends, in an odd sort of way. We were, after all, competitors in the same crazy game. As for Warren Beatty, I only saw him on one further occasion and that was by chance. We came face to face while we were both out shopping along the immorally expensive Rodeo Drive. We smiled, but neither of us spoke.

That day, as every day, I was with Stuart. The man I had needed to fill the hours was there, but after the first rush of excitement, things started to go wrong. Stuart soon appeared to me as the typical spoiled Jewish boy. He had been paid through college and medical school and while he had gone on to become a psychiatrist, deep down he wanted to be a pop star or a movie actor. He talked about getting into television and wanted to have a psychiatry quiz show, with himself as the host. Stuart saw me, I think, as a sort of way to the stars, and I saw Stuart as the way to recapture the happiness I had known when I was married to Mike King, perhaps!

It wasn't perfect, but there was a big plus on the credit side that I had to consider. Sean and Stephen, now nine and eight years old, took to Stuart immediately. I had dragged them around the world since they were babies and they deserved the security Dr Stuart Lerner promised to provide.

I had so much to think about that I did the only sensible thing and forgot about it.

Stuart, though a doctor, still didn't know I was pregnant and I was soon too busy to set the record straight. I had signed months earlier for *Some Call It Loving* and filming started in February at the John Paul Getty mansion, in Malibu.

It was a bizarre story filled with contradictions and had me cast as Scarlett, the mother superior in a place where a man's fantasies become a reality. James B. Harris, the producer and director, also wrote the script for what was essentially an adult fairy tale that explored unconventional sexual and emotional behaviour; or, as Hollis Albert put it in the *Saturday Review*: '... a film that has some of the most elegant eroticism yet seen on the screen.'

As a fantasy, the plot wasn't always easy to follow and though the underlying theme was aimed at the intellect, the more obvious, perhaps more exposed, aspects reached cinema audiences. My wardrobe shifted between the extremes of a nun's habit and a collection of garish, flesh-revealing gowns; a religious fanatic and a provoking object of desire.

The man living out his fantasy was Zalman King; Tisa Farrow was the young and often naked novitiate and Richard Pryor, as a terminally sick alcoholic, drank himself into a daily stupor, just to get into the part. One of the scenes was set in a local church but after Richard's first blasphemous display the minister threw us out. I thought we were tempting providence, and to confirm those fears, in a later scene, a large wooden crucifix fell from the wall and pinned me to the floor. I wasn't badly hurt, but a few days later Tisa wasn't so lucky. She took a tumble and broke her arm. We were plagued with minor accidents and delays. Finally, I became too ill to work. I had pains in my stomach and it wasn't morning sickness.

It was then that I told Stuart I was pregnant and it was then that Stuart said he wanted us to get married.

He wanted to get married, but he wanted me to have an abortion first. He didn't mind taking on a movie star mother who was six years his senior, but another man's child was out

255

of the question. He explained why it was necessary and, though I have since forgotten what he said, it made sense at the time.

The operation was simple and within a matter of days I was back on set. There were no more pains in my stomach, but there was an emptiness that lasted for a long time. I didn't want anything to do with men and now only talked to Tisa, comforting her while she faced a dilemma I knew so well. Her arm was fine in its plaster cast, but she was pregnant and unsure whether or not to have the baby.

The film was completed without further interruptions and April arrived with everything but showers. My birthday hit the point of no return: I was twenty-nine. Jo Janni's *Made* had opened to rave reviews in London and, on the 26 April, I became Mrs Stuart Lerner. It was all kept very simple with just a few friends. Sean and Stephen were happy, but I remained in that empty space. My lips moved and I said, 'I do', but the voice inside was shouting, 'I don't, I don't'. I knew it was a mistake before the ceremony was over. We went out to lunch, I got blind, belting drunk and I fell face-first into an artichoke. I had avoided such excess for more than a year and my wedding turned out to be the beginning of the biggest bender of them all.

It was two months later that my mum was taken into hospital. She had smoked three packs of cigarettes a day all her life and she now had a cancer spot on her lungs. A month later, in July, I flew back to London. Stuart and the boys were with me.

In those few short weeks, mum's condition had become much worse. She was now paralysed and lying in a mental hospital, a psychological reaction, the doctors said, to my father's illness. Their life together had been one long battle, but they had a love for each other that I envied. I sat at my mother's bedside for hours. She had always been such a beautiful woman, the source of strength in the background of my life, but the toil and torment of those last few years were etched now in the lines that marked her face. She was far away from me and from everyone, but during her clear moments, she held my hand and those lines became a smile.

I wanted to stay with my mother, but Stuart had to return to work and, when it was time for him to go, I went with him. The months that took us to Christmas were slow and vacant and though I had my own problems, they appeared petty by comparison when I saw my mother again. She had been in hospital, but she was allowed home for the holiday. I had never seen anyone deteriorate so fast. She was just a shadow, her face pale and her skin like parchment as it stretched across her sunken cheeks. She was lying in bed, her hands comforting each other on the white of the turned-down sheet.

I had twice tried to take my own life, but death remained a foreigner to me. Now it was there, in my mother's room. I felt vulnerable and transient, so sad for my mother, but determined to find contentment in my own life. I decided to make a real go of my marriage to Stuart, to support him, even if I had to give up my own career to do so.

While mum tried hard to get up and be with the family, dad couldn't understand what was happening. His brain tumour operation had been a success, but he had never really recovered. He became angry and demanding; he wanted a Christmas like he remembered from the past. Those days had gone forever.

We remained in London for less than a week and shortly after our return to Los Angeles mum was back in hospital. The cancer in her lungs had spread through her whole body and the doctors now gave her just nine months to live. Their estimate was morbidly accurate.

Mum died on 16 October. We flew immediately to London, but I still felt guilty for not having been there at the end. Dad sat at the graveside in his wheelchair, a lost and lonely man, though friends from far and wide attended the funeral and created a nostalgic, almost festive atmosphere.

257

The gathering after the ceremony was a bit like a wake and I'm sure that mum would have approved. She loved parties and dressing up, good clothes and expensive jewellery; she had a strong and forthright personality and, like my dad, she had always been there when I needed her, my security in a world so far from Hammersmith. Mum had lived her life to the full and I feel certain she had no regrets.

It was the next day that I realised that my father would never get over mum's death. He sat in his wheelchair and watched the traffic go by in the street below. His expression was blank and his eyes had lost their colour.

I had tried hard to make my marriage work, but my effort was just a sandcastle against the tide. In London, we had stayed at the home of that 'friend indeed', John Davis. Stuart had persuaded me to sell my own house in Fulham, and that was typical of the compromises I was prepared to make. Stuart said we would never need the house and though I knew it was stupid to get rid of it I did so to keep him happy.

Stuart worked long hours to be the top man in his profession. He had left his position at the university, but in opening a private practice in Beverly Hills, his patients and our social life became indivisible. Our home in the Benedict Canyon became the scene for the Hollywood weirdos, people hung-up on drugs and using a psychiatrist to dry out. I was surrounded by coke whores and dealers, jazz musicians and wealthy rockstars who were there because they weren't anywhere else.

Hollywood in the mid-seventies was a plastic replica of London in the sixties. The faces were the same, but the driving force had gone. Life was too easy, the days were tediously long and most of my friends had exchanged the books of Hermann Hesse for the *Wall Street Journal*. We alleviated our boredom with wild, extravagant parties, gatherings of musicians and movie stars, with their casual designer clothes and fabulous jewellery – the tribal trappings of success.

At first, I avoided the drug scene, as well as many of the old faces who had been there before, but I made up for it by being shamefully self-indulgent. Champagne flowed through the house like water, the table was filled with European delicacies and that year I stuffed the Christmas turkey with minced veal, instead of sausage meat.

I was bored. Stuart worked and Sean and Stephen had the time of their lives. They were kept amused by a throng of visitors and house guests: Keith Moon, a real-life loony, and Ringo Starr. Songwriter Al Stewart, a latecomer to the scene, was almost out of place amongst the drop-outs and the same goes for Harry Nilsson. He was an intellectual giant, just like Stuart, who gave up his career when John Lennon was killed in 1980. He became, and still is, a vehement campaigner for gun control.

Life was one long cocktail party and I grew to hate it. I had turned down numerous TV and film offers to be with Stuart and he repaid me by giving all his time to his psychiatry practice. It was ages before I came to terms with this and, when I did, I became so depressed that I turned to the same escape hatch as everyone else. I tried cocaine and I liked it. I didn't think I would get hooked, but every day I wanted more. On some days, I became so high I had to take Valium to bring me back down to earth. I took diet pills to lose weight, the result of a drinking spree that started on my wedding day; I took Quaaludes to relax and sleeping pills to block out everything.

From that first snort of cocaine, it was downhill all the way.

I had been faithful to Stuart since the day we met, but now I just wanted to enjoy myself. Cathy Bach, one of the leggy ladies in the *Dukes of Hazzard*, introduced me to a young skier and when he invited me for a holiday in Aspen, Colorado, I packed my bags and went. The show business

259

crowd all thought Mick was a professional sportsman. When he turned out to be a big wheel in the organisation that smuggled the raw cocaine crystals from South America, I didn't even care. I was a denizen of the twilight zone and getting kicks was all that mattered.

Stuart seemed unconcerned by my fickle moods, but paid me back in his own subtle way. We both filed for divorce in April 1974, about the same time as that trip to Colorado, but we remained together right up until the time it came through two years later. Stuart hated the idea of letting go – I was his possession, his chattel – while I wanted it to work for the sake of my children. They were both doing well at school and, despite their unusual lifestyle, they were both normal, healthy boys. I had a lot to be grateful for.

It was back to the game-playing syndrome I had left behind with Paul Burke, only Stuart's games were far more complicated.

I was always being tested. Stuart did strange things, just to see my reaction, his behaviour patterns changed, he disappeared and reappeared, asking me questions, as if I were his personal guinea pig and he was researching something profound. Stuart Lerner had an IQ that rated him a genius, but I had inherited an innate strength from my parents and only rarely did I fall beneath his psychological attacks.

One of Stuart's experiments took me to John Mayall's house of insanity on the Laurel Canyon Boulevard. I entered the room, expecting to meet the usual crowd, but the room was in darkness and I was leapt up on by a gang of silent men. It was a mock rape, like a scene from a morality play, and although I wasn't hurt, I found the experience anything but funny.

If my psychiatrist husband was trying to drive me out of my mind, he had chosen the perfect setting.

The house was like a nightmare on acid. Ugly and exotic masks stared down from every corner, instruments of pain

260

and humiliation clung to the walls, music blared from batteries of speakers and porno-flicks ran constantly from the miniature cinema. There was a sewing room where John made frilly and fanciful costumes, and in the grounds there were small guest lodges that recreated John's sexual fantasies: the Victorian room, the Japanese room, the room of mirrors and the chamber of horrors.

It was at John's house that I got to know Keith Moon, though we didn't climb into bed together, but into each other's heads. It had been the same with John Lennon and Brian Jones. Now they are all dead. My relationship with the glittering Rod Stewart was more down to earth, but our brief flirtation never left the slopes of the Laurel Canyon. Rod believed so fervently in his own ego that it was impossible to see the man behind it. The parties were endless and so are the memories that remain fragmented in my mind, names that are known the world over with faces that decorate my soul: Eric Clapton, John McVie, the dour and silent sages of Pink Floyd, Yes and Genesis. They all passed through and left something of themselves in John Mayall's private hallucination, although now the whole trip has passed into legend.

The house burnt to the ground in the great fires that swept through the Hollywood Hills in 1979. John Mayall lost everything – but his talent. We met again this year and, although he isn't playing himself, he manages a punk band fronted by a girl singer, a blonde and blue-eyed angel not long out of high school.

The parties, though ultimately destructive, were a relief from the monotony of Stuart's games. I still believed our marriage could work, but while I continued to turn down the movies I was offered, my eternal second self stared hopelessly upon a career so static it was growing moss.

Made still collected its fair share of favourable reviews, but it didn't have the results that Jo Janni had expected. *Some Call It Loving* had a certain cult following, but it reached few people on a linear level. The erotic sequences overshadowed its greater merits, or as one cynic put it: '. . . like *Last Tango in Paris* without the butter.'

The film was completed in April 1972 and more than two years had since gone by. It was the longest period I had ever gone without working. My life was in a mess and it was still there at Christmas, when my father arrived for his first and only visit to the United States. He had long ago lost the will to live, yet he was still concerned for me. He sat in his wheelchair, the paralysis making his speech almost incoherent, but I could see by the fear in his pale blue eyes that he knew what was wrong with me: he knew I was on drugs and only by leaving Stuart Lerner would I find the strength to set my life straight.

I wanted to tell him that I was still his little girl, that everything was temporary, that it would all work out for the best. I knew that it didn't matter how despondent I became, it was just a test, that destiny for me was not in an empty bottle of sleeping pills. I was not going to be a star who ended it all in a moment's panic, for life had to be lived with all its pain and for all its pleasures. I was back in that long lonely tunnel, yet a tiny light flickered in the distance. I didn't say anything to dad, but I held his frail and useless hands and prayed that he, too, could see that light.

While I spent Christmas with my father, the rest of the family seemed so far away, though one of my brothers was actually in the United States, across country in Virginia. Joe White Jnr. had finally decided to settle down with his girlfriend, Terri, a stewardess with British Airways. They were married on Christmas Day.

I didn't get to see them both until the following summer, when I went back to England to spend some time with dad. His condition was much the same, but communication was even more difficult. Joe and Terri had now produced Kelly, their daughter, but my dad wanted another grandson and, in his mind, she was always a boy. I left London at the end of the summer and I never saw my father again.

262

My father had been rushed to hospital while I was working on *Daddy's Gone a Hunting* in 1968. He had fought a losing battle against the illness for eight long, miserable years and he finally died at the Brompton Hospital in February 1976. The funeral this time was a family occasion, but although I was with the people who meant the most to me, with both my parents gone, I had never felt more alone in my life.

Since dad's visit to my home in Los Angeles, I had made a more determined effort to kick the drug habit and get back to work. There were a lot of offers floating around Hollywood, but I didn't consider anything seriously until the agent Roz Chatto introduced me to Michael Apted, during my stay in London in 1975. We had, in fact, met before at Barbara Steel's house in Malibu and, with the reforging of old links and fond memories, Michael offered me the lead in *The Squeeze*, which was going into production the following year.

It was the offer I had been waiting for. Hollywood movies earned me more money, but the films I made in England always had greater artistic value and I usually found myself with a nomination for at least one award.

In the twelve months that passed, I finally left Stuart and moved in with the producer Si Litvinoff, a man whose house on the beach was always filled with the biggest names in the movie industry, but where I still didn't find the sense of balance that had been missing from my life for so long.

My escape from Stuart did at least lift the shroud-like depression from my shoulders and the people I now met offered an interesting assortment of diversions . . . lunch with Raquel Welch, a surprise meeting with the folk singer, Donovan, parties with Jack Nicholson, Ryan O'Neal, Candy Clarke, Jenny Agutter and an actress who formed one whole piece in the jigsaw puzzle of the past:

Her name was Julie Christie.

We had been on the payroll of the same film studio as teenagers, we knew the grief of loving that complex man Warren Beatty and, it was true, we even looked alike. Our lives had run on the same set of parallels and they finally met at Si's house in Malibu. We looked at each other apprehensively, the doubts became a smile and, suddenly, it was so easy to become friends. We had both had our share of losing and in those matching smiles lay all the frustration that belonged to another time. We walked together that night, the ocean pulling gently against the sand and our voices growing soft in the vastness of so much space.

I found an empathy with Julie Christie that I rarely shared with women; one that I certainly didn't share with Si's French maid. She was over six feet tall, as mad as a March hare and she said she was in love with me. It turned out to be harmless, another of those 'interesting diversions' and it helped to pass the time while I was waiting to start work on *The Squeeze*.

My arrangement with Si Litvinoff was very open-ended and I divided my time between his house and what I now thought of as Stuart's house, the home of my two growing sons. They weren't upset by my comings and goings and had reached an age when they had their own separate lives; junior high school in the United States is, in fact, a separate world. While I wasn't living with Stuart, it was easier for us to be friends, and as soon as we were friends, we wanted to try again.

It was during one of the periods when we were making 'one last go of it', that I met up with Dudley Moore, another refugee from the sixties seeking fame and fortune in Hollywood. He was waiting for the break that so rarely comes, although when it did come for Dudley, it couldn't have happened to a nicer person.

He turned up at a session of group analysis therapy, it's very fashionable in Beverly Hills, and bumped into producer Blake Edwards, whose problem was finding the right man to play opposite the freshly cast screen goddess Bo Derrick in her movie debut *10*. The film, which also starred Blake's wife, Julie Andrews, was enormously successful and Dudley then went on to top the bill in *Arthur*, which made him a millionaire and the most unlikely sex symbol ever to invade California.

Dudley as a megastar is just as funny and just as cuddly as he was that night we went out to dinner, even though it didn't turn out according to plan.

He wanted us to go out alone, but I would only agree if I could take a friend.

'Sure, why not, as long as your friend's not a psychiatrist,' Dud said with a smile. He had obviously had enough of group therapy.

'That's exactly what he is,' I replied and, although Dudley's mouth fell open, we made a time and dined together later that week, all three of us.

The exchange between Oxford graduate Dudley Moore and superbrain Stuart Lerner was memorable, to say the least, so memorable, in fact, that it was still on Dudley's mind when he met Jane Seymour in Hollywood two years later. He invited her out for dinner and much to his surprise, like me, she wanted to take a friend.

'This could be habit forming,' Dud joked. 'I just hope your friend isn't a psychiatrist.'

'... that's exactly what he is,' Jane replied.

'Next you're going to tell me it's Stuart Lerner!'

I'd give an Academy Award, just to have seen the look on Dudley Moore's face.

Jane Seymour's friend was indeed Stuart Lerner, not that the affair lasted very long.

Eighteen

THE SUMMER of 1976 arrived like a reprieve from a jail sentence. Sean and Stephen were with their nanny and step-dad and I flew to London to start work on *The Squeeze*.

It was to be my last fling, a safari along those time-worn circles in search of scenes that had once been joyful. The spirit of the sixties was with me, a pale and dusty ghost, and together we breathed the thin air of the past. I wanted to fill my days with as much fun as possible, my desire embracing a harmless naïveté that did not exist in Los Angeles. All innocence was lost in that terrible city and, as I left, it felt as if I had escaped from Sodom and Gomorrah; Lot's wife without the slightest desire to look back.

The national newspapers advertised my unaccompanied return in their gossip columns and once I moved into a suite at the Kensington Hilton, the telephone never stopped ringing.

I had tried hard to be faithful to Stuart, but with the divorce being finalised, our contract had come to an end. We owed each other nothing. There had been a time when I really did love Stuart, but our marriage had been a disaster from the start. There had been advantages for us both, although we had never been particularly happy. I had given up my career and immersed myself in Stuart's personality, but that in itself was alien to the real me and my release through the use of drugs was unavoidable. I was an actress and I had to perform, yet while life is what happens between roles, for me, the four years that had passed since the completion of *Some Call It Loving* had been wasted. I had been treading water and I was anxious to make up for lost time.

My fling that sizzling hot summer began not with a telephone call, but a late night knock on the door. It was that man of many faces Freddie Starr, who was playing the part of an amiable petty thief in *The Squeeze* and who happened to be staying at the Hilton. He had a bottle of iced champagne waiting in his suite, the lights and music were low ...

Freddie's excessive ardour created some tension on set next day, although when we started working, I realised that even the script was excuse enough for his lack of charm.

Michael Apted had chosen a project with those ingredients that appeared to be essential for a film to have any sort of box office success. It came in the wake of *Death Weekend* and *The Texas Chain-Saw Massacre* and like them, a proportion of its running time was devoted to bloody beatings and the sexual humiliation of its female characters. It was a sad indictment of the movie industry, although, as *The Times* said when the film was released: '... such horrors are not imposed on the public by some malevolent private agency; they are provided because the public demonstrates by paying to see them that they are what it desires.'

The Squeeze, too, was a little different from most in its genre and balanced the violence with an unusually good story line. I was in the centre of the plot as the victim of a kidnapping and the sides of good and evil drew upon the talents of Stacy Keach, David Hemmings, Edward Fox and Stephen Boyd, who died tragically soon after filming was completed.

It seemed unfortunate that such gifted performers should have to lend their art to a film lacking social value, but then, the elements had conspired that summer to make philosophical discussions all but impossible.

The summer wasn't just hot, it was scorching: the highest temperatures on record, the highest, I'm sure, since planet Earth evolved from out of the primeval soup. I was pleased to be working, even though fate had chosen to place me in the worst of locations. My scenes nearly all took place with me either in the back of a van, or a claustrophobic, barred and shuttered room in Ladbroke Grove. It was like going to work each day in an oven. I had to appear distresed for most of those scenes and, naturally, it wasn't very difficult.

Apart from the joy I felt simply being back in front of the cameras, there was another positive effect from the conditions: the extra weight I had put on just fell away. I lost thirty pounds in six weeks.

After my little contretemps with Freddie Starr, I avoided further entanglements with the men I worked with and it remained that way until a boiling and breathless weekend, when I joined David Hemmings for an excursion into the country. We went to a hotel, showered and found a small restaurant. The only trouble was, we left the windows open at the hotel and the lights had attracted a swarm of moths. When we arrived back at the room, any romantic notions we may have had went straight out of the window, unlike the moths. They were still coming in.

We never managed to find another free weekend and, although the rumour that David and I were having an affair found its way all over London, it never came to pass.

It may have done, but the hours were short and my social life was abundantly full. I went out with Michael Apted, record chief John Adrian, my fun-loving first husband Mike King and my old friend Albert Finney, who talked about my dad and read me poetry.

Albert was appearing in a season of Shakespeare at the National Theatre and the words he learned during the day, he rehearsed in his sleep at night. It was strange to wake up and hear him performing a monologue, but he did it so well I started to enjoy it.

It is only roles in the theatre that find their way into your subconscious and I hadn't experienced it since my years at the Corona Stage School. I found myself thinking about

268

those long lost days and in doing so, one of its heroes came sailing back into my life.

I went to a reception for the actress Elaine Stritch with Mike King, but when I saw Richard O'Sullivan, it seemed in that first fleeting glimpse that we had been waiting for each other all our lives. We both edged our way through the smoke and evening-dress-clad people to join hands and travel the Time Machine back to a dancing class, Richard in his pea-green ballet tights, the smell of Kiwi shoe polish, the wall bars all gleaming from the sweat of a million tiny fingers.

We remained motionless for two decades, our words stuck and our memories a collage of disjointed thoughts. I remembered Richard kicking through the leaves in Ravens-court Park, the pleasure in his eyes when I got the lead role in *Never Let Go*, the day after years of waiting that we ran hand in hand through the park and made love beneath the trees. Richard represented all the happy times, the innocent joy that can only be felt as a child. We had gone too far and learned too much to recapture that feeling but, for a second, we managed to leap through the barriers of time and space and we were children again.

Once we had found each other, we wanted to remain together, although that night it wasn't possible. I was with Mike and Richard was with Tessa Wyatt, his co-star from the TV series *Robin's Nest*. She was married to disc jockey Tony Blackburn, but was going through a divorce to be with Richard.

It was typical.

The Carol White Triangle.

Richard and I started to see each other, but it was all done in secret and the dishonesty soon bored me. Richard had the same old twinkle in his eye; he was full of high spirits and I couldn't understand his fatal attraction to Tessa Wyatt. She was a pretty little blonde thing, but she didn't sparkle.

The weeks passed, but in the end my dates with Richard O'Sullivan served only to reveal the emptiness of my life. I had the same feeling when I was with Mike King. We had shared so much that our lives were irreversibly joined together, but while the conditions for a lasting reunion were almost perfect, they weren't perfect enough. I wouldn't compromise and that left me in the usual empty space.

Work on *The Squeeze* continued in the crackling, glistening heat and while my fruitless love life limped cautiously along, the social scene never contained a dull moment. I had 'confessed' to the press that I no longer believed in marriage and, since the interview, journalists and women's rights campaigners had been hounding me for my views on free love, abortion and a dozen other issues. I did a commercial for French television, some radio talk shows and I went on endless shopping sprees all over the West End. Beverly Hills contains just as many nice stores, but the atmosphere isn't the same.

The parties and receptions all glazed into a momentary Shangri-la and the one night I still remember was the première of the Led Zeppelin classic *The Song Remains the Same*, at the Odeon, Leicester Square. The red carpets were out and so were rock's royalty. Paul McCartney turned up with Wings; Roy Harper was there, as funny and as angry as always; Robert Plant and the producers; the arrangers and all the musicians who had survived the years and the drugs. I went with the film's director, Peter Clifton, and it was on his arm that I remained for the rest of the evening.

After the film, we went on to a party at the Green Room, in Covent Garden, where the music blared, the inevitable three-paper joints revolved in endless circles and the spinning crystal ball captured the history of sixties rock in its diamond-shaped chips of glass. It was like a revival, faces from long disbanded Mersey groups appearing through the flashing lights, record critics, with their bald heads and gaudy clothes, the first punks with their safety pins and serious faces. Everyone danced in one great throbbing mass, as if the flood tides of a new era were climbing up the walls, the drinks were spiked with acid and guitarist Jimmy

McCullough tried to throw himself from a balcony. Someone who was a little less stoned managed to stop him just a second before he leapt. But ultimately he too died this year from an overdose of heroin.

People stood in the streets below, waiting to catch a glimpse of their idols, as if the musicians were gods and the Green Room had transformed into Olympus. The hours passed, the music grew louder and the party didn't break up until that awful moment when the body is about ready to crush in on itself. My companion was in a worse state than I was and by the time we got back to Blake's Hotel, in South Kensington, he was unconscious. I left Peter Clifton on his bed and retreated back into the warm summer night, the sky was clear and filled with stars and the words of the Pink Floyd song *The Dark Side of the Moon* droned in my skull ...

The words belonged to Pink Floyd lyricist Roger Waters, who I was to meet the following year, and although we did no more than join eyes across the frenzy of a riotous party, I felt the subtle aura of a kindred spirit.

When I left Peter Clifton with his acid-coloured dreams, I set off for my suite at the Hilton, but I didn't want to spend the night alone and somehow, I managed to wake up the next day with Richard O'Sullivan.

The première and the crazy gathering that followed were a suitable end to that crimson-lit summer. I was skinny and exhausted; work on *The Squeeze* was almost over and, although there was talk of my going to Rome to make another film, it would be one long party and that wasn't what I wanted. I thought about all the things I might do and then the telephone rang and helped me make up my mind.

It was Stuart Lerner.

He had bought a six-bedroomed mansion house on the beach at Malibu, business was obviously on the up and up, and he wanted me to join him.

271

'I've missed you so much, Carol,' he said. 'This time it will be different.'

'I'm not sure. I don't think we're right for each other, Stuart, and anyway, I don't want to give up my career.'

'Of course not. That's what went wrong last time,' Stuart added. 'I know that you have to work and I've employed a full-time maid so that she can take care of the boys. They really miss you, you know.'

'That's blackmail.'

'But it's true.'

I remained thoughtful and silent and then Stuart dropped his bombshell.

'I want us to get married again, Carol, I want us to get married and start it all properly.'

'Married!!!' I replied. 'We've only just got divorced.'

'I know, but I love you and I want to make up for the bad times in the past.'

Marriage I certainly wasn't sure about, but I had a desperate need to be with Sean and Stephen and they were the tie that tilted the balance.

The new London fashions, a year ahead of anything in California, filled my suitcases and, like a migrating bird, I fled the coming autumn to pick up the threads of my life with Stuart Lerner.

The house he had bought was wonderful, the downtown pollution not invading the beach, the sea breezes rippling the pool and the days soon passing like sand through an hourglass.

During the next few months, Stuart tried hard to make our relationship work, so hard, in fact, that he even befriended Mike King when he turned up in Los Angeles. Mike was in the city to negotiate a deal with one of the television networks and rather than him stay in an hotel, he moved in with us. It was strange to be living with not one, but two ex-husbands, but nothing in my life had ever been ordinary and it actually worked out very well. For Sean and Stephen, it was a case of having their cake and eating it, too.

They were with their dad, their step-dad, they had everything teenage boys could ever want and were both spoiled rotten.

I didn't think it was such a bad thing. There had always been plenty of money, but it was the first time they'd had a permanent home for several years. They were doing surprisingly well at school, they took extra music classes and they intended following their father's footsteps into the recording business.

For a while, I was happy. I knew it couldn't last, but I kept faith with the Alcoholics Anonymous little adage and took life: One day at a time.

Mike King was a calm and patient man, a self-possessed Buddha who created a peaceful influence in the house. While he was there, Stuart and I got on fine, but when he left, things started to go wrong. Our new romance was a delicate flower and, one by one, the petals began to fall. I must have been incredibly optimistic, but while I thought there was a vague chance of us staying together, I was prepared to put up with almost anything. It remained precarious for several weeks, but then Stuart had some reason to go through my belongings and, in doing so, he found a note from John Adrian. It wasn't exactly a love letter, but the inference was clear enough.

Stuart was incensed and even though my affair with John had taken place after the divorce and while Stuart was squiring an assortment of English actresses, his ego was inflamed and our delicate flower was crushed beneath its heel.

'Get out and don't come back,' he yelled and I felt too weary to lift my voice and fight back.

I packed my bags, I took my children and I left.

It was Christmas Eve 1976 and I was out on the streets, the character in *Cathy Come Home* haunting my life and adding a seasonal twist to Jeremy Sandford's tale.

We took a taxi into town and, after a few desperate calls, we were offered the use of a house in the Beverly Hills, by the producer Alan McKeown, the man who started out as Elizabeth Taylor's hairdresser and, more recently, produced

Elton John's TV show in Russia, *From Russia with Elton*.

We remained there for three weeks and before Stuart Lerner changed his mind and asked me to return, I flew with the boys to London. I rented a mews house in South Kensington, the boys went to the American school and while the British film studios lay in dormant hibernation, I set out to rebuild my career.

England was cold and I missed my mum and dad.

I spent each morning in the kitchen, watching the stones in the garden revolve in their cycle of life: dewy wet and glistening with the morning damp; dry and dusty as the winter sun lifted ponderously above the back fence; polished to glassy mirrors in the late afternoon. I listened as the gas flames licked at the kettle, I read the newspapers and I thought about my life.

The whole of our culture, the movies, the drugs, the new attitude towards love and sex, all were the backdrop to our ideas; yet so blinded were we by the scenery, that we missed the point of the plot: our own inner feelings. I tried to see myself as I really was, but the exercise was confusing and I gave up. I was a product of the times, yet for all the peace, love and freedom, there was a price that had to be paid. We were the first generation not to march away to war, but the liberty had grown into barricades and prison walls and we tortured ourselves by seeking some greater reason for it all.

I thought about all the men I had ever loved and I realised that while the influences on our generation had brought us together, they had in some ways always torn us apart.

The days passed like exhausted steam trains, the weeks became months and the reality of Britain's economic malaise stole into my life. There was the usual selection of television parts, but I needed to get my teeth into a movie and there weren't any going into production. I listened to the news on the radio, a disjointed fairy tale where the pound was sinking, the stock market was up three points and the weather would be fine tomorrow; abroad now and fighting continued in the streets of Tehran, the EEC was selling chunks of its butter mountain to the Soviet Union and thousands were dead as the droughts spread across the deserts of Central Africa.

I tried to be thankful for what I had, but while the winter rain eased the colour from my cheeks and the world about me appeared to be crumbling, it was hard to think about anything but my own neurosis.

Winter became spring and London yawned its way back to life. A new season of parties got under way, but I avoided the men from the past and chose boyfriends who, like me, were wary of emotional ties. One of these was Jimmy Bain, the bass guitarist in Rainbow, whom I met at a surprise party at the Fulham home of June and Marc Bolan. Marc was the founder of the legendary band T. Rex and June was one of the first friends I ever had.

We had shared the same desk at the St Paul's Church of England Primary School, in Hammersmith.

The gathering consisted of another Who's Who in British rock, with the musicians from Rainbow, UFO and Pink Floyd; the music thundered on through the night and, though I enjoyed Jimmy Bain's company, I somehow felt alone and isolated. I had tried to shake it, but a vast malignant depression had built up through the months and there was only one thing that prevented me from toppling into another nervous breakdown: Sean and Stephen.

They missed their friends and their life in Malibu; they were both unhappy and they wanted to go home.

Nineteen

WHEN I finished work on *The Squeeze* in the summer of 1976, Stacy Keach introduced me to the *I Ching*, the ancient Chinese book of divination.

Under Stacy's guidance, I tossed three brass coins a total of six times, while he drew a formation of broken and solid lines. The resulting pair of hexagrams contained the extremes that were natural to my life: a nightmare lay in the immediate future, but beyond and more important, were the calm waters of Positive Changes.

Fire-spouting dragons would mark my path and I had to follow the example of the wise old fox, who walked slowly on the thin ice.

My slip back into the drug scene was written in the stars. It was necessary for me to sink to the deepest depths of depression and uncertainty before I could rise and be reborn.

Sean and Stephen were overjoyed when we arrived back at the mansion house on the beach, but I just sat by the pool and watched the sky. I drank champagne from breakfast until bedtime and clung to the twilight world of valium, Mellaral, Thorazine; the drugs that had but one exit: death. I no longer wanted to work, my usual cure, and slowly I became a prisoner: a prisoner of my ex-husband, but worse, a prisoner of my own apathy. In a moment of panic, I checked into the state hospital at Camarillo and it was only through the faith of a young English psychiatrist that I managed to get out.

I wasn't crazy; I was lost.

What happened next brings me back to the beginning of my story.

Michael Arnold was there, waiting for me when I returned from that out-of-body experience and he was still at my side in the autumn of 1977, when I flew back to London to take part in the *Evening News* annual film awards. I had been nominated as best actress and although I lost the award to Billie Whitelaw, for her performance in *The Omen* it didn't matter. I was deliriously happy. I had fallen in love with Michael the second he poured me that first glass of orange juice and my feelings just grew stronger with each passing day.

He was the strength that had been missing from my life, the strong arm when I needed support and the Gemini air that fanned my Arien flames. Since the day that I had split up with Mike King, I had tried to recapture the innocence of our young love. It had never been the same with anyone else, but suddenly, it didn't need to be; suddenly it was new and vital, the past had been chopped away like an unwanted burden and the present was all that mattered.

When we attended the *Evening News* awards' dinner, the guests were all serious and stern, with their evening clothes and professional faces. We sat at a large table with Christopher Plummer, Micky Dolenz, Billie Whitelaw and a scattering of executives and their wives. Roasted legs and wings of chicken were served and, while everyone picked gingerly at their meal with blunt knives and forks, Michael instantly used his fingers. I kicked him under the table, but he just smiled and it wasn't long before our companions followed his example.

It was typical. Michael cared nothing for star systems, etiquette and the movie bullshit that had always been in the background of my life. He liked sixties rock, he wanted to build his own boat and he knew nothing about the film industry. He was the breath of fresh air that I needed to face the future and it seemed completely natural that we decided to get married. I was thirty-four and Michael Arnold was only twenty, but he had a maturity beyond his years and I was still in the process of growing up. We talked about it for a long time, but we saw no harm in the age gap.

Autumn in London was beautiful. The trees in Hyde Park were burning in shades of bronze, copper and orange; we walked the changing streets of Hammersmith and on 25 November, we were married at the Registry Office in Kensington.

The press were there in force and so were the fans, but I was too happy to open my eyes, in case the dream came to an end.

But it didn't end. Each day my life became more real, more filled with reason. I had no need to take drugs and now that I was cured from the alcohol habit, I enjoyed a few glasses of champagne at receptions and wine when we went out for a meal. I was a new person, at the height of my awareness as a woman and at the height of my ability as an actress.

It didn't come easily, but time and Michael's love were the cure. After our marriage, we left London to visit Michael's parents, Dorothy and Richard, in the Boston township of Whitman, a place, according to Michael, inhabited by some of the craziest people in the world, but where he had escaped through his desire to succeed in the music business. From Boston, we went for our honeymoon at Martha's Vineyard Island, where the Kennedy family have their summer retreat. That honeymoon lasted for twelve months. Michael fished with his friends and I grew vegetables and cooked big meals. Show business was far away and the only reminder came through the frequent visits of Joe Delaney, one of the finest jazz pianists in the world and a man whose biggest ambition was to play for Frank Sinatra. He found it hard to believe that Frank was one of the dearest friends I had.

I had a small twinge of sadness when I thought about Sean and Stephen, three thousand miles away on the west coast, but they were happy where they were and that was all that really mattered.

We might have remained on the island forever, it was the haven that Warren Beatty had never found, but my agent in Hollywood was eager to get me back to work. Michael remained silent for, as he said, it was my decision. He was in the process of starting up a building firm, but he knew instinctively that, as an actress, I would have to return to work. When I decided that it was time to go west, he asked me if there was any hurry.

'No, I suppose not. Why?'

'I thought it might be a good idea to drive.'

And it was a good idea.

Michael passed on his building orders to a couple of friends, we bought a new car and, on a snowy winter's day in 1978, we left for the Promised Land. We took our time and the journey had such a calming effect that I didn't feel in the least bit depressed when that famous, white-lettered sign appeared above the hills:

HOLLYWOOD

We pulled off the Ventura Freeway, the Pasadena suburbs like a carpet behind us. The snaking U-turns of the Laurel Canyon Boulevard led through a forest of tall pines and suddenly I was back in filmstar city.

I had set out from Martha's Vineyard Island for a 'definite' part in a science fiction movie ... 'All we've got to do is sign the contract,' one of my agents assured me; but like so many definite things in the movie world, the company putting up the money for the project had gone bust and all work on the production had ceased.

It didn't really matter. The offer had put an end to my long vacation and, once the casting directors knew I was back in town, I was soon busy with the usual round of guest appearances and television work, parts that weren't always rewarding, but were important while I waited for the right movie. It doesn't matter how good you are as an actress, you have to spend time in front of the cameras to keep your craft at its peak.

Micheal hated to be idle and, in starting a small building company, he found himself designing new offices for those movie moguls George Lucas and Steven Spielberg; the arms of the film studios reached out and embraced my life, one way, or another.

It was on one of the occasions when he was out that I found this poem that he had written to describe our relationship:

The White Knight

She's got culture, diamonds and pearls
She comes from a whole different world
There's no way to cut the cake
For she'll take all that you bake
She's got culture, diamonds and pearls
She comes from a whole different world
In the morning when it breaks to dawn
She fills my sails and I'm gone
Goodnight to Beverly. The hills were not for me.
It's the ocean that sets me free
The White Knight is like a veil
She fills each and every sail
She's got culture, diamonds and pearls
She comes from a whole different world.

The house we rented in Sherman Oaks had wonderful views and plenty of spare room for the boys when they came visiting with their friends. It was an odd situation. Sean and Stephen still living with their step-father, but they were well-adjusted and I could see no point in making changes.

As for Stuart Lerner, he may have been a good psychiatrist, a good doctor, even a kind and thoughtful parent, but as husbands go, he was lousy. I was too happy to bear any grudges and in the five years that have gone by since our parting, all wounds have healed and we now have a marginal, telephone friendship.

My work in Hollywood lacked the satisfaction I always found in London, but now that life outside the studios was full, what happened on set didn't matter. I maintained an icy reserve off camera and the only persistent admirer I had was the ten-year-old child prodigy Gary Coleman. When I co-starred in his show *Different Strokes*, I discovered that his hands were as quick as his tongue.

There were a number of movie offers during this period, but I had long since decided to be more selective and the roles that came up didn't fit with the course I had chosen.

Life was and had always been a pattern of wheels within wheels, the greater, all-encompassing circle too vast to see or understand. Michael Arnold was the thread that tied so many of my life's loose ends, but it was somehow inevitable that whatever I did in the United States would only be temporary.

Me; my life; my career. They all belonged to London.

We returned briefly at the end of 1980 to work on a series of newspaper articles, but timing is the essence of success and the time wasn't quite right.

It was right in January 1982.

Stephen had reached his eighteenth birthday and graduated from high school. Sean, now nineteen, was at the University College of Los Angeles, and with the boys setting out with their band for a series of night club and party appearances, I left them in charge of our Hollywood apartment and flew with Michael into the cold, real and exhilarating world where it had all begun.

I signed to star with Joan Collins in a new film entitled *Nutcracker* and I went into rehearsals for the award-winning play *Steaming*. It opened to packed houses at the West End's Comedy Theatre in March. I hope the people came to see a highly acclaimed production – not Carol White without any clothes on.

That aspect of the production was worrying, but nudity on stage differs from the cinema screen and it was obviously the right role for me to be playing. My first love at drama school had been the theatre, and my return after twenty years in the movies was to a play written by Nell Dunn, one of my oldest friends and the author of *Poor Cow*, the film that made me a star. To make the nostalgia even more complete, the play was directed by Roger Smith, the story editor on *Cathy Come Home* and *Up the Junction*.

I have lived a full, fast and exciting life, a life balanced with its fair share of heartaches and good fortune. I am and always will be a child of the sixties and, with the influence of those powerful years behind me, I have the strength to carry me through the challenges of the future.

There was never any doubt that Carol would finally Come Home.

Twenty

WITH MY life having turned full circle, I can't say that I would do it all again, because I wouldn't.

I have made a lot of wrong choices in my life, but while I have done the same in my career, the differing roles have helped to stretch me to the limits of my own potential. I lost millions of fans when I broke away from the mould of a working-class hero. Those films and plays that underlined Britain's social problems made me the glamorous mouthpiece for the old and the poor, but as an actress, the real test was in the parts beyond those confines.

Some of the films I then made were considered controversial. The scenes of sadism and mild pornography didn't fit with my public image, nor of the image I had of myself, but though it would have been easy to stay in the rut of that old winning formula, life is a process of change and I could do nothing but meet it head-on.

Nobody likes to lose something they love and, though I missed the fans as much as they missed me, the road to fame, wealth and Hollywood was an essential part of the path that was to lead me back home to London.

The same, in some ways, applies to my experiences with drugs. I had to touch upon every aspect of the culture in which I lived, if only to learn that drug-taking would ultimately close more doors than it opened.

That brings me to my book's conclusion and its dedication to a Los Angeles photographer named Cynthia. She was twenty-two, she worked for the magazine *Rolling Stone* and, with everything to live for, she died of a brain haemorrhage following an overdose of heroin and cocaine.

Using these two drugs is the latest craze for the fast-set in Hollywood. The cocaine is taken after being passed through ether, a ritual they call free-basing, and that is followed by a snort of heroin.

It killed Cynthia. It killed the actor John Belushi, found dead with a hooker in a hotel bedroom. If my story prevents others from living the same life and going the same way, then the writing of it has all been more than worthwhile.

I am now thirty-eight, I am happily married and I love my husband.

My sons, Sean and Stephen are working hard to succeed in the music business and it was only a diary full of bookings that stopped them from being with me at the opening night of *Steaming*. They would have joined the rest of my family, my husband Michael, my dear and close friend Mike King and co-writer Clifford Thurlow, who has followed me across the world to listen to my words and help to write this chronicle of the times.

It is, I hope, not just an autobiography, but more a brief, almost historical, glimpse of a star's life in the sixties – a star who survived to tell the tale.

Book
Tokens

Give them
the pleasure of choosing

Book Tokens can be bought
and exchanged at most
bookshops in Great Britain
and Ireland.

NEL BESTSELLERS

T51277	'THE NUMBER OF THE BEAST'	*Robert Heinlein*	£2.25
T50777	STRANGER IN A STRANGE LAND	*Robert Heinlein*	£1.75
T51382	FAIR WARNING	*Simpson & Burger*	£1.75
T52478	CAPTAIN BLOOD	*Michael Blodgett*	£1.75
T50246	THE TOP OF THE HILL	*Irwin Shaw*	£1.95
T49620	RICH MAN, POOR MAN	*Irwin Shaw*	£1.60
T51609	MAYDAY	*Thomas H. Block*	£1.75
T54071	MATCHING PAIR	*George G. Gilman*	£1.50
T45773	CLAIRE RAYNER'S LIFEGUIDE		£2.50
T53709	PUBLIC MURDERS	*Bill Granger*	£1.75
T53679	THE PREGNANT WOMAN'S BEAUTY BOOK	*Gloria Natale*	£1.25
T49817	MEMORIES OF ANOTHER DAY	*Harold Robbins*	£1.95
T50807	79 PARK AVENUE	*Harold Robbins*	£1.75
T50149	THE INHERITORS	*Harold Robbins*	£1.75
T53231	THE DARK	*James Herbert*	£1.50
T43245	THE FOG	*James Herbert*	£1.50
T53296	THE RATS	*James Herbert*	£1.50
T45528	THE STAND	*Stephen King*	£1.75
T50874	CARRIE	*Stephen King*	£1.50
T51722	DUNE	*Frank Herbert*	£1.75
T52575	THE MIXED BLESSING	*Helen Van Slyke*	£1.75
T38602	THE APOCALYPSE	*Jeffrey Konvitz*	95p

NEL P.O. BOX 11, FALMOUTH TR10 9EN, CORNWALL

Postage Charge:

U.K. Customers 45p for the first book plus 20p for the second book and 14p for each additional book ordered to a maximum charge of £1.63.

B.F.P.O. & EIRE Customers 45p for the first book plus 20p for the second book and 14p for the next 7 books; thereafter 8p per book.

Overseas Customers 75p for the first book and 21p per copy for each additional book.

Please send cheque or postal order (no currency).

Name ....

Address ....

....

Title ....

While every effort is made to keep prices steady, it is sometimes necessary to increase prices at short notice. New English Library reserve the right to show on covers and charge new retail prices which may differ from those advertised in the text or elsewhere.(7)